Jeffrey Andrew Barash

Shadows of Being

Encounters with Heidegger in Political Theory and Historical Reflection

Studies in Historical Philosophy

ISSN 2629-0316

1 *Dustin Peone*
Memory as Philosophy
The Theory and Practice of Philosophical Recollection
ISBN 978-3-8382-1336-1

2 *Raymond Barfield*
The Poetic Apriori: Philosophical Imagination in a Meaningful Universe
ISBN 978-3-8382-1350-7

3 *Jennifer Lobo Meeks*
Allegory in Early Greek Philosophy
ISBN 978-3-8382-1425-2

4 *Vanessa Freerks*
Baudrillard with Nietzsche and Heidegger: Towards a Genealogical Analysis
ISBN 978-3-8382-1474-0

5 *Thora Ilin Bayer and Donald Phillip Verene*
Philosophical Ideas
A Historical Study
ISBN 978-3-8382-1585-3

6 *Jeffrey Andrew Barash*
Shadows of Being
Encounters with Heidegger in Political Theory and Historical Reflection
ISBN 978-3-8382-1485-6

Jeffrey Andrew Barash

SHADOWS OF BEING

Encounters with Heidegger in Political Theory and Historical Reflection

ibidem Verlag

Bibliographic information published by the Deutsche Nationalbibliothek
Die Deutsche Nationalbibliothek lists this publication in the Deutsche Nationalbibliografie; detailed bibliographic data are available in the Internet at http://dnb.d-nb.de.

Bibliografische Information der Deutschen Nationalbibliothek
Die Deutsche Nationalbibliothek verzeichnet diese Publikation in der Deutschen Nationalbibliografie; detaillierte bibliografische Daten sind im Internet über http://dnb.d-nb.de abrufbar.

Cover picture: © copyright 2021 by the Estate of Paul Jenkins
Phenomena Anvil Wedge, 2008, acrylic on canvas
205.7 cm x 325.1 cm

ISBN-13: 978-3-8382-1485-6

Printed in the United States of America

Contents

Contents

Introduction

In a review of Karl Jaspers's early work, *Psychology of Worldviews* (*Psychologie der Weltanschauungen*, 1919), composed several years before the publication of his book *Being and Time*, Martin Heidegger suggested that the philosophical orientations of his period had made a wrong turn and skirted by the fundamental path of thought. He claimed that instead of retrieving a heritage of original questions, his contemporaries had become preoccupied with secondary matters, positing as essential what was in fact only incidental.[1] During the years that followed, Heidegger's promise to reorient philosophy in terms of the *Seinsfrage*, the question of Being, exercised a well-known influence on successive generations of thinkers on a global scale. The present book delves into the philosophical sources of this influence and raises the question whether Heidegger indeed made good on the promise to reveal for thought what is truly fundamental. In proposing this investigation, I assume that Heidegger should not be taken at his word, but that it is necessary to scrutinize what he posits to be fundamental in light of its broader implications—above all for ethico-political judgment and for historical reflection. After addressing this question in the first part of the book, the second part examines the significance of Heidegger's reorientation of philosophy through the prism of its critical reception in the thought of Ernst Cassirer, Hannah Arendt, Emmanuel Levinas, and Paul Ricœur.

Each chapter in this book was written independently of the others and can be understood separately from them on the basis of the arguments it presents. Taken as a group, all of the chapters nonetheless fit together as a whole, since each of them examines the broader implications of Heidegger's thought from a different perspective. Although the different chapters in this book were initially written in different periods over the course of three decades of reflection, all have been reformulated and rewritten, not only in the perspective of the book as a whole, but of important analyses of Heidegger's thought and its reception that have appeared in recent years.

The chapters of the first part of this book directly interpret Heidegger's thought and its legacy, and they analyze it in the period of

1 Martin Heidegger, "Anmerkungen zu Karl Jaspers 'Psychologie der Weltanschauungen'," in *Wegmarken*, *GA*, vol. 9, ed. Friedrich-Wilhelm von Herrmann (Frankfurt am Main: Klostermann, 1976), p. 5. Hereafter *GA* will designate the *Gesamtausgabe*, Heidegger's collected works.

Being and Time (*Sein und Zeit*, 1927), while also extending the interpretation of his œuvre well beyond the scope of this early period. Following interpretation of *Being and Time* and other contemporary writings, they focus on Heidegger's works during the period of Nazi rule in Germany and afterward. Here I take into consideration the numerous course lectures and writings that have been published for the first time in recent years, including the *Contributions to Philosophy: On the Event* (*Beiträge zur Philosophie: Vom Ereignis,* 1936–38),[2] the different course lectures of this period, and the *Black Notebooks* (*Schwarze Hefte*), which have substantially modified our understanding of Heidegger and of the meaning of his endeavor.

The chapters in the second part of this book deal with the critical reception of Heidegger's work by thinkers who to my mind stand among his most profound interpreters. They include analyses of Heidegger's thought by Ernst Cassirer, Hannah Arendt, Emmanuel Levinas, and Paul Ricœur who each grappled with the ethico-political and historical implications of his philosophy, above all in *Being and Time*, and with the significance for its interpretation of his political engagement in favor of the Nazi regime as rector of the University of Freiburg im Breisgau in 1933–34.

As Heidegger often reiterated, his thought in all of its periods was centered on one principal theme: the question of Being or *Seinsfrage*. From

2 Unless otherwise indicated, all translations are my own. It is well known that the question of how to best translate Heidegger's terminology in the different periods of his thought has given rise to all manner of differences of opinion. In what follows, I have chosen to translate Heidegger's terms as simply as possible, especially where their meaning in contemporary German is straightforward. This is the case for the word *Ereignis*, event, in modern German. In their translation of Heidegger's *Beiträge zur Philosophie*, Parvis Emad and Kenneth Maly have rendered *Ereignis* into English as "enowning," which seems to me to substitute for a straightforward German term a neologism that is hardly clear in standard English. David Farrell Krell and Gregory Fried who, among Heidegger's recent interpreters, produce what are to my mind the most accurate and readable translations of Heidegger's difficult terminology, have preferred to translate Heidegger's *Ereignis* as "appropriating event" (Fried) or as "(ap) propriating event" (Krell). I can appreciate the logic of their arguments, which each defends in his respective works. Nonetheless, as with other instances of Heideggerian terminology, I have chosen to stick to the clearest translation possible, since I consider that Heidegger's terminology is sufficiently complex in itself and the creation of neologisms or interpretative departures from the strict sense of the words themselves can only add to the difficulty. See Martin Heidegger, *Contributions to Philosophy: (From Enowning)*, trans. Parvis Emad and Kenneth Maly (Bloomington and Indianapolis: Indiana University Press, 1999); David Farrell Krell, *Ecstasy, Catastrophe. Heidegger from Being and Time to the Black Notebooks* (Albany, NY: SUNY Press, 2015), p. 56, 195; Gregory Fried, *Heidegger's Polemos: From Being to Politics* (New Haven and London: Yale University Press, 2000), p. 70.

different vantage points in the period of *Being and Time* and his later works, he posed the *Seinsfrage* as an essentially *historical* query. The fundamental significance of this question in its historical articulations had, in different ways, continually been obscured for Heidegger by the great representatives of the Western metaphysical tradition.

The ten chapters in this book will examine in detail modulations in the orientation of Heidegger's *Seinsfrage* and in his interpretation of the forgetfulness of Being underlying Western metaphysical traditions in the earlier and later periods of his thought. In pursuing the *Seinsfrage*, Heidegger presupposed in all of these periods that this question itself and its obfuscation by Western metaphysical traditions constituted the fundamental task for thought to which all other forms of historical reflection where entirely subordinate. In enunciating this assumption, he set in place a specific strategy of interpretation permitting him to identify his own endeavor as a monumental point in the movement of Western thought. In accord with this strategy in the different periods of his work, he engaged a dialogue with the towering figures of Western philosophy, from Plato and Aristotle to Leibniz, Kant, Hegel, and Nietzsche, while setting aside from consideration all forms of historical analysis and of ethico-political reflection that deviated from the path he designated.

The critical examination I propose of Heidegger's legacy, in investigating Heidegger's claim to have revealed what is truly fundamental for thought, intentionally departs from Heidegger's own method of interpretation and of self-interpretation; it seeks to establish an independent vantage point from which to set the implications of this claim in clear relief. Only in this way, as I argue, is it possible to uncover omissions, inconsistencies, and biases that are inherent to his perspective, which his conception of thought may lead us to overlook.

***

During the years of elaboration of these different studies, I benefitted from the encouragement, advice, and counsel of a number of scholars whose help was indispensable to me. I would like above all to recall to thankful remembrance those whose insight was of lasting importance: Werner Beierwaltes, Tobias Brocher, Reinhart Koselleck, Leonard Krieger, Paul Oskar Kristeller, John Michael Krois, Ada Löwith, Werner Marx, Otto Pöggeler, Paul Ricœur, Rainer Rochlitz, Jacques Rolland, Hans Saner, and Philippe Soulez. I also extend my heartfelt thanks to Sophie-Jan Arrien, Ronald Beiner, Hans-Helmuth Gander, Jean Greisch, Alexander and Maria Gungov, Wolfgang Holl, Paul and Suzanne Jenkins, Servanne Jollivet, Ethan Kleinberg, Jerome Kohn, Reinhart Mehring, Hans Ruin, Klaus Stichweh, Donald Phillip Verene, and Peter Welsen.

Part I

Politics, Myth, and History in Heidegger

Chapter 1

The Legacy of Martin Heidegger in Contemporary Perspective

The legacy Martin Heidegger bequeathed to future generations is at once profound, wide-reaching, and disturbing. In this introductory chapter I will examine different facets of Heidegger's reception that began to resonate on a broad scale following the publication of *Being and Time* (*Sein und Zeit*) in 1927.

During the years before and just after World War II, *Being and Time* constituted the primary source of Heidegger's legacy. Over the decades that followed, however, Heidegger steadily published new philosophical works and it became evident that this work was only the first—albeit among the most important—expressions of Heidegger's thinking spanning six decades of continuous productivity. If these decades witnessed numerous twists in Heidegger's thought and a significant turn in his orientation during the 1930s and 1940s, upon which I will have occasion to comment below, the Freiburg thinker nonetheless often emphasized the continuity of his endeavors in relation to the central query to which, from *Being and Time* onward, he addressed ever and again: the *Seinsfrage*, or question concerning the meaning of Being. According to Heidegger's own interpretation, the *Seinsfrage* served as the *leitmotiv* that revealed the different topics of his work as so many perspectives oriented toward a single backdrop, whether they dealt with the foundations of Western metaphysics, the origin of the work of art, the essence of language and poetic expression, technology and the Western scientific heritage or any other of the manifold themes of his investigations.

In view of the seemingly recondite character of this *leitmotiv* unifying Heidegger's endeavors, the reception of his thinking on a global scale may seem puzzling. Few questions, indeed, would seem farther removed from the standard discourse of philosophy in the post-World War II period than the question of Being. In what terms, therefore, might one characterize the meaning of Heidegger's endeavors in the perspective of his global reception since the late 1920s?

In this introductory chapter I shall propose a brief response to this question. The reception of Heidegger's thought has been closely tied to the publication of the collected edition or *Gesamtausgabe* of his works, which began in 1975. This collected edition, which Heidegger himself initially helped to edit in the years before his death in 1976, comprises a total of 102 volumes. If, over the past decades, this collected edition has rapidly become the chief source for interpretation of Heidegger's thought, the publication among the last volumes of the *Gesamtausgabe* of five volumes of Heidegger's *Schwarze Hefte*, or *Black Notebooks*, caused a considerable uproar due to the highly controversial and overtly anti-Semitic character of his utterances. As I will have occasion to examine in more detail below, these notebooks and other publications in the framework of the collected works will undoubtedly play a significant role in the future reception of Heidegger's work.[3]

The clamor aroused by the publication of the *Black Notebooks* between 2014 and 2018 constituted the latest in a successive series of scandals that have surrounded his philosophy since his engagement in favor of the Hitler regime as rector of the University of Freiburg im Breisgau in 1933–34. If his official support for the Nazi regime was short-lived, his heretofore unpublished course lectures and documents and the *Black Notebooks* illustrate that his complicity with the Nazi ideology and the Nazi war effort was deeper and more extensive than was previously believed. Clearly, Heidegger's actions in this period and his later political leanings, which I will return to below, only render more complex the already problematic question of his legacy. After all, what possibly could be the *meaning* of such a recondite query as the *Seinsfrage*, which Heidegger's political attitude would seem to place in a dubious light?

Since Heidegger rose to philosophical prominence in Germany well before these political sympathies became manifest, I will examine his early philosophy before turning to the problem of its political implications and to the legacy of his later thought. In the framework of this introduction, I propose to analyze Heidegger's legacy under the following three headings: 1. The deconstruction of Western intellectual and cultural traditions; 2. Heidegger in political perspective; 3. Heidegger and the heritage of scientific rationality.

3 On the politics of the publication of the *Gesamtausgabe*, see above all Theodor Kisiel, "Edition und Übersetzung. Unterwegs von Tatsachen zu Gedanken, von Werken zu Wegen," in Dietrich Papenfuss and Otto Pöggeler, eds., *Zur philosophischen Aktualität Heideggers*, vol. 3, *Im Spiegel der Welt: Sprache, Übersetzung, Auseinandersetzung* (Frankfurt am Main: Klostermann, 1992), p. 89–107; Reinhard Mehring, *Heideggers "Grosse Politik." Die semantische Revolution der Gesamtausgabe* (Tübingen: Mohr/Siebeck, 2016). On the policies of the editors of the *Gesamtausgabe*, see F.-W. von Herrmann, "Wirkungen der Martin-Heidegger-*Gesamtausgabe*," in Markus Happel, ed., *Heidegger – neu gelesen* (Königshausen und Neumann: Würzburg, 1997), pp. 87–96.

I
The Deconstruction of Western Intellectual and Cultural Traditions

In the years after 1919, and before envisaging the full implications of his appeal in light of the question of Being, Heidegger began to call for a "deconstruction" (*Abbau*) and alternately a "destruction" (*Destruktion*) of Western intellectual and cultural traditions.[4] In his review of Karl Jaspers's book *Psychology of World Views* (*Psychologie der Weltanschauungen*, 1919), which Heidegger sent to Jaspers at some point between 1919 and 1921 but which was not published until 1973, the Freiburg thinker proposed that Western intellectual traditions might have unwittingly strayed from the fundamental themes which stood at their origin and, through an "unwarranted concern to save culture," had mistaken merely secondary matters for fundamental problems.[5] Such a concern to "save culture" proved wholly inadequate for the purpose of retrieving the original meaning of the past, just as did all approaches to the past in terms of objectified categories—like the "ideal of humanity" or the cultivation of "personality"—that a declining tradition had bequeathed.[6]

At the outset of a biting attack against the contemporary interpretations of the cultural task of philosophy in the 1923 Freiburg course lecture *Ontologie (Hermeneutik der Faktizität) [Ontology: (Hermeneutics of Facticity)]*, Heidegger stipulated that "philosophy as such has no warrant to concern itself with universal humanity (*allgemeine Menschheit*) and culture (*Kultur*)." He then called for a reinterpretation of this task from the vantage point that later became *Being and Time*'s central focus: he

---

4 Martin Heidegger, "Anmerkungen zu Karl Jaspers (Psychologie der Weltanschauungen)," *Wegmarken, GA*, vol. 9, pp. 3–6; Martin Heidegger, *Phänomenologie der Anschauung und des Ausdrucks. Theorie der philosophischen Begriffsbildung, GA*, vol. 59, ed. Claudius Strube (Frankfurt am Main: Klostermann, 1993), p. 29–41. In regard to the topic of "destruction" and "deconstruction," see also Heidegger's letter to Karl Löwith, dated 19.8.1921, in Martin Heidegger, Karl Löwith, *Briefwechsel, 1919–73*, ed. Alfred Denker (Freiburg/Munich: Alber, 2017), pp. 52–56. Löwith initially referred to Heidegger's notion of "destruction" in this correspondence in an article published in *Les Temps Modernes* shortly after World War II; see Karl Löwith, "Les implications politiques de la philosophie de l'existence chez Heidegger," in *Les Temps Modernes*, vol. 2, 1946, pp. 343–60. On the topic of destruction in Heidegger's early philosophy, see the insightful analysis of Sophie-Jan Arrien, *L'inquiétude de la pensée. L'herméneutique de la vie du jeune Heidegger (1919–1923)* (Paris: Presses Universitaires de France, 2014).

5 Ibid., p. 5.

6 Ibid., p. 34.

proposed that the "destruction" or "deconstruction" of intellectual traditions should proceed from a reexamination of the original Greek interpretation of Being, which had been completely misunderstood because of the influence of a long historical tradition that culminated in more recent academic styles of analysis.[7]

Well before the publication of *Being and Time* in 1927, Heidegger rose to prominence in Germany on the basis of his reputation as a teacher. A number of his former students—including Karl Löwith, Hannah Arendt, and Hans-Georg Gadamer—have attributed his renown to the originality of his attempt to disengage interpretation of the seminal thinkers of the past from the conventional assumptions of contemporary academia. As these former students have emphasized, Heidegger's critical appraisal of traditional, culturally oriented contemporary philosophy was warmly received among students and younger professors who, following the devastation wrought by World War I, questioned the soundness of the Western cultural heritage and the purport of any attempt to evaluate philosophy in relation to its contemporary cultural significance.[8]

In the years following World War I, Heidegger's deconstruction of intellectual and cultural traditions directed particular attention not only toward the attempt to adapt philosophy to a cultural role but also toward the more specifically philosophical connotation that the term "culture" had acquired during the course of the nineteenth century. What was the purpose of this critique? What was the precise relation between the "destruction" of cultural traditions and the more original interpretation of the question of Being he sought to elaborate?

A closer inspection of Heidegger's early Freiburg and Marburg lectures (1918–28), published during the years of gestation of the central themes of *Being and Time*, enables us to place these questions in a more comprehensive perspective. Among his central targets, Heidegger's deconstruction of contemporary ideas of "spirit" (*Geist*), "tradition" (*Tradition*), and of "culture," (*Kultur*) challenged the historical and historicist orientations responsible for the elaboration of these ideas since the late

7 Martin Heidegger, *Ontologie (Hermeneutik der Faktizität)*, *GA*, vol. 63, ed. Käte Bröcker-Oltmanns (Frankfurt am Main: Klostermann), 1988, pp. 51-77, 91, 108.

8 Hannah Arendt, "Martin Heidegger at Eighty," *New York Review of Books*, vol. 17, 6, 21 October, 1971, pp. 50–54, reprinted in Michael Murray, ed., *Heidegger and Modern Philosophy* (New Haven: Yale University Press, 1978), p. 293–303; Karl Löwith, Appendix to *Heidegger. Denker in dürftiger Zeit. Zur Stellung der Philosophie im 20. Jahrhundert*, *Sämtliche Schriften*, vol. 8, (Stuttgart: Metzler, 1984), pp. 294–96; H.-G. Gadamer, Introduction to Martin Heidegger, *Der Ursprung des Kunstwerkes* (Stuttgart: Reclam, 1962), pp. 102–107.

nineteenth century. From Heidegger's standpoint it was these orientations that obstructed the approach to the past requisite for the reformulation of the originary question of Being. This is why the debate concerning historical consciousness evoked by terms like "spirit," "tradition," and especially "culture" is so closely bound to the interpretation of Heidegger's *Seinsfrage*. Let us turn to Heidegger's early lectures in which he examined the idea of historical consciousness that the term "culture" had come to represent over the course of the nineteenth century. From there I will proceed toward an elucidation of Heidegger's *Seinsfrage* through an analysis of its relation to the "deconstruction" of cultural and intellectual traditions in his writings of the 1920s.

Heidegger provided a detailed analysis of the idea of "culture" or of "historical culture" in the 1919 course lecture, "Phenomenology and Transcendental Philosophy of Values" ("Phänomenologie und transzendentale Wertphilosophie"). Here he explained that the idea of "culture" or "historical culture" served as the basis for interpretation among German thinkers, which was most specifically elaborated in relation to the theme of historical consciousness from the period of Johann Gottfried Herder and Friedrich Schlegel onward.[9] In the course of the nineteenth century, "culture" in this sense, according to Heidegger, had come to signify an "accomplishment" (*Leistung*) and an "achievement" (*Errungenschaft*) in a long process of historical development. This idea of historical development, as Heidegger noted, was most immediately spurred by the emergence of scientific consciousness and by the ensuing progress of natural science and technology.[10]

What stood most directly in question in this and other lectures Heidegger presented in the 1920s was not so much the emergence of modern historical consciousness or of science and technology *per se*; he sought above all to reveal how a one-sided focus on the development of culture had tended to obscure other interpretative possibilities which could not be readily measured in terms of cultural values. Heidegger directed his polemics of this period at philosophers who had most strongly influenced the idea of culture that had marked contemporary German thought: the Marburg neo-Kantians, above all Hermann Cohen, and the Baden neo-Kantians Wilhelm Windelband and Heinrich Rickert. Heidegger labeled the "philosophy of culture" (*Kulturphilosophie*) of Windelband and Rickert

---

9 "Phänomenologie und transzendentale Wertphilosophie," *Zur Bestimmung der Philosophie*, *GA*, vol. 55/56 (Frankfurt am Main: Klostermann, 1987), pp. 133–34.

10 Ibid., pp. 130–31.

(the latter of whom had directed Heidegger's doctoral thesis and habilitation at Freiburg) as "the typical philosophy of the nineteenth century."[11] Heidegger did not hesitate to take to task other thinkers, most notably Max Weber and Ernst Troeltsch, in so far as they shared similar ideals.[12] Even the contemporary "philosophy of life" (*Lebensphilosophie*) came under fire for its affirmation of the ideal of universal validity (*Allgemeingültigkeit*) in the study of objectifications of cultural life, in spite of the fact that Dilthey's "philosophy of life" seemed to Heidegger to anticipate a more radical interpretation of human existence toward which he himself was groping at this time.[13]

In the context of these early years of the Weimar Republic, the broad appeal of Heidegger's critique of intellectual traditions and of "culture" might seem to bear a certain resemblance to other contemporary expressions of radical doubt in the Western heritage. In this regard, one need only think of the enormously popular work of Oswald Spengler, *The Decline of the West* (1918). On the basis of an all-encompassing typology of cultural forms, Spengler interpreted the waning of Western spiritual values and religious faith in favor of the pragmatic and technological orientation of a materialistic civilization as the unmistakable sign of the West's impending decline. If Heidegger reproached what he took to be the dilettantism of

---

11 Ibid., p. 131.

12 On Heidegger's critique of Weber see "Anmerkungen zu Karl Jaspers," pp. 40–41 and Martin Heidegger, *Grundprobleme der Phänomenologie* (1919/20), *GA*, vol. 58, ed. Hans-Helmuth Gander (Frankfurt am Main: Klostermann, 1993), pp. 189–95. Heidegger expressed his critical attitude toward Ernst Troeltsch in an early letter to Heinrich Rickert in November, 1917, in which he wrote: "I expected from Meinecke, Troeltsch and from the spiritual centers (*geistige Zentren*) of Heidelberg University the emergence of spiritual and evaluative positions concerning the problem of German existence (*Problem der deutschen Existenz*)." Four years later, on 15 March 1921, Heidegger wrote to Rickert that he considered a debate with Troeltsch to be urgently necessary, and he alluded to the critical attitude he adopted toward Troeltsch in his seminar in Freiburg. "Troeltsch's Hegelianism," as Heidegger wrote, "did not sufficiently spring from an original motivation (*zu wenig ursprünglich motiviert zu sein*)." Martin Heidegger, Heinrich Rickert, *Briefe (1912–33) und andere Dokumente*, ed. Alfred Denker (Frankfurt am Main: Klostermann, 2002), p. 45, 53–56. See also Martin Heidegger, "Einleitung in die Phänomenologie der Religion," and "Augustinus und der Neuplatonismus," in *Phänomenologie des religiösen Lebens*, *GA*, vol. 60, ed. Matthias Jung, Thomas Regehly, and Claudius Strube (Frankfurt am Main: Klostermann, 1995), pp. 19–30, 160–62. On Troeltsch's thought in this period, see especially Robert E. Norton, *The Crucible of German Democracy. Ernst Troeltsch and the First World War* (Tübingen: Mohr/Siebeck, 2021).

13 Martin Heidegger, *Phänomenologische Interpretationen zu Aristoteles. Einführung in die Phänomenologische Forschung* (1921–22), *GA*, vol. 61, ed. Walter Bröcker and Käte Bröcker-Oltmanns (Frankfurt am Main: Klostermann, 1994), pp. 7, 79–89; Heidegger, "Anmerkungen zu Karl Jaspers," *Wegmarken*, *GA*, vol. 9, pp. 1–44.

Spengler's historical method, he nonetheless heartily applauded the boldness of Spengler's prediction. It demonstrated nothing more clearly, for Heidegger, than the groundlessness of historical methods in the human sciences in their attempt to elaborate objective, universally valid criteria of judgment as a basis for comparison of typical patterns of cultural expression.[14]

Much closer than Spengler to Heidegger's own concerns in this period stood a group of young neo-orthodox Protestant theologians who berated nineteenth and twentieth century liberal theology for what they took to be its too-exclusive focus on the cultural role of religion in the historical world. In the context of these years immediately following World War I, the polemics that theologians like Karl Barth, Friedrich Gogarten, and Rudolf Bultmann directed against Adolf von Harnack and Ernst Troeltsch, whose orientation had been deeply influenced by the neo-Kantian *Kulturphilosophie*, ran directly parallel to the early philosophical critique enunciated by Heidegger. Indeed, Heidegger himself evoked the theological implications of his endeavors in his early Freiburg course lectures, above all in "Introduction to the Phenomenology of Religion" ("Einleitung in die Phänomenologie der Religion," 1920–21) and in "Augustine and Neoplatonism" ("Augustinus und der Neuplatonismus," 1921). In these lectures Heidegger, like his neo-orthodox associates, directed his concern toward the eschatological, otherworldly striving at the heart of the pristine religiosity of the original Christian community; like these theologians, he censured a long tradition of interpretation of the essence of Christianity in terms of the objective manifestations of the Christian contribution to the development of culture.[15] It is this affinity between philosophical and theological concerns which enables us to comprehend the close collaboration

14 Heidegger, *Ontologie (Hermeneutik der Faktizität)*, pp. 35–57.

15 See for example Rudolf Bultmann, "Die liberale Theologie und die jüngste theologische Bewegung" (1924), *Glauben und Verstehen, Gesammelte Aufsätze*, vol. 1 (Tübingen: Mohr, 1933), pp. 1–25. On the orientation of this group of neo-orthodox theologians, Heidegger wrote to Löwith on 24 August 1925: "What still manifests 'life' is the Barth-Gogarten movement that in Marburg is independently and prudently represented by Bultmann." Martin Heidegger, Karl Löwith, *Briefwechsel*, p. 128; for a closer analysis of this theological background to Heidegger's early philosophical orientation see my book *Martin Heidegger and the Problem of Historical Meaning* (New York: Fordham University Press, 2003), pp. 132–156. See also the analyses of Sylvain Camilleri, *Heidegger et les grandes lignes d'une phénoménologie herméneutique du christianisme primitif* (Cham, Switzerland: Springer, 2017) and of Christian Sommer, *Heidegger, Aristote, Luther: Les sources aristotéliciennes et néo-testamentaires d'Être et temps* (Paris: Presses Universitaires de France, 2015).

between Heidegger and Bultmann during the Marburg years (1923–28) when Heidegger was engaged in the composition of *Being and Time*.

An interpretation of Heidegger's aim to deconstruct Western intellectual traditions might well be extended to encompass affinities that Heidegger shared with other authors and with a broader climate in the post-World War I years of social and political unrest, of radical critique of tradition, and of cultural concerns of an earlier period. In order to account for the meaning of Heidegger and for the magnitude of his influence, we might also search for a sociological basis to his orientation by attempting to trace it to a given ideological milieu. As suggestive as such methods might be for the comprehension of Heidegger's intellectual biography, they would hardly seem to indicate how the deconstruction of the historical "consciousness" or "spirit" bequeathed by cultural traditions might be related to the *philosophical* meaning of the question of Being at the heart of *Being and Time*.

Nonetheless, even a superficial reading of *Being and Time* illustrates the difficulty involved in the designation of this relation: as central as the question of Being is to this work, Heidegger hardly ever referred in it to the concept of "culture," which had been a focus of his earlier critique and, more generally, of radical doubt in Germany during the decade following World War I. Indeed, two years after the appearance of *Being and Time*, during the celebrated public debate at Davos in 1929 with Ernst Cassirer, Heidegger insisted that one should not attempt on the basis of that work to understand "culture" and the "realms of culture": "When one asks this question in such a way, it is absolutely impossible to say something from what is given here."[16]

This deliberate neglect of a philosophical concept, the significance of which Heidegger himself had underscored in his early Freiburg lectures, by no means indicates a suspension of Heidegger's critical thrust in this direction, but rather a broadening of its focus. Indeed, one of the principal tasks of *Being and Time* was to encompass the deconstruction of "culture" and of the related topics of the historically-oriented philosophies of the post-Hegelian world—such as "history of the spirit or intellect" (*Geistesgeschichte*) and "world history" (*Weltgeschichte*)—in a broader deconstruction of traditional metaphysics.[17] The originality of Heidegger's

16 Ernst Cassirer, Martin Heidegger, "Davoser Vorträge. Davoser Disputation," appendix to *Kant und das Problem der Metaphysik*, *GA* vol. 3, ed. Friedrich-Wilhelm von Herrmann (Frankfurt: Klostermann, 1991), p. 284.

17 See in this regard Martin Heidegger, *Der Begriff der Zeit* (1924), *GA*, vol. 64, ed. Friedrich Wilhelm von Herrmann (Frankfurt am Main: Klostermann, 2004), p. 120; Martin

interpretation stems from his elucidation of modern philosophies of history and of historical consciousness in view of what he took to be their tacit affirmation of presuppositions inherited from a long tradition of thought concerning the meaning of Being. Since to Heidegger's mind the predominant contemporary philosophies of history and of culture had unwittingly imbibed the presuppositions of traditional metaphysics, deconstruction of the metaphysical residue at the basis of these philosophies aimed toward a fundamental reinterpretation of the past—and, above all, of the question of Being it had bequeathed—from a vantage point that, by virtue of their very dependence on the presuppositions of traditional metaphysics, these philosophies had thoroughly obstructed.

This attempt to designate the post-Hegelian philosophies of history and of culture as the unwitting exponents of traditional metaphysical presuppositions may indeed seem strange to readers familiar with the works of the theoreticians against whom Heidegger's polemics were directed in *Being and Time* and in course lectures of the late 1920s. Here, as in the early 1920s, Heidegger's critique was leveled at theories of objectivity and universal validity (*Allgemeingültigkeit*) in the works of the Baden neo-Kantians Wilhelm Windelband and Heinrich Rickert, as well as in those of Max Weber, Georg Simmel, and Wilhelm Dilthey. But what could be farther from traditional ontology or metaphysics than these theories, which have in large measure provided the methodological foundations for present-day social or human science? Had these authors, after all, not redefined such terms as "culture" (Windelband, Rickert) and "spirit" (Dilthey) as a means of critically refining them by separating them from the metaphysical presuppositions of the Hegelian philosophy of history? In spite of all the differences between these thinkers, were they not united, as Heidegger himself stressed in his early Freiburg lectures, in the pursuit of a "critique of historical reason,"[18] for which the historical contingency of consciousness—the rootedness of its grasp of truth in a singular historical and cultural perspective—precluded knowledge of an ultimate truth beyond the limits of any given perspective and capable of encompassing the ultimate metaphysical meaning of history as a totality? Was not the much touted relativism of the human sciences in general, and of modern historical methods in particular, a direct result of the abandonment of metaphysical claims to an ahistorical, absolute foundation for truth?

Heidegger, *Die Grundprobleme der Phänomenologie* (1927), *GA*, vol. 24, ed. Friedrich-Wilhelm von Herrmann (Frankfurt am Main: Klostermann, 1975), p. 241; Martin Heidegger, *Sein und Zeit*, *GA*, vol. 2, ed. Friedrich-Wilhelm von Herrmann (Frankfurt am Main: Klostermann, 1977), pp. 236, 501, 522.

18 Heidegger, *Ontologie (Hermeneutik der Faktizität)*, pp. 68–69.

The answer to these questions depends upon what one identifies as *traditional* in the history of metaphysics. For Heidegger the claim to have uncovered ultimate metaphysical knowledge of the world in itself constituted only one aspect of this tradition. Indeed, according to Heidegger's argument in *Being and Time*, this claim to ultimate knowledge of the world in itself is rooted in another, more significant characteristic of metaphysics: the presupposition of the temporal permanence and perdurability of Being that ultimate knowledge designates, which was originally introduced into the Western metaphysical tradition by the Platonic claim to eternity of ideas and the Aristotelian doctrine of the ongoing presence of substantial forms.

From the standpoint of *Being and Time*, this identification of Being with permanence and unperishing presence constitutes the fundamental presupposition of the Western metaphysical tradition, whatever its historical variations. This presupposition re-emerged in the predominant interpretations of Being that oriented the concept of truth in the ancient, medieval, and modern periods of Western intellectual history. And, in each period, this identification was founded on a tacit, unexamined omission: the question of Being, of what truly "is," overlooked, or set aside as insignificant for consideration, the temporal finitude of the questioner. It was this supposedly insignificant omission that Heidegger sought to take into consideration as fundamentally constitutive of the interpretation of Being and of truth throughout the Western intellectual tradition.

According to the renowned argument of *Being and Time*, the identification of permanence and continual presence with the very criteria of Being in Western intellectual traditions, far from constituting a merely theoretical hypothesis, derives from an all-pervasive though usually hidden quest rooted in *Dasein*'s (finite human) everyday being-in-the-world: *Dasein*'s quest to interpret its existence in terms of a semblance of perdurability and permanence as a tacit means of dissembling the finitude of its own being as being-toward-death. In a complex series of finely-constructed arguments which cannot be reproduced here, Heidegger supported the argument that the ultimate criteria of Being acknowledged by the predominant strands of the Western metaphysical tradition were theoretical expressions of *Dasein*'s everyday attempt to seek refuge from the finitude of its own mortal being.

A mountain of literature since the 1950s has widely popularized Heidegger's analyses of human finitude in relation to the Western intellectual heritage. But what of the line of argumentation which will enable us to interpret these analyses in light of Heidegger's deconstruction of the "spirit" and the historical consciousness present in contemporary cultural traditions?

Heidegger advanced this line of argumentation in his interpretation of world history (*Weltgeschichte*), and in this manner he placed his earlier critique of culture in a more comprehensive framework in *Being and Time*. In spite of modern insight into the historical character of human understanding, rooted in variations of historical viewpoint relative to evolving cultural perspectives, the idea of world history as a broad framework of cultural and spiritual continuity shared one essential presupposition with earlier metaphysical assumptions it had supposedly superseded: setting aside any consideration of human finitude in the elaboration of the criteria of truth, the modern idea of world history located the source of historical meaning in the continuity of processes of development. Like earlier metaphysical traditions, with their emphasis on the eternal and immutable character of truth, modern historical reflection had adopted continuity and perdurability as *the* criteria of truth *per se*. And, nowhere was the predominance of these criteria more evident than in the ideal of fixed scientific "objectivity" and "universal validity" posited by all the post-Hegelian philosophies of history. This ideal involved the identification of criteria capable of subsisting beyond the temporal finitude of singular, mortal beings, providing a permanent standard to encompass the resolute historicity of human existence. It signified to Heidegger nothing less than an unspoken attempt to overcome the finite perspective of temporal and historical existence through the comforting illusion of the fixed presence of the past in its uniform, "objective" accessibility. And precisely here the modern methodologies of the social and human sciences revealed their unacknowledged debt to an ancient way of positing the meaning of Being.[19] For Heidegger, the deconstruction of the ontological tradition was tantamount to unveiling the illusory character of this attempt in order to delve beyond the objective interrelation of cultural and world-historical processes and to reveal the finite temporality of *Dasein* as the primary source of historical truth.

In the decades following Heidegger's critique, and partly due to his influence, it has become a commonplace of intellectual life to posit the dissolution of the subject, spirit, or consciousness as a uniform structure underlying historical continuity; in light of the historical variability of the ground of experience, the idea of an essential historicity of interpretation

19 Heidegger, *Sein und Zeit*, pp. 512–533.

has become a standard presupposition in the hermeneutically oriented human sciences. At the same time, the human sciences have been faced since then with the problem of the relativism of truth, which the "crisis of historism" brought to the fore in the early twentieth century. Heidegger himself accounted for this crisis due to what he took to be the untenable position of the human sciences themselves in their belief that cultural processes and continuity in the development of the human spirit constitute, in the idiom of Dilthey, Burckhardt, or Meinecke, the generative matrix of historical meaning.[20] At the same time, the question of the implications of Heidegger's radical challenge to the criteria of truth such as "objectivity" or "universal validity" bequeathed by Western intellectual traditions and adopted by the contemporary social and human sciences has been set in a highly problematic light by his engagement in the domain of politics. This engagement raises the question concerning the relation between his critique of Western intellectual traditions and contemporary conceptions of truth in the human sciences and his willingness to succumb to the "temptation of Nazism" and the arbitrary ideology that oriented the Hitler regime.[21] Let us turn to this question which will permit us, in the third part of this chapter, to set in a more complete perspective our scrutiny of the legacy of his philosophical interpretation for the broad heritage of scientific rationality.

II
Heidegger in Political Perspective

An unavoidable question that arises in regard to Heidegger's thought and its legacy concerns his relation to National Socialism in the years after 1933. Scholars interested in Heidegger's work have long been aware of his engagement at the beginning of the Hitler period in the official capacity of

20 Ibid., p. 523; Heidegger, *Phänomenologie der Anschauung und des Ausdrucks*, *GA*, vol. 59, p. 154; Heidegger, *Ontologie (Hermeneutik der Faktizität)*, *GA*, vol. 63, p. 42. In his classic work, *Der Historismus und seine Probleme* (*Werke*, vol. 3 [Tübingen: Mohr, 1922], p. 4) Ernst Troeltsch referred to the contemporary crisis, not so much in the historical disciplines themselves as in "the general philosophical bases and elements of historical thought, in the conception of historical values in terms of which we think and construct the cohesion of history (*Zusammenhang der Geschichte*)." On the genesis of the crisis of historicism see the insightful analysis of Servanne Jollivet, *L'Historisme en question. Généalogie, débats et réception (1800–1930)* (Paris: Honoré Champion, 2013).

21 I adopt the concept of "Nazism as temptation" from the apt characterization by Fritz Stern; Fritz Stern, "Der Nazionalsozialismus als Versuchung," in Hans Jonas, Fritz Stern, *Reflexionen finsterer Zeit* (Tübingen: Mohr, 1984).

rector of Freiburg University, of his speeches in favor of the "departure" (*Aufbruch*) of 1933, and of his attempts to lend credibility to the Nazi ideology through the language of the fundamental ontology of *Being and Time*.[22] It would seem, however, that in 1934 Heidegger became convinced of the futility of efforts on the part of the universities to "guide the Führer" (*den Führer führen*), to employ Karl Jaspers's perceptive expression.[23] Nonetheless, this familiar account of Heidegger's complicity with the Nazi regime has been supplemented in recent years by revelations in Karl Löwith's posthumously published autobiography, as in works by Hugo Ott, Otto Pöggeler, and by numerous other authors, including the books of Victor Farias, and of Emmanuel Faye, which each sparked an uproar when it was published.[24] Above all, as noted above, the appearance in the *Gesamtausgabe* of a number of Heidegger's heretofore unpublished writings of the 1930s and 40s, the publication of correspondence with his colleagues, the work *Beiträge zur Philosophie* and the volumes of the *Schwarze Hefte* provide new insight into Heidegger's political attitude during the somber years of Nazi domination of Germany.[25] These sources,

---

22 See in this regard volume 16 of the *Gesamtausgabe* in which Heidegger's political speeches and other documents of the Nazi period have been reprinted: Martin Heidegger, *Reden und andere Zeugnisse eines Lebensweges, 1910–1976*, ed. Hermann Heidegger, *GA*, vol. 16 (Frankfurt am Main: Klostermann, 2000).

23 See Otto Pöggeler's review article on this topic, "Den Führer führen? Heidegger und kein Ende," *Philosophische Rundschau*, vol. 32, 1985, pp. 26–67, and more recently on Heidegger's political engagement, Reinhard Mehring, *Heideggers "Grosse Politik." Die semantische Revolution der Gesamtausgabe*, pp. 147–228.

24 Karl Löwith, *Mein Leben in Deutschland vor und nach 1933. Ein Bericht* (Stuttgart: Metzler, 1986); Hugo Ott, *Martin Heidegger. Unterwegs zu seiner Biographie* (Frankfurt/M: Campus, 1988); Otto Pöggeler, *Philosophie und Politik bei Heidegger* (Freiburg: Alber, 1972); Alexander Schwan, *Politische Philosophie im Denken Heideggers* (Wiesbaden: VS Verlag, 1989); Victor Farias, *Heidegger et le nazisme* (Paris: Verdier, 1992); Emmanuel Faye, *Heidegger, L'introduction du nazisme dans la philosophie. Autour des séminaires inédits de 1933–1935* (Paris: Albin Michel, 2005).

25 Among the many volumes that deal with the political implications of Heidegger's *Schwarze Hefte* see: Sophie-Jan Arrien and Christian Sommer, eds., *Heidegger aujourd'hui. Actualité et postérité de sa pensée de l'événement* (Paris: Hermann, 2021); Donatella Di Cesare, *Heidegger e gli ebrei. I "Quaderni neri"* (Torino: Bollati Boringhieri, 2014); Ingo Farin and Jeff Malpas, eds., *Reading Heidegger's Black Notebooks, 1931–1941* (Cambridge, MA: MIT Press, 2016); Hans-Helmuth Gander and Magnus Striet, eds., *Heideggers Weg in die Moderne: Eine Verortung der "Schwarzen Hefte"* (Frankfurt am Main: Klostermann, 2017); Marion Heinz and Sidonie Kellerer, eds., *Martin Heideggers "Schwarze Hefte." Eine philosophisch-politische Debatte* (Frankfurt am Main: Suhrkamp, 2016); Friedrich-Wilhelm von Herrmann and Francesco Alfieri, *Die Wahrheit über die Schwarzen Hefte* (Berlin: Duncker and Humblot, 2017); David Farrell Krell, *Ecstasy, Catastrophe. Heidegger from Being and Time to the Black Notebooks*; Eugenio Mazzarella, *Il mondo nell'abisso. Heidegger e i Quaderni neri* (Milan: Neri Pozza, 2018); Andrew J. Mitchell and Peter Trawny, eds.,

which will be discussed at length in the different chapters of the present book, attest to Heidegger's early partiality toward the Nazi ideology, which persisted in writings of the war years in spite of his political isolation and his disappointment regarding the direction the regime had taken.[26]

My purpose in this introductory chapter is not to investigate the shifts and turns in Heidegger's complex attitude toward the Nazi regime during the years before, during, and after World War II. I will focus, rather, on another question, which is more directly elicited by Heidegger's thought itself: what might Heidegger's philosophy from the period of *Being and Time* onward reveal in regard to his initial willingness to embrace the Nazi ideology? What aspect of Heidegger's thought might help us understand his affirmation of the politics of National Socialism and, even after his disappointment in its orientation, his ongoing partiality toward the Germanic ideology and his complicity with the Nazi war effort which, as I will examine more fully below, the *Black Notebooks* clearly reveal?

Since Heidegger's engagement in favor of Hitler in 1933, a variety of commentators have regarded the Freiburg philosopher's partiality toward Nazism as a direct consequence of the philosophy of *Being and Time*. Is it possible, however, to derive Heidegger's politics in 1933–34 from his philosophical affirmations in this publication of 1927 without grossly oversimplifying the reflection in this work? Might the complexity of his critique of culture, and of the aim to deconstruct Western metaphysical traditions promoted by it, be adequately accounted for in terms of the ideology of the revolutionary right?

If this were the case, it would seem impossible to comprehend the broad reception of Heidegger's thought among the German intelligentsia of the Weimar period. Many of the intellectuals who enthusiastically

Heidegger's *Black Notebooks: Responses to Anti-Semitism* (New York: Columbia University Press, 2017); Peter Trawny, *Heidegger und der Mythos der jüdischen Weltverschwörung* (Frankfurt am Main: Klostermann, 2015); Judith Werner, *Poesie der Vernichtung: Literatur und Dichtung in Martin Heideggers Schwarzen Heften* (Stuttgart: Metzler, 2018).

26 Heidegger summarized his attitude toward the Nazi regime in the period following his resignation from his functions as rector of the University of Freiburg in a revealing statement written in a letter he addressed to his friend and colleague Kurt Bauch on 9 August, 1935: "It seems to me that Ernst Jünger's vision is confirmed beyond or beneath what passes as a 'movement,' and is becoming ever more *petit bourgeois* (*kleinbürgerlich*) in character. This 'simplification' of existence (*Dasein*), which on the whole is yet manifestly something new, will be necessary, if our world is to prevail (*wenn unsere Welt gelingen soll*), which evidently is something entirely different than a spiritual addition—as spiritual, it must be fitted out in a completely different way than what today is passed around as a 'Weltanschauung'." See Martin Heidegger – Kurt Bauch, *Briefwechsel, 1932–1975*, ed. Almuth Heidegger (Freiburg im Breisgau: Alber, 2010), p. 22.

greeted *Being and Time* identified his cultural critique and deconstruction of Western intellectual traditions with anything but the ideology of the revolutionary right. For example, as paradoxical as this might seem in light of later events, in 1929 Heidegger's radical questioning won the approval of Jewish theologian and philosopher Franz Rosenzweig. In one of this author's last essays, written after Heidegger's Davos debate with Ernst Cassirer, Rosenzweig went so far as to relate Heidegger's investigations to the later writings of Hermann Cohen, and most notably to Cohen's doubts as to whether one might consider "the intellectual transport on the eternity of culture" as the ultimate purpose of the human individual.[27]

From a completely different vantage point, the young Herbert Marcuse, in a 1928 article entitled "Contributions toward a Phenomenology of Historical Materialism" ("Beiträge zu einer Phänomenologie des historischen Materialismus"), focused on the theme of the "destruction" of Western intellectual traditions. In this early article Marcuse attempted to reinterpret the Heideggerian notion of historicity in relation to Marx's historical materialism.[28] From a still different perspective, and a number of years later, Karl Löwith attempted to comprehend the significance of "destruction" in *Being and Time* for him and for other members of his generation. Underlining Heidegger's critique of permanence and uniformity as standards of evaluation of the past, Löwith referred to a "positive" meaning of destruction for his generation,

> "because the conviction lived in one's consciousness that nothing remaining could remain if it had not been fundamentally placed in question and renewed."[29]

If, as these examples suggest, *Being and Time* represented a good deal more than a simple prelude to a later political decision, how is that later decision to be understood in relation to Heidegger's philosophy? The broader perspective provided by the Freiburg and Marburg course lectures, published for the first time during the past decades in the *Gesamtausgabe*, enables us to reformulate this question in what I believe to be more adequate terms: might it be that Heidegger's *Seinsfrage* itself, in its insistence

27 Franz Rosenzweig, "Vertauschte Fronten," in *Zweistromland. Kleinere Schriften zu Glauben und Denken, Gesammelte Schriften,* vol. 3 (Dordrecht: Nijhoff, 1984), pp. 235–37.

28 Herbert Marcuse, "Beiträge zu einer Phänomenologie des historischen Materialismus" (1928), *Der deutsche Kunstlerroman. Frühe Aufsätze, Schriften*, vol. 1 (Frankfurt/M: Suhrkamp, 1978), pp. 347–384.

29 Karl Löwith, appendix to *Heidegger—Denker in dürftiger Zeit*, in *Sämtliche Schriften*, vol. 8, p. 294.

on the fundamental role of finitude for the constitution of human historical being, obscured possibilities of historical reflection which would have been capable of revealing a tacit relation between Heidegger's ontological mode of analysis and the historical situation of the times in which it emerged? Was it not precisely such a relation that became most glaringly evident during the period of Heidegger's adhesion to the Nazi movement? Moreover, in spite of Heidegger's claim to provide more fundamental insight into human historical being than could contemporary historical circumstances, did his ontological deconstruction of cultural traditions and of the ideal of their universal, world historical significance not lend itself to an all-too-timely breakdown in the traditional lines of resistance to the totalitarian solution to Germany's problems proposed by extremist movements like Nazism?

One of the continuous lines running between Heidegger's philosophy in *Being and Time* and his later political engagement in favor of National Socialism becomes visible, I believe, through a closer scrutiny of Heidegger's reflection on history and historical culture in the period between 1918 and 1934. Because of its proximity to political themes Heidegger later addressed, an examination of this reflection reveals the magnitude of the philosophical problem that his politics posed. For the purpose of this examination let us consider from a different vantage point Heidegger's critique of the nineteenth century philosophies of culture articulated in the 1919 lecture series "Phenomenology and Transcendental Philosophy of Values" ("Phänomenologie und Transzendentale Wertphilosophie"), to which I briefly referred in the previous section.

In this lecture series, as we have seen, the young Martin Heidegger dealt with the eighteenth- and nineteenth century sources of the "typical" philosophy of the nineteenth century, characterized according to him by Windelband's and Rickert's philosophy of values with its focus on historical culture. Heidegger's consideration of two eighteenth- and nineteenth-century sources of this "typical" philosophy is particularly revealing in regard to his later understanding of politics. Heidegger identified the first source as the historical thought of the Enlightenment. The Enlightenment, as he remarked, approached culture as a goal of development and thus "elaborated for the first time in basic clarity the idea of universal history." The Enlightenment's "universal ideal of thought" thus "extended its vision above and beyond the Nations."[30] The second source, represented by

30 Heidegger, "Phänomenologie und transzendentale Wertphilosophie," *Zur Bestimmung der Philosophie*, *GA*, vol. 55/56, p. 132.

Herder's thought, inaugurated a shift in emphasis in the historical consciousness of modernity by breaking with one-sided notions of continuity and development according to the "linear orientation toward progress" of the eighteenth century. Herder recognized "above all" the "autonomous intrinsic value of each nation and of each epoch."[31] This historical insight proved fruitful for the entire nineteenth century, not only for the historical thought of Friedrich Schlegel, Barthold Georg Niebuhr, Friedrich Karl von Savigny, and Friedrich Schleiermacher but also for the very different orientation proposed by Hegelian idealism, which encompassed the individuality of national cultures within a philosophical system. By mid-century, and in important measure in reaction against such speculative systems, Ranke's presupposition of the individuality of national cultures and of their place in the narrative of world history (*Mär der Weltgeschichte*), aimed to glean world history in its "genuine universal-historical cohesion (*in ihrem echten univeral-geschichtlichen Zusammenhang*)." This provided an "orientation for the future."[32]

In the decades following Hegel's death, Ranke's idea of the individuality of national cultures too multifarious to be comprehended within a uniform rational system but nonetheless assured of their ultimate significance in the inscrutable, providentially-sustained cohesion of world history, did indeed provide an orientation for future thought. Here we find, as Heidegger stipulated, a cardinal source of later ideas of universal cohesion of the historical process that, as we saw in the previous section, he traced in course lectures of the 1920s and then in *Being and Time* to one predominant quest: the quest for "timelessness in the historical, or beyond the historical, [...] in a developed, concrete culture."[33]

But was this quest for "timelessness in the historical" the only consideration involved in the postulation of a universal dimension beyond the particularity of national cultures, or did Heidegger's own philosophical method lead him to see matters exclusively in this way? A history of reflection among German thinkers since the Enlightenment, indeed, suggests another perspective in which this theme might be placed. From this perspective, the quest for the universal or world-historical significance of a

31 Ibid., p. 133.

32 Ibid., p. 135.

33 Heidegger, *Ontologie (Hermeneutik der Faktizität)*, *GA*, vol. 63, p. 42; Heidegger later repeated this same critique in *Logik: Die Frage nach der Wahrheit* (1925–26), *GA*, vol. 21, ed. Walter Biemel (Frankfurt am Main: Klostermann, 1976), pp. 91–92. In both instances Heidegger cited Eduard Spranger's article "Über Rickerts System," in *Logos*, vol. 12, 1923–24, p. 198.

national culture evokes the different, eminently political problem of identifying meaning in world history beyond the mere particularity of nations and their brute pursuit of power. It can hardly be a matter of indifference that Heidegger placed the political implications of this problem entirely beyond the purview of the *Seinsfrage* in *Being and Time* and of the deconstruction of cultural and intellectual traditions it engaged.

German intellectual history, above all since the Enlightenment, has been profoundly marked by a dichotomy between the particularity of national identity and universal or world historical ideals, signified by notions of the "world-spirit," the ideal of "Humanity," or of culture in its broadest sense, encompassing an acquisition for humanity as a whole. Heidegger was undoubtedly justified in the course lectures *Ontology (Hermeneutics of Facticity) [Ontologie (Hermeneutk der Faktizität)]*when, in relation to Kant's *Religion within the Limits of Religion Alone*, he traced the ideas of "Humanity" and of "personality" to theological sources.[34] The ideas of "culture and Humanity" in Herder's *Letters Toward the Advancement of Humanity* (*Briefe zu Beförderung der Humanität*) as of "Humanity," "Religion," and the historical "world-spirit" in Schleiermacher's *On Religion* (*Über die Religion*), give ample testimony to the theological inspiration that so often gave rise to the quest for a universal, supranational source of ideals. From a different standpoint than that of Kant's critical philosophy or, from still another perspective, of the neo-humanist approach in Wilhelm von Humboldt's *Ideas Concerning the Attempt to Determine the Limits of the Activity of the State* (*Ideen zu einem Versuch, die Gränzen der Wirksamkeit des Staates zu bestimmen*), these works shared their clear awareness of the contradiction between these ideals and unrestrained state power-politics, even where, as in the case of Schleiermacher, this ideal increasingly gave way to the new nationalist sentiment of the early nineteenth century.[35] If the later Schleiermacher could claim that the State was "culture raised to its highest potential," this is because he was convinced

34 Heidegger, *Ontologie (Hermeneutik der Faktizität)*, pp. 26–27.

35 Immanuel Kant, *Die Religion innerhalb der Grenzen der blossen Vernunft*, in *Die Metaphysik der Sitten*, *Werkausgabe*, vol. 8, ed. Wilhelm Weischedel (Frankfurt am Main, Suhrkamp, 1982), pp. 680–88, 770–777; Wilhelm von Humboldt, "Der Endzweck des Menschen," "Der Staat und das Wohl der Bürger," "Staat und Religion," *Ideen zu einem Versuch, die Gränzen der Wirksamkeit des Staates zu bestimmen*, *Werke*, vol. 1 (Stuttgart: Cotta, 1960), pp. 56–94, 110–130; J. G. Herder, *Briefe zu Beförderung der Humanität*, *Werke*, vol. 7, ed. Hans Dietrich Irmscher (Frankfurt am Main: Deutscher Klassiker Verlag, 1991), see especially letters 25 and 57; Friedrich Schleiermacher, *Ueber die Religion: Reden an die Gebildeten unter ihren Verächtern* (Hamburg: Meiner, 1958), see especially the fourth discourse.

of the "universal validity" (*Allgemeingültigkeit*) dwelling in the individuality of the state and—as he noted in his last period—of the ethical and supranational significance of cultural development.[36] If I must confine my examination of this theme to such examples, it should nonetheless also be noted that in a mid-nineteenth century conservative context, Leopold von Ranke shared Schleiermacher's enthusiasm for individual national principles whose universal significance could not be reduced to rational formulas. Ranke nonetheless evinced a sharp sensitivity to the danger to universal ideals represented by the more recent drive to national sovereignty. In his lectures "On the Epochs of Modern History," ("Ueber die Epochen der neueren Geschichte," 1854), Ranke called attention to the "destructive potential of the quest for national sovereignty." To his eyes this quest represented a danger to "culture und Christianity," which derived their significance from a more universal order.[37] With the conservative mentality of the Restoration period in mind, Friedrich Meinecke, in his work *Machiavellism: The Doctrine of Raison d'Etat and its Place in Modern History* (*Die Idee der Staatsräson in der neueren Geschichte*, 1924), identified a "Christian-universalist and ethical ideology in the nineteenth century, which consciously inhibited the drive for sheer power."[38]

In the case of each of the thinkers mentioned, the idea that particular states incarnate a universal historical significance—transcending any simple political categorization in terms of "liberal" or "conservative," or of "proto-liberal" and "proto-conservative"—may well have drawn inspiration from what Heidegger identified as the metaphysical quest for "timelessness in the historical." Be this as it may, the identification of an uninhibited drive for state power as a danger for universal ideals, in the very different perspectives from which that identification was made in the course of the late eighteenth and nineteenth centuries, was also motivated by ethico-political ideals that were not merely subordinate to this metaphysical presupposition.

In the decades following German unification, this ideal of universal significance beyond the particularity of the German national identity lost both its theological persuasiveness and its central place in scholarship in

---

36 Friedrich Schleiermacher, *Brouillon zur Ethik* (1805–06) (Hamburg: Meiner, 1981), p. 33; F. Schleiermacher, *Die Lehre vom Staat. Aus Schleiermachers handschriftlichem Nachlass*, *Sämtliche Werke*, vol. 8, 3 (Berlin: Reimer, 1845), pp. 154–57.

37 Leopold von Ranke, "Ueber die Epochen der neueren Geschichte," *Geschichte und Politik*, ed. H. Hofmann (Stuttgart: Kröner, 1940), p. 344.

38 Friedrich Meinecke, *Die Idee der Staatsräson in der neueren Geschichte*, *Werke*, vol. 1 (Munich: Oldenbourg, 1963), pp. 487–88.

the human sciences. This is not the place to trace the complex movement, extensively analyzed by Meinecke, from the cosmopolitanism of the late eighteenth century to the growth of German national consciousness. However, I may recall in passing an important sign of the political fragility of universalist ideals brought to light during the years prior to World War I in the work of Friedrich Naumann, whose attempt to find a "national and above all a social adjustment" (*zu einer nationalen und vor allem sozialen Einstellung zu finden*) Heidegger claimed he had in mind when he accepted the position of rector in 1933.[39]

In his influential work, *Central Europe* (*Mitteleuropa*, 1915) Naumann described the universalist or "international idea" as one which, over the course of centuries, had shifted from a religious and philosophical conviction to an ideal of economic internationalism, championed first in the guise of English free-trade and later, in a different form, through socialism.[40] In the context of Naumann's theory, the economic embodiment of this "international idea" clearly reflected its fragility in a period of increasing nationalism: its survival, as Naumann himself stipulated, depended upon the reconciliation of socialist internationalism with the requisites of nationalism in the context of the economic struggle for existence among forward-striving national cultures.[41] Far from advocating the demise of this ideal, however, Naumann, who shared many of the political goals of Max Weber, refused to glorify naked power for its own sake or to endorse anti-Semitism. All the more disingenuous, therefore, appears Heidegger's later claim to have sought a national and social "adjustment" (*Einstellung*) in 1933–34 similar to what Naumann had proposed![42] Clearly Heidegger was receptive to an extremist orientation that had little use for Naumann's theories, still anchored in the German strain of intellectual and political liberalism.

Nonetheless, the *philosophical* sources of Heidegger's radicalism, inspired by thinkers like Søren Kierkegaard, Friedrich Nietzsche, and Franz Overbeck, are hardly compatible with Heidegger's enthusiasm for a violently nationalistic movement like Nazism. It is true that Heidegger, as

39 Martin Heidegger, "Spiegel-Gespräch mit Martin Heidegger (23 September 1966)," *Reden und andere Zeugnisse eines Lebensweges*, *GA*, vol. 16, p. 655; Eng. trans: "'Only a God Can Save Us': The *Spiegel* Interview" (1966), trans. W. Richardson, *Heidegger: The Man and the Thinker*, ed. Thomas Sheehan (Chicago: Precedent, 1981), p. 48.

40 Friedrich Naumann, *Mitteleuropa* (Berlin: Reimer, 1915), pp. 165–173.

41 Ibid., p. 173.

42 Heidegger, "Spiegel-Gespräch mit Martin Heidegger," *GA*, vol. 16, p. 655; Eng. trans., p. 48.

early as 1923, tended to downplay the philosophical significance of what he took to be Kierkegaard's theological resolution of existential problems.[43] All the more attentively did he respond to the radical atheism of Nietzsche and to the Christian skepticism of Franz Overbeck and to their respective critiques of attempts to legitimate the quest for meaning in universal historical processes by means of the Christian faith. But Heidegger's attentiveness to the radicalism of the "two friends [...] Nietzsche and Overbeck"[44] underscores precisely what is most troubling in his thought: in spite of the profundity of his interpretation of the ideas of these two thinkers, Heidegger remained blind to the *untimely* concern that infused their respective works and that nourished their friendship. Living in an age of jingoist nationalism and of the first serious outbreak of anti-Semitism in the new German *Reich*, Nietzsche, after sounding the swan song of the Christian faith, held on all the more dearly to the universalist ideal which it had traditionally nurtured. After rebuking all forms of narrow cultural philistinism, Nietzsche held up the ideal of true *Kultur* in the broadest cosmopolitan sense, and noted the danger that the quest for state power represented to it. "Culture and the state are antagonists," he wrote, "[...] the one lives from the other, the one thrives at the expense of the other."[45] And Nietzsche prided himself with being a "good European," "beyond all merely locally or nationally determined perspectives."[46]

Overbeck, who wrote from a theologian's viewpoint while paradoxically questioning the meaningfulness of theology, interpreted the term *Kultur* in a more negative vein; anticipating the neo-orthodox theology of Karl Barth and of Heidegger's later Marburg associate, Rudolf Bultmann, he castigated modern attempts to subordinate Christian otherworldliness to merely cultural aims and to derive the meaning of the Christian faith from its world-historical role. All the more fervently did Overbeck seek to maintain the universalist outlook of what he took to be a more original Christian religiosity. All the more resolutely did he reject any attempt to

43 For example, Heidegger, *Ontologie (Hermeneutik der Faktizität)*, *GA*, vol. 63, p. 42.

44 Martin Heidegger, "Phänomenologie und Theologie" (1927), *Wegmarken*, *GA*, vol. 9, pp. 45–46. In a letter dated 30 June, 1925, Heidegger wrote to Löwith: "There is a lot of vacuity and readiness for compromise behind the theologians, and as long as Overbeck is not 'refuted,' everything remains artificial and a way of escape." See Martin Heidegger – Karl Löwith, *Briefwechsel 1919–1973*, p. 125.

45 Friedrich Nietzsche, "Was den Deutschen abgeht," *Götzen-Dämmerung*, *Kritische Studienausgabe*, vol. 6, ed. Giorgio Colli and Mazzino Montinari (Berlin/New York: DTV/de Gruyter, 1988), p. 106.

46 Friedrich Nietzsche, *Ecce homo*, *Werke*, vol. 3, ed. Karl Schlechta (Frankfurt am Main: Ullstein, 1979), p. 519.

lend Christian respectability to a chauvinist orientation, including the hyper-nationalism and anti-Semitism of his comrade from his student days, Heinrich von Treitschke.[47]

Given these roots of Heidegger's philosophical radicalism and of his cultural critique, one can readily understand Karl Löwith's surprise in 1933 upon learning of the political activity of his former professor. In reaction to Heidegger's use of the terminology of *Being and Time* in a 1933 newspaper article to glorify Leo Schlageter, a man from Heidegger's own *Heimat* who had become a Nazi martyr, Löwith wrote:

> "In 1927, when Heidegger's *Being and Time* appeared, not one of us indeed would have arrived at the idea that the radical singularization through a death which is 'each time my own' might be restyled six years later in order to herald the glory of a National Socialist hero."[48]

It is not difficult to understand Löwith's surprise and dismay. Indeed, as Nazi ideologues like Ernst Krieck later noted when criticizing Heidegger, the topic of race or of other such merely "ontic" distinctions did not enter into the question of Being at the heart of *Being and Time*.[49] Moreover, if this ontological query aimed to uncover modes of *Dasein*'s temporal and historical being more fundamental than the ways in which humanity exists in the contexts of culture and of world-history, then nationalism and the power politics of the *Machtstaat* could no more enter into the field of ontological analysis than could considerations of race. In this regard Heidegger asked the following question in the course lectures presented in 1929–30, *Grundbegriffe der Metaphysik*:

> "Who then are we? How do we comprehend ourselves now, when we say 'us'? [...] This history of the spirit—is it only a German or Western and furthermore a European occurrence? Or, should we widen the circle within which we are standing?"[50]

---

47 On the topic of nationalism and culture Franz Overbeck wrote: "European Christianity is currently a miserable protective barrier against the dangers through which nationalism among the particular peoples, also among the Germans, threatens their culture." *Christentum und Kultur. Gedanken und Anmerkungen zur modernen Theologie*, ed. Carl Albrecht Bernoulli (Basel: Schwabe, 1919), p. 257.

48 Karl Löwith, "Der politische Horizont von Heideggers Existenzialontologie" (1940?), *Der Europäische Nihilismus: Betrachtungen zur geistigen Vorgeschichte des europäischen Krieges*, *Sämtliche Schriften*, vol. 2, *Weltgeschichte und Heilsgeschehen* (Stuttgart: Metzler, 1983), p. 523.

49 Ernst Krieck, "Germanischer Mythos und Heideggersche Philosophie," *Volk im Werden*, vol. 2, 1934, p. 247.

50 Martin Heidegger, *Die Grundbegriffe der Metaphysik. Welt – Endlichkeit – Einsamkeit* (1929–30), *GA* 29/30, ed. Friedrich-Wilhelm von Herrmann (Frankfurt am Main: Klostermann, 1983), p. 103.

At the conclusion of this section of the lecture, Heidegger, far from admonishing his students to become German nationalists, gave the following answer:

> "We must locate ourselves, so that we tie ourselves to our *Dasein* and that this *Dasein* becomes that alone which binds us."[51]

But precisely this response sets the full scope of the problem in relief. In the last analysis, what insight can one attain into human collectivities, whether small communities or nation-states, on the sole basis of the ontological analysis of singular *Dasein*? Certainly Heidegger provides lengthy descriptions of the inauthentic dimension of human collectivities bound together in the "they-self" (*Das Man*), or the inauthentic quest to displace the burden of finite existence. When it is a question, however, of designating the authentic collectivity, Heidegger proposes only the barest elaboration in terms of *Dasein*'s "generation" and "people" (*Volk*).[52] In this interpretation of the authentic collectivity, Heidegger avoided the objectifications of collective experience—culture, the public realm (*Öffentlichkeit*), humanity (*Humanität*), world history—which traditionally grounded the singular nation in a broader supranational community. The domains in which a supranational ideal had traditionally been envisioned gave way to this reconstitution of collective authenticity solely in terms of singular generations and particular peoples derived from the radically singular being of finite mortal *Dasein*.

But in what way does this specific problem posed by Heidegger's ontological analysis of history in *Being and Time* relate to his later political decision? In what way might an interpretation of Heidegger's ontology of history in light of the historical situation in which it emerged clarify the relation between that ontology and his later political engagement?

It is tempting to respond to these questions by designating a direct relation between Heidegger's deconstruction of cultural and world history and the political subversion of such supranational ideals under Nazi rule. Indeed, in the 1920s authors of the pre-war generation like Ernst Troeltsch and Friedrich Meinecke had already expressed concern over both the political and cultural implications of contemporary doubt in the universal significance of cultural values and supranational ideals. In a 1922 lecture, entitled "Natural Right and Humanity in World Politics" ("Naturrecht und Humanität in der Weltpolitik"), presented at the Deutsche Hochschule für

51 Ibid., p. 116.
52 Heidegger, *Sein und Zeit*, pp. 382–387.

Politik shortly before his death, Troeltsch underlined the historical significance of supranational ideals of human rights, and hoped for a "return to universal-historical thought and life-sentiment" (*Rückkehr zu universalgeschichtlichen Denken und Lebensgefühl*).[53]

Nonetheless, Heidegger's philosophical critique of liberal intellectuals like Troeltsch for their emphasis on universal processes as the ultimate source of meaning in history by no means accounts for the Freiburg author's later partiality toward Nazism. Indeed, a considerable number of German intellectuals who, on the basis of traditional humanist values, did not share Heidegger's philosophical radicalism were willing to collaborate with the Nazis.[54] But if we are hardly warranted in reducing to an ideological program Heidegger's deconstruction of the cultural and world historical domains in which a supranational ideal had traditionally been envisioned, this does not mean that his later political decision bears no relation to his earlier philosophy. Heidegger's own pronouncements in 1933 make this eminently clear.

In the speech he gave upon assuming the functions of rector of the University of Freiburg on May 27th 1933, titled "The Self-Assertion of the German University" ("Die Selbstbehauptung der deutschen Universität") Heidegger raised the same question concerning the identity of his hearers that, as we have seen, he examined in 1929. He asked: "Do we know then who we are?" In the course of his speech his audience learned that the singular *Dasein* to which he referred was now framed in terms of the "necessities and torments" of the "folkish-state *Dasein*" (*volklich-staatliches Dasein*), which "wills that the people should fulfill its historical mission."[55]

With this shift in analytic emphasis to "folkish-state" *Dasein*, Heidegger did not hesitate to reintroduce his earlier critique of culture. Here, however, in the hiatus left by the earlier deconstruction of the supranational sphere traditionally constituted by culture, humanity, or world history, there emerged a glorification of "earth- and bloodlike forces" that resonated with the ideology of power politics of the state. In Heidegger's words:

---

53 Ernst Troeltsch, "Naturrecht und Humanität in der Weltpolitik," *Deutscher Geist und Westeuropa. Gesammelte Kulturphilosophische Aufsätze und Reden*, ed. Hans Baron (Aalen: Scientia, 1966), pp. 22–24; Friedrich Meinecke, "Einige Gedanken über Liberalismus" (1927), *Politische Schriften und Reden, Werke*, vol. 2, ed. Georg Kotowski (Darmstadt: Toeche-Mittler, 1958), pp. 414–17.

54 Fritz Stern, "Der Nazionalsozialismus als Versuchung," pp. 3–59; Raymond Klibansky, "Das Sagbare hat seine Grenzen. 50 Jahre Reichspogrommnacht," *Unispiegel* (Universität Heidelberg), June, 1988, pp. 3–4.

55 Martin Heidegger, "Die Selbstbehauptung der deutschen Universität," *Reden und andere Zeugnisse eines Lebensweges, GA*, vol. 16, pp. 115–17.

> "And the spiritual world of a people is not the superstructure of a culture, as little as it is the armory for useable knowledge and values, but it is the power of the deepest preservation of its earth- and bloodlike forces (*erd- und bluthafte Kräfte*) as the power of the innermost arousal and the broadest trembling of its *Dasein*."[56]

During the semester following his resignation from the rectorship at Freiburg in 1934, Heidegger reflected more directly on the state as a political problem. He addressed this theme above all in a 1934–35 seminar on Hegel's *Philosophy of Right* which, on the basis of Heidegger's notes and student transcripts, has been published in the *Gesamtausgabe*.

In this seminar, in which the jurist Erik Wolf participated, Heidegger proposed a metaphysical interpretation of the political sphere in light of Hegel's *Philosophy of Right*. In one significant passage toward the end of this seminar, Heidegger provided insight into his own idea of the political through his critique of one of the most influential apologists of the Nazi regime, Carl Schmitt. In his work, *The Concept of the Political* (*Der Begriff des Politischen*, 1932), written before the Nazi era, Schmitt heralded the eclipse of the "liberal" universalist ideal. Against this ideal, Schmitt defined the fundamental political relationship as that opposing friend and foe, pitting against each other the vital interests of different groups. In this conflict, fundamental group convictions and the values they bring to expression are instrumentalized as ideological arms that are wielded in struggle. In light of this assumption, Schmitt sought to demystify the "ethical and humanitarian forms" of the ideal of humanity, which he portrayed as so many expressions of a hidden, underlying interest, constituting a particularly effective way of promoting economic imperialism.[57]

It is this conception of the political that Heidegger sharply contested in his seminar on Hegel's *Philosophy of Right*. In direct reference to Schmitt's *The Concept of the Political*, Heidegger criticized the notion that the essence of the political lies in the "friend-foe relationship" for its neglect of the more fundamental theme of the origins of our political heritage in the Greek polis. In reexamining this theme in relation to Hegel's reflection on the state, Heidegger affirmed Hegel's genuinely "metaphysical" retrieval of the political which, far from the tradition of individualistic "liberalism" and abstract, transcendental (*am Himmel hängende*) political theories, founded the idea of Right solely on the state's historical existence. It was precisely here, according to Heidegger, that Hegel proved to be the

56 Ibid., p. 112.

57 Carl Schmitt, *Der Begriff des Politischen* (Berlin: Duncker and Humblot, 1963), p. 55; English translation, *The Concept of the Political*, trans. Tracy Strong (Chicago: University of Chicago Press, 1996), p. 54.

genuine precursor of National Socialism. "It has been said," as Heidegger wrote, "that Hegel died in 1933; on the contrary, it is in 1933 that he began to live."[58]

Whatever his criticism of Carl Schmitt, Heidegger's interpretation of politics here, as in his rectoral address, resembles that of Schmitt by the absence of reflection on the supranational scope of the European heritage which in spheres such as religion, art, science, or politics could only wither under pressure from the hypernationalism of the Nazi ideology. However different they might have been from one another, their respective positions left little room for any idea of fundamental historical truth beyond the brute power politics of the particular state. If there was little room in Hegel's own system for reflection on the dangers represented by the drive to state power, this was because of the depth of Hegel's confidence—so typical of his period—that this power ultimately depended upon the state's capacity to embody universally valid ethico-political and religious principles. And it is precisely this dimension of Hegel's thought which was set aside by Heidegger, just as the problem of universal ideals was deflated in *Being and Time*. It was all the easier to neglect any question of danger in the uninhibited drive for state power—a neglect motivated in Heidegger's case, as in Schmitt's, not by ready confidence in the universal significance of national principles in their difference from the arbitrary decrees of power politics, but by a total eclipse of the problem posed by this difference *per se*.

It would indeed be possible to deny the relevance of Heidegger's interpretation of the state in 1933–34 to the earlier fundamental ontology of *Being and Time*. One might discount Heidegger's intentions in 1933, when he couched his support of the Hitler regime in the language of his philosophy, and treat his later political reading of *Being and Time* as merely one among many possible approaches to this work. If, as Heidegger believed, ontology is more fundamental than all merely ontic political and historical themes it underlies, such an interpretation might well marshal support from Heidegger's own statements.

And yet, can the ontological analysis of history in *Being and Time* be so readily disentangled from the historical situation in which it emerged and to which it in some measure responded? If there is no necessary reason to derive Heidegger's politics in 1933 from his philosophy in 1927, there

58 Martin Heidegger, "Hegel, Rechtsphilosophie, WS 34/35," Transcription Wilhelm Hallwachs, in *Seminare, Hegel – Schelling*, Appendix 2, *GA*, vol. 86, ed. Peter Trawny (Frankfurt am Main: Klostermann, 2011), p. 606; concerning Heidegger's seminar on Hegel's *Rechtsphilosophie*, see Peter Trawny, "Heidegger und das Politische: Zum "Rechtsphilosophien"-Seminar," in *Heidegger-Studies*, vol. 28, 2012, pp. 47–66.

are lines of relation between them which, I believe, may be placed in relief only in light of the historical context of Heidegger's thought. Only in that light is it possible to understand Heidegger's rejection of precisely those strong points of the German heritage which stood in direct contradiction to what the Nazi "revolution" represented.

In harmony with this interpretation, the clearest line of relation between the philosophy of *Being and Time* and Heidegger's politics in 1933–34 reveals itself in the following way: in the ready transfer of the impact of this philosophy from the critique of cultural values and of the "ideal of humanity," which is capable of laying claim to universal truth, to an undermining of traditional political values transcending the brute particular existence of the state. The facility of this transfer becomes comprehensible above all in relation to the eclipse of earlier concerns of German thought in the course of German intellectual history since the Enlightenment.

Although Heidegger maintained a certain critical distance from the Nazi ideology during the years following his resignation from his official function as rector of the University of Freiburg in 1934, I alluded earlier to the fact that publication over the last decades of his course lectures dating from the years of Nazi rule and, more recently, of the *Black Notebooks*, reveals a deeper affinity of his thought with the Germanic ideology favored by the Nazi regime and a greater complicity with the Nazi war effort than had previously been known. Indeed, the *Black Notebooks* bring to expression his conviction that "only the Germans can express Being in a novel and original way," since they alone have maintained the original determination bequeathed by the Greeks (*anfängliche Bestimmung des Griechentums*) and have retained an intimation of the historical (*Ahnung des Geschichtlichen entfaltet*).[59] In the depths of World War II, Heidegger retained his belief in the unique mission conferred upon the Germans, even if the Germans still lacked the courage to dominate "from out of the calm conferred by the supreme struggle in Being itself." Heidegger conceived of this struggle in wholly mythical terms, as that of the "preserved origin of the last god (*das der aufbewahrte Ursprung des letzten Gottes ist*)."[60]

59 Martin Heidegger, *Überlegungen II–VI (Schwarze Hefte 1931–1938)*, *GA* vol. 94, ed. Peter Trawny (Frankfurt am Main: Klostermann, 2014), §71, p. 27; letter to Kurt Bauch, 1 May 1942, in Martin Heidegger – Kurt Bauch, *Briefwechsel, 1932–1975*, ed. Almuth Heidegger (Freiburg im Breisgau: Alber, 2010), p. 78.

60 Martin Heidegger, *Überlegungen XII–XV (Schwarze Hefte, 1939–41)*, *GA*, vol. 96, ed. Peter Trawny (Frankfurt am Main: Klostermann, 2014), § 27, p. 48. On the mythological dimension of Heidegger's thought that came clearly to light in his *Beiträge zur Philosophie*, see the insightful analysis of Alexander Schwan, "Heideggers 'Beiträge zur

Heidegger's political outlook in this period of Nazi dictatorship was broadly consonant with its principles of political organization. In the *Black Notebooks*, Heidegger espoused nothing but contempt for the principles of popular sovereignty and democracy, and he favored dictatorial rule which he took to be more conducive to the accompanying of modernity to "the consummation of its supreme essence." This consummation heralded another beginning and the birth of a new intimation of the sacred.[61] I will save a more detailed analysis of the different aspects of Heidegger's political ideology during these dark times for the later chapters of this book and I will address the question at this point of the lasting significance of Heidegger's challenge to Western scientific rationality.

III

Heidegger and the Heritage of Western Scientific Rationality

In the opening paragraph of the *Collected Essays on the Sociology of Religion* (*Gesammelte Aufsätze zur Religionssoziologie*), Max Weber raised a question to which he responded in the body of that work, providing a noteworthy interpretation of the emergence of Western rationalism. Weber inquired how the criteria of rationalization, once they made their appearance in the particular historical context of classical antiquity, could lay claim over the course of centuries to universal validity characteristic of modern science. Weber wrote:

> "What concatenation of circumstances led to the emergence of cultural phenomena (*Kulturerscheinungen*) in the West, and only here, which nonetheless—as we at least like to think—assumed a developmental orientation of universal significance and validity?
>
> [...] Only in the West is there 'science' at the level of development which we today recognize as valid."[62]

Philosophie' und die Politik," in *Zeitschrift für philosophische Forschung*, vol. 43, 1989, pp. 593–617.

61 Martin Heidegger, *Überlegungen VII–XI (Schwarze Hefte, 1938–39)*, *GA*, vol. 95, ed. Peter Trawny (Frankfurt am Main: Klostermann, 2014), § 47, p. 404. The theme of the "other beginning" is also evoked in Heidegger's *Contributions to Philosophy. On the Event.* For an insightful discussion of this theme, see Hans Ruin, *Enigmatic Origins. Tracing the theme of Historicity through Heidegger's Works* (Stockholm: Almqvist and Wiksell International, 1994), pp. 247–273.

62 Max Weber, *Gesammelte Aufsätze zur Religionssoziologie*, vol. 1 (Tübingen: Mohr, 1947), p. 1.

In his response to this question in the *Religionssoziologie*, as in his writings on the theory of science, Max Weber expressed a salient presupposition which he shared with a number of the most prominent philosophers of his generation, whatever their differences in epistemological orientation might have been. Like Heinrich Rickert, Ernst Cassirer, and Edmund Husserl, Weber assumed that the validity of scientific truth reaches beyond the historical contingency that has marked its development, and thus beyond the accidental historical variation to which the elaboration of scientific method has been subject and the arbitrary paths this elaboration has occasionally pursued. Whether conceived in terms of the development of the "spirit" or of the Kantian and neo-Kantian "consciousness in general," continuity in the historical course of scientific rationality ultimately derived from the universal scope of the faculties of meaning-constitution underlying the cultural emergence of the West.

Heidegger directed his critique of the tradition of Western scientific rationality precisely at this idea that continuity in the development of rational approaches to truth presupposed their foundation in the universally valid meaning-constituting faculties of the subject. On what grounds did he articulate this critique? Following his resignation from the rectorship of the University of Freiburg in 1934 and the subsequent *Kehre* or shift in the orientation of the *Seinsfrage*, the critical thrust of his reflection was redirected. The significance of this later challenge to the tradition of scientific rationality comes into view above all in relation to Heidegger's altered perspective regarding the possibility of a new philosophical foundation for science on the basis of the ontology of *Being and Time*. Let us examine his earlier view of the philosophical foundations of science more closely and, in relation to that, his subsequent quest to set in relief what he took to be the limits of Western scientific rationality *per se*.

Heidegger's thoughts on rebuilding the philosophical foundation of the sciences came to light in the 1925 course lectures *Prolegomena to the History of the Concept of Time* (*Prolegomena zur Geschichte des Zeitbegriffs*).[63] The main points of this reflection on the sciences were subsequently included in the introduction to *Being and Time*. At the outset of this lecture series, Heidegger alluded to the widespread doubt (*Verzweifelung*) among the younger students concerning the meaningfulness of the sciences prompted by the discussion surrounding Max Weber's speech on this theme—a reference, apparently, to Weber's 1920 lecture in

63 Martin Heidegger, *Prolegomena zur Geschichte des Zeitbegriffs*, *GA*, vol. 20, ed. Petra Jaeger (Frankfurt am Main: Klostermann, 1979), pp. 1–10.

Munich, *Science as a Vocation*.[64] In the context of this discussion, Heidegger's call for a deconstruction of intellectual and cultural traditions in *Being and Time* brought into question the presupposition of continuity in the development of the sciences in harmony with general faculties of meaning-constitution underlying "consciousness" or the epistemological "subject." Once the foundation of scientific discovery was shifted to the finite temporal and historical being of *Dasein*, such a presupposition of continuity appeared to mask what Heidegger, in a complex chain of arguments, sought to establish: the fundamentally bothersome quality of the original and radically singular, which recalls to *Dasein* the finite singularity of its own being and leads to its everyday tendency to appropriate originality within the framework of the standard and the general. From this viewpoint, discovery is interpreted less in terms of a logic of scientific progress than as a recovery, in an ever unique historical dimension, of fundamental truths which have ever and again been obscured. "The history of mankind," as Heidegger wrote in the course lectures *The Fundamental Concepts of Metaphysics* (*Grundbegriffe der Metaphysik*, 1929–30), "is arranged in such a way as to take care that what has been seen anew is, in its own time, buried once again."[65] With the thought of the periodic recovery of fundamental truth and its projection to orient the unique outline of a possible future, Heidegger evoked in similar terms in *Being and Time* the theme of historical discontinuity which comes to expression in what he termed "crises" and "scientific revolutions."[66]

As a direct consequence of the critique of what he designated as traditional presuppositions of continuity in the epistemological elaboration of scientific method, Heidegger's notion of "crises" and of "scientific revolutions" aimed at a fundamental redefinition of the relation between philosophy and the ontic sciences. Since traditional philosophy of science assumed the universal validity of the logic of analysis underlying existing scientific practice, its task had been identified with a logical elucidation of contemporary scientific methodology, considered to be the cumulative result of an historical process of elaboration. Heidegger's deconstruction of the subject, and the wide margin of discontinuity involved in the "crises" and "scientific revolutions" it introduced, placed in question this assumption that existing scientific practice might provide the model for philo-

---

64 Ibid., p. 3.

65 Heidegger, *Die Grundbegriffe der Metaphysik*, *GA*, vol. 29/30, p. 378.

66 Heidegger, *Prolegomena zur Geschichte des Zeitbegriffs*, p. 4; *Sein und Zeit*, pp. 11–14; Eng. trans., pp. 28–31.

sophical investigation of the development of the logic of the sciences. By casting doubt on the continuity of scientific truth grounded in the uniform, meaning-constituting faculties of the subject, he undercut all assurance that scientific method had surmounted the merely contingent and accidental aspects of its historical development. From this perspective, the philosophy of science could only be misguided when, in typically neo-Kantian fashion, the methodologies elaborated in the historical development of the ontic sciences serve as the focus of its analysis, since this logic provides no guarantee that the sciences have set themselves on a primary route of discovery given the secondary paths into which they have traditionally strayed. The problem for philosophy becomes not simply one of describing the procedure of the existing sciences, but of anticipating their development in what Heidegger terms "the process of originary logic," which, according to him,

> "was brought to light by Plato and Aristotle—in any case within very narrow boundaries. Since then the concept of logic has reached an impasse and has no longer been understood."[67]

Given that Heidegger admits the fact of scientific discovery in spite of what he takes to be shortcomings in scientific logic, such a reference to the logic of Plato and Aristotle in the period of Einsteinian physics may seem surprising. Heidegger did not, however, advocate a revival of ancient scientific theories. Rather, he attempted in light of ancient ways of questioning to displace the focus of philosophical analysis from an investigation of the logic of accepted scientific practice to what he took to be more important role of the researcher's presuppositions in interpreting the fundamental concepts science deploys. Certainly the neo-Kantians had appreciated the theoretical importance of the researcher's presuppositions, rooted in the values of his or her culture—above all in the human sciences. The very purpose of Heinrich Rickert's theoretical reflection on the cultural disciplines had been to examine the possibility of eliminating arbitrary presuppositions introduced by the researcher's own cultural values in interpretations of a foreign or past culture. Heidegger's insistence that the primary source of presuppositions or "preconceptions" lay not in cultural values but in an ontology of finite existence led to a far more radical notion of the role of preconceptions in orienting the researcher's mode of "being in" and structuring the world. Only such an ontology might be capable of interpreting the precedence of these preconceptions which, in their

---

67 Heidegger, *Prolegomena zur Geschichte des Zeitbegriffs*, p. 5.

capacity to obscure as well as to reveal the meaning of available "data," resemble anything but universally valid logical standards underlying an advancing process of development. Indeed, rather than a process of development or of scientific progress, Heidegger was convinced that,

> "[…] Every science […] is historical not only in its progress and results, but just as much in the regressions in its mode of questioning. The regressions of a science are for the most part inconspicuous, yet they are more central than its progress."[68]

In his works of the late 1920s and early 1930s, Heidegger applied his claim concerning the central role of preconceptions in the logic of scientific discovery to contemporary practice in both the historical and natural disciplines. A closer consideration of the grounds of this claim will enable us to set in relief the broad significance of Heidegger's early philosophy of science and the terms of his subsequent shift in perspective.

Heidegger's considerations concerning the central role of preconceptions in orienting analysis in the human sciences were developed for the most part in *Being and Time*. As I have noted, he placed in question there the traditional idea of the meaningfulness of the human historical world derived from the universal validity of objective processes in the context of cultural or world history. In displacing the basis of analysis from the continuity of world history to the finite singularity of *Dasein*, Heidegger emphasized how the researcher's way of being orients a given approach to human existence through which it may either be made meaningful in light of future possibilities, or else obscured. In the scope of historical investigation, Heidegger emphasized the cardinal importance of the historian's way of temporal and historical being as a condition of the possibility of bringing to light meaning in the past which would otherwise remain hidden. If in *Being and Time* Heidegger credited Nietzsche with having expressed the essential with regard to the "use and abuse of history for life," there is indeed a striking parallel between Heidegger's historical reflection and Nietzsche's thoughts on the opacity of what is uniquely meaningful in the past to the typical standards of historical analysis.[69] Although Heidegger did not allude to this specific aspect of Nietzsche's reflection on the "use and abuse of history" until later lectures on Nietzsche's thought, it had nonetheless marked a decisive moment in historical reflection in Europe, directly anticipating Heidegger's displacement of the locus of historical meaning from objective, world-historical processes to the

68 Heidegger, *Die Grundbegriffe der Metaphysik*, p. 277.
69 Heidegger, *Sein und Zeit*, pp. 396–397.

preconceptions governing the mode of appropriation of the past. In this vein Nietzsche had written: "The saying of the past is always an oracular saying: only as architect of the future, only as knower of the present, will you understand it."[70]

Heidegger's course lectures of the late 1920s and early 1930s that have been published in the *Gesamtausgabe*, above all *The Fundamental Concepts of Metaphysics* (*Die Grundbegriffe der Metaphysik*), provide insight into Heidegger's reflection concerning the role of preconceptions in the logic of discovery of the natural sciences. A lengthy section of these course lectures deals, for example, with the theories of contemporary biology and zoology, which Heidegger considered in relation to the then-prominent orientations of Hans Driesch and of Jakob von Uexküll. Interpreting certain aspects of their theories, Heidegger argued against predominant nineteenth century work in these fields which to his mind had been misled by inappropriate preconceptions derived from mechanics and physics and—in the case of Darwinian biology—from principles of economics. Adapting insights from the biological research of von Uexküll in the perspective of his own concept of world (*Welt*) and of environment (*Umwelt*), Heidegger questioned Darwin's conception of self-preservation (*Selbsterhaltung*), which applied the same preconceptions to humans and other animals and assumed that in all cases biological adaptation took place in the framework of a uniform concept of "world." Following Uexküll, he argued for a differentiated concept of adaptation to the environment that posited a more radical distinction between the worlds of animal life and of human existence that to his mind Darwin's uniform conception of competition in the process of natural selection had obscured.[71]

In the somewhat later lecture series *What is a Thing?* (*Die Frage nach dem Ding*, 1935–36), Heidegger provided a penetrating philosophical analysis of the difference between Aristotelian and Newtonian physics. Through an examination of the ancient Greek notion of *tà mathémata*, Heidegger proposed to underscore what was unprecedented in the idea of

---

70 Friedrich Nietzsche, "Vom Nutzen und Nachteil der Historie für das Leben," second of the *Unzeitgemässe Betrachtungen*, in *Die Geburt der Tragödie, Unzeitgemässe Betrachtungen 1–4, Nachgelassene Schriften, 1870–73, Sämtliche Werke, Kritische Studien Ausgabe*, vol. 1, ed. Gigio Colli and Mazzino Montinari (Berlin/New York: DTV/de Gruyter, 1988), p. 294. For a more detailed analysis of this point see my article "Ueber den geschichtlichen Ort der Wahrheit. Hermeneutische Perspektiven bei Wilhelm Dilthey und Martin Heidegger," in *Martin Heidegger: Innen- und Aussenansichte*, ed. Peter Rohs, Siegfried Blasche, Wolfgang R. Köhler, Wolfgang Kuhlmann (Frankfurt/M: Suhrkamp, 1989), pp. 58–74.

71 Heidegger, *Die Grundbegriffe der Metaphysik*, pp. 377–385.

mathematics deployed by the modern experimental method. Here the Freiburg philosopher examined what he took to be the implicit preconceptions governing the scientist's way of envisaging and organizing reality to demonstrate that the development of science from Aristotle to Newton involved a transformation in the basic presuppositions concerning nature, which could not be adequately grasped when represented in terms of the progress from mere speculation to genuine science. If, indeed, modern mathematical methods made it possible to set sharply in relief certain areas of investigation that had previously remained obscure, insistence that the emergence of these methods characterizes genuine science *per se* tends to ignore the fact that the most fundamental problems concerning the nature of space, time, force, or matter remain very much unresolved. Such insistence has tended to neglect investigation of the limits of the claim to truth advanced by the modern mathematical conception of science in areas where it overlooks the source of "fundamental representations" (*Grundvorstellungen*) that have oriented this claim less in relation to a methodological ideal than to the criteria of economic and technological success.[72]

In his writings of the 1920s and 1930s, Heidegger's aim to redefine the relation between philosophy and the ontic sciences was not limited to the examination of the role of preconceptions in orienting research. He simultaneously advanced a far bolder claim according to which fundamental ontology was to serve as the basis of a new unity of the empirical sciences. Again and again Heidegger stated his critique of what he considered to be the disunity—indeed the anarchy—in the methodological relation of the different disciplines, first in the 1929 lecture "What is Metaphysics?", then in the 1933 rectoral address, and in his *Introduction to Metaphysics* (*Einführung in die Metaphysik*, 1935), and finally in his later account of his aims in the early 1930s presented in the 1966 *Spiegel* interview.[73] To Heidegger's mind, this disunity represented nothing less than an eclipse of the essential purpose of science, which it was the task of a metaphysics of finite *Dasein* to redefine. In "What is Metaphysics?" Heidegger claimed that

72 Martin Heidegger, *Die Frage nach dem Ding. Zu Kants Lehre von den transzendentalen Grundsätzen* (1935–36), *GA*, vol. 41, ed. Petra Jaeger (Frankfurt am Main: Klostermann, 1984), pp. 94–95.

73 Martin Heidegger, "Was ist Metaphysik?", *Wegmarken*, *GA*, vol. 9, p. 121; Heidegger, "Die Selbstbehauptung der deutschen Universität," *GA*, vol. 16, p. pp. 111; Martin Heidegger, *Einführung in die Metaphysik* (1935), *GA*, vol. 40, ed. Petra Jaeger (Frankfurt am Main: Klostermann, 1983), p. 37; Heidegger, "Spiegel-Gespräch mit Martin Heidegger," *GA*, vol. 16, p. 654.

> "Only when science exists on the basis of metaphysics is it capable of continually renewing its task, and this not only in the sense of a collecting and ordering of its conceptions, but of the revealing of the entire area of truth of nature and of history, which always remains to be re-accomplished."[74]

In what specific way, however, might the analysis of *Dasein* serve as a foundation on which to unify the ontic disciplines? Notwithstanding Heidegger's suggestive remarks concerning crisis and revolution in the sciences, the broad implications of the *Seinsfrage* for the transformation that might bring about such unity remained exceedingly vague. Moreover, when it was explicitly oriented toward political propaganda in the 1930s, Heidegger's critique of the idea of scientific progress took on a particularly dubious character, which his claims to scientific seriousness can hardly dispel.[75]

Whatever the difficulties inherent in Heidegger's early philosophy of science, its impact is undeniable. His analysis of human finitude has been particularly fruitful in regard to the problem of interpretation in the human sciences. Among his contemporaries, the theology of Rudolf Bultmann, the literary criticism of Emil Staiger, the hermeneutics of Hans-Georg Gadamer, and the existential psychology of Rudolf Binswanger provided some of the most creative, and in each case independent expressions of Heidegger's influence. Furthermore, in a 1949 volume entitled *Heidegger's Influence on the Sciences* (*Heideggers Einfluss auf die Wissenschaften*), to which among others Staiger and Binswanger contributed, the physicist C.W. v Weizsäcker spoke of the pertinence for theoretical physics of Heidegger's critique in *Being and Time* of the traditional Cartesian notion of space.[76] The physicist Werner Heisenberg also maintained a lively interest in Heidegger's thought.[77]

The decade of the 1930s witnessed the shift or "Kehre" in Heidegger's formulation of the question of Being.[78] The significance of

---

74 Heidegger, "Was ist Metaphysik?", *Wegmarken*, *GA*, vol. 9, p. 121.

75 See for example the speeches pronounced by Heidegger in Heidelberg on 30 June, 1933, "Die Universität im neuen Reich," and in Freiburg on 15 and 16 August 1934, "Die deutsche Universität," Heidegger, *Reden und andere Zeugnisse eines Lebensweges*, *GA*, vol. 16, pp. 761–63, 285–307.

76 Carlos Astrada, ed., *Heideggers Einfluss auf die Wissenschaften. Aus Anlass seines sechsigsten Geburtstags* (Bern: Francke, 1949).

77 Werner Heisenberg, "Grundlegende Voraussetzungen in der Physik der Elementarteilchen," *Martin Heidegger zum siebzigsten Geburtstag* (Pfullingen: Neske, 1959), pp. 291–97.

78 Heidegger's thought is unified in all of its articulations through its focus on the *Seinsfrage*. Nonetheless, Karsten Harries seems to me to go too far when he concludes that there is "not really" a *Kehre* in Heidegger's thought. He identifies a basic continuity in

this shift, which coincided with Heidegger's growing disenchantment with the direction Nazi politics were taking, became gradually manifest in his work from the mid-1930s onward, most notably in books such as the *Beiträge zur Philosophie*, *Nietzsche*, *Vorträge und Aufsätze*, and then in *Holzwege*, *Der Satz vom Grund*, and *Identität und Differenz*. At the same time, a number of Heidegger's course lectures of the period between 1933 and 1945 have helped clarify the transformations in Heidegger's standpoint during these dark years, including *Grundfragen der Philosophie*, *Hölderlins Hymne "Andenken," Hölderlins Hymne "Der Ister," Parmenides*, and *Heraklit*.

Subsequent to the period of the "Kehre," Heidegger no longer referred to his way of posing the *Seinsfrage* as "fundamental ontology," for he abandoned the attempt to found a more original ontology on the basis proposed in *Being and Time*. Whereas in works following *Being and Time*, such as the course lectures *The Metaphysical Foundations of Logic from Leibniz Onward* (*Metaphysische Anfangsgründe der Logik im Ausgang von Leibniz*, 1928) and *Kant and the Problem of Metaphysics*, he referred to existential analytics as a "metaphysics" of finite *Dasein*, the shift in his perspective in the mid-1930s is signaled by a change in his use of the term "metaphysics": in works after this period he no longer referred to his orientation in terms of "metaphysics," but reserved this term exclusively to denote that aspect of the Western tradition which it was a question of overcoming.[79] With this abandonment of the attempt to found a finite

all of the periods of Heidegger's work and he sums up what he considers to be "the development [...] of an ever clearer awareness of the need for some transcendent logos to descend into the visible." Karsten Harries, *Art Matters. A Critical Commentary on Heidegger's "The Origin of the Work of Art"* (Berlin/New York: Springer, 2009), p. 191. I will leave aside the question concerning the appropriateness of the qualification of Being in any period of Heidegger's thought in terms of "some transcendent logos." From a very different perspective, I have argued in my book *Martin Heidegger and the Problem of Historical Meaning* that an understanding of the important change in his position in the 1930s, which occurred against the backdrop of a series of sharp criticisms that were directed against the ontological claim of *Being and Time* by both theologians and philosophers, is of primary importance for interpreting the dead end which that work faced and the genesis of his later position. On Heidegger's own interpretation of this reversal in his thinking, see Martin Heidegger, Preface, William J. Richardson, *Through Phenomenology to Thought* (New York: Fordham University Press, 2003), pp. viii–xxiii.

79 Martin Heidegger, *Metaphysische Anfangsgründe der Logik im Ausgang von Leibniz*, *GA*, vol. 26, ed. Klaus Held (Frankfurt am Main: Klostermann, 1978), p. 186; Heidegger, *Kant und das Problem der Metaphysik*, *GA*, vol. 3, pp. 233–34. On Heidegger's conception of a metaphysics of *Dasein* see François Jaran, *La métaphysique du Dasein: Heidegger et la possibilité de la métaphysique (1927–30)* (Bucharest: Zeta Books, 2010).

metaphysics, the locus of the *Seinsfrage* shifted from the temporal and historical being of *Dasein* in its singularity to what Heidegger came to qualify as the epochs of the history of Being (*Seinsgeschichte*), manifested in metamorphoses in language and in the ways of conceiving of truth since Greek antiquity.

At the same time, it was in terms of this shift that Heidegger presented his later challenge to the heritage of Western rationality and to the modern idea of science that had emerged within it: from Heidegger's later perspective this heritage and the modern scientific criteria of truth were excrescences of the metaphysical tradition that it was a question of overcoming. Heidegger related Western rationality to metaphysics in this way because he redefined metaphysics to encompass what he took to be the modern historical outcome of ancient forgetfulness of the limits of human reflection. This is the original metaphysical forgetfulness that Plato inaugurated with the presumption that Being can be adequately known on the basis of ideas of beings or entities (*die Seienden*) constituting human experience. In an elaborate series of analyses of the historical metamorphoses of truth and of the language which designates it, Heidegger portrayed the central *leitmotiv* that unifies the history of Being in the diversity of its epochs: the deepening forgetfulness of the opacity of Being beyond the limits of human cognitive capacities. What is most important in this assertion from our standpoint is that for Heidegger this forgetfulness is not overcome but, on the contrary, is only reinforced with the emergence of modern science and its renunciation of any claim to ultimate metaphysical knowledge. Forgetfulness of the limits of human representation—which is the obverse of forgetfulness of the opacity of Being beyond these limits—comes to its ultimate expression for Heidegger once the only acknowledged truth is that which can be revealed on the basis of psychological, sociological, historiographical, or other purely human modes of explanation. From this modern perspective, human representations give the only adequate account of reality. Every possible "explanation" which does not correspond to the human world-image (*Weltbild*) is *a priori* discounted.[80]

Considered from the vantage point of the human sciences themselves, this account of the modern outcome of the history of Being may seem to represent nothing more than a renunciation of rigorous standards

80 Martin Heidegger, "Platons Lehre von der Wahrheit," *Wegmarken*, *GA*, vol. 9, pp. 109–144; Martin Heidegger, *Nietzsche: Der europäische Nihilismus*, *GA*, vol. 48, ed. Petra Jaeger (Frankfurt am Main: Klostermann, 1986); Martin Heidegger, "Die Zeit des Weltbildes," *Holzwege*, *GA*, vol. 5, ed. Friedrich-Wilhelm von Herrmann (Frankfurt am Main: Klostermann,1977), pp. 69–104.

and a retreat into quasi-mysticism. Moreover, this view of Heidegger has only been reinforced by the rather obscure terminology he coined in his last years which (often in very approximate translation) has become the hallmark of many of the disciples his teachings have attracted.

Be this as it may, it is another matter to believe that we might simply dispense with the problem Heidegger again and again articulated concerning the historicity of our criteria of truth. This is the problem Heidegger identified in our inability adequately to represent the source of the historical metamorphoses of truth—truth in art, for example, or in faith, or in science itself—embodied in the continuous transformations in the language we employ to characterize ourselves and our world. It was Heidegger's constant task in later years to point out what he took to be the shortcomings of that attitude in the human sciences which holds that such truths are grasped only when reduced to a sociological, economic, or psychological context in a system of influences attributable to the acts of human consciousness and to the cultural and intellectual history supposedly fabricated by these acts. This indeed was the ultimate challenge that Heidegger raised to traditional ideas of the subject and of a cultural milieu as the medium of production of meaning serving as the constitutive source of the history it traverses. In his later attempt to designate the limits of the claim of Western rationality to surmount the particular circumstances of its historical emergence and to represent a universally valid acquisition, he now sought a more comprehensive indication of the possibility that to his mind this assumption of universality had set aside: that of an historical transformation of humanity, elicited by the metamorphoses of truth, so radical as to render essential dimensions of the past impermeable to the particular criteria of a present "cultural milieu." And, for Heidegger in later years, the deepest indication of such impermeability lay precisely in the criteria of scientific rationality themselves. By narrowing down the basis of explanation to what can be objectified in relation to psychological, sociological, or political causes, such criteria not only lose sight of the truths affirmed by a radically different past humanity, the essential meaning of which tacitly evades such modern forms of representation; more important still, they foster the illusion, fundamental to the fully developed technological procedure of rationalization, of being able to orient their own historical transformation—which, however, they are incapable of dominating or even adequately representing. The self-evidence of the criteria of rationality, far from confirming the universal scope of truth, gives testimony only to the persuasive force of this particular image of the world (*Weltbild*) in the period we call modernity.

In considerably different terms than those proposed by Heidegger, Max Weber's argument concerning the universal validity of modern scientific rationality also envisaged a critique of historical reductionism, above all that of Karl Marx, which derived past assertions of truth, qua ideology, from socio-economic processes. But Weber simultaneously sought to assure a certain measure of autonomy of consciousness, however limited, as a source of continuity and cohesion in the movement of a history which human beings could hardly hope to master. If, as Weber believed, fundamental historical transformation is in some measure based on conscious human acts, yet the purposefulness of these acts is neither given *a priori*, nor established as the result of a purely cumulative process, then an understanding of the truths that are affirmed in history depends on the reconstruction of the traditions in which such assertions emerged and the context to which they responded.

In positing the dependence of truth on a *Seinsgeschichte* beyond the purview of human acts as of all socio-economic processes, the later Heidegger, if often only indirectly, has perhaps nowhere been more profoundly influential than in his resolute opposition to the contextual methods of the human sciences. In proclaiming the death of nineteenth century models of "Ideen- und Geistesgeschichte" à la Weber, Burckhardt, or Dilthey, the later Heidegger displaced the center of analysis from ideas and concepts to the language of their embodiment. Far from the expression of the deep structures of a linguistic subject, or of humans as anthropological beings, language for Heidegger—expressing the metamorphoses elicited by the call of Being—constitutes the historical margins within which different kinds of experience become possible over time, engendering the historical ways in which humans experience themselves, and thus establishing *who* they are. In this manner, linguistic metamorphoses could denote something beyond the historical development of a *Volksgeist* in the sense of Herder or of Wilhelm von Humboldt, of a symbolic form anchored in the acts of consciousness in the sense of Cassirer, and beyond a simple empirical transformation of words to be compensated by the act of translation. In Heidegger's later perspective, language—"the house of Being" (*Das Haus des Seins*)[81]—tacitly emerges from the zone of fracture between past and present, marking the locus of discontinuity between historical epochs.

81 Heidegger, "Brief über den Humanismus," *Wegmarken*, *GA*, vol. 9, p. 145.

Whatever conclusions one might draw in regard to Heidegger's analysis, and to the aporias which it inevitably faces, it must be recognized that his affirmations concerning humanity and history ultimately rest on the basic assumptions he adopted. The task I have assigned myself in this volume lies in a laying bare for critical analysis of the implications of Heidegger's assumptions for both political theory and historical reflection.

Chapter 2

Heidegger and the Metaphysics of Memory

In this chapter I will focus on Heidegger's interpretation of the theme of memory as it developed from the period of his Freiburg lectures in the years after World War I up to *Being and Time* (1927) and his works of the late 1920s. During these years Heidegger's understanding of this theme shifted its focus and I will examine the differences in his approach to it that come to light in the 1921 Freiburg course lectures, "Augustine and neo-Platonism," in *Being and Time* (1927), and finally in the 1928 lectures, *The Metaphysical Foundations of Logic from Leibniz Onward* (*Metaphysische Anfangsgründe der Logik im Ausgang von Leibniz*) and in the book *Kant and the Problem of Metaphysics* (1929). The changes in Heidegger's manner of interpreting memory in these works, as I will argue, are of interest not only for the light they shed on the internal development Heidegger's thinking, but above all for the elucidation they permit of memory as a central facet of the metaphysical tradition he brought into question. In this elucidation, as I will illustrate, the deeper implications of Heidegger's deconstruction of Western metaphysics may be placed in relief.

If we compare Heidegger's course lecture "Augustine and neo-Platonism," which he presented during his first Freiburg period, with the later work *Being and Time*, it is remarkable that his early examination of the thought of St. Augustine concentrated on book ten of the *Confessions* that deals with memory, and not on book eleven concerning temporality, which was a central topic of Heidegger's own analyses in the years that followed. Moreover, in the context of *Being and Time* itself, when Heidegger interpreted the question of being in relation to the finite temporality of *Dasein*, he barely evoked the theme of memory he had examined in "Augustine and neo-Platonism" and in other early course lectures.[82] As the analysis of

82 As early as 1919–1920, in his Freiburg course lectures, *Grundprobleme der Phänomenologie*, Heidegger alluded to the philosophical importance of the theme of memory which he analyzed a year later in "Augustine and neo-Platonism." Heidegger wrote in this regard: "The fundamental character of factical life, which I find expressed in experience (*Erfahren*) itself, becomes more clearly visible when factical life (*das faktische Leben*) remembers itself. In remembrance (*Erinnerung*) the articulation of life (*Artikulation des Lebens*) and its relations lift themselves onto me and in this way the character of experience becomes visible (*sichtig*)." Martin Heidegger, *Grundprobleme der*

finite temporality became more prominent in *Being and Time*, the theme of memory, *Erinnerung*, receded into the background.[83] What is the significance of this apparent change in Heidegger's focus?

Let us begin our analysis by making some preliminary remarks about the idea of memory that St. Augustine elaborated in the *Confessions*. A cursory reading of book ten of the *Confessions* illustrates that this part of the work marks a significant break in its organization as a whole, since Augustine's autobiographical recollections in the earlier parts of the work lead here to the broader question he raises concerning the *meaning* of memory as such. To respond to this question, he does not interpret memory as a simple *capacity* of the soul. Far from considering *memoria* to be one faculty among others, Augustine identifies it with the soul itself. As he himself emphasizes at various points in the course of book ten:

> "But [...] the spirit is memory itself (*cum anima sit* etiam *ipsa memoria*)" or "it is memory that we call the spirit (*ipsam memoriam vocantes animum*)."[84]

Augustine's identification of memory with the soul itself indicates the *interiority* of memory, which radically distinguishes the soul from a world of sensuous things. As a large and infinite sanctuary (*penetrale amplum et infinitum*),[85] the soul is capable of rising from the images it retains of sensuous things to their intelligible ground, which is rooted exclusively in the soul and marks its independence from the material world. Here we recognize Platonic and neo-Platonic presuppositions concerning memory as *anamnēsis*, reminiscence as the ground of knowledge of true intelligible being which, as Heidegger stipulates, Augustine attempted to reconcile with motifs arising from early Christian religiosity. It is noteworthy that Augustine's identification of memory with the immaterial soul in light of his Christian orientation inspired his interpretation of its relation to the *temporal* realm. And, as I will illustrate, this examination of memory in book ten of the *Confessions* in relation to the soul's temporality, prior to Augustine's direct analysis of time in book eleven of this work, would prove to be of particular importance for Heidegger.

Phänomenologie (1919/20), *GA*, vol. 58, p. 252–253. An earlier version of this chapter was published in *Studia Phenomenologica*, 8 (2008), pp. 401–409.

83 During this early period of his work Heidegger made no terminological distinction between the two German words for memory *Erinnerung* and *Gedächtnis*.

84 St. Augustine, *Confessions*, vol. 2, X, § 14, translated by W. Watts (Cambridge, MA: Loeb Classical Library, Harvard University Press, 1988), p. 111–113 (translation modified).

85 *Ibid.*, § 8, pp. 98–99.

On the basis of his broad identification of memory with the soul itself, Augustine distinguished his inquiry from the tradition bequeathed by Aristotle and Cicero, which identified memory with the capacity to recognize experience of the past. According to this tradition, past experience retained by memory may then be related to present understanding and to deliberation concerning future action. Augustine's identification of memory with the soul marked a wholly different approach to its temporal being: through memory, for Augustine, the soul does not only extend backwards to become aware of past experience; rather, it becomes *present* to itself. If the past continues to exist in our recollection, memory at the same time configures the present: it assures the presence of images and of reflections flowing from the past which constitute the interior experience of the soul. Without memory, as Augustine insists, "I could not say anything [...] and I could not even name myself."[86] It is thus in drawing on the treasures of *memoria* that the soul encompasses all of the dimensions of time: from past experience it brings the present into being and anticipates the future.

At the heart of these reflections on memory in book ten, Augustine adumbrated the theme of temporality which he would fully elaborate in the following book of the *Confessions*, where he analyzed the synthetic power of the soul in terms of the *distentio animi* and of the bond that the soul forges between past, present, and future. I cite this key passage in book ten that Heidegger evoked in "Augustine and neo-Platonism":

> "All this do I within, in that huge court of my memory. For there have I in a readiness the heaven, the earth, the sea, and whatever I could perceive in them, besides those which I have forgotten. There also meet I with myself; I recall myself, what, where, or when I have done a thing; and how I was affected when I did it. There be all whatever I remember, either upon mine own experience, or on others' credit. Out of the same store do I myself combine fresh and fresh likelihoods of things, which I have experienced, or believed upon experience: and by these do I infer actions to come, events and hopes: and upon all these again do I meditate, as if they were now present."[87]

Given Heidegger's later reflection on the temporalizing modes of *Dasein* that bring together the ekstases of time, it is noteworthy that he did not dwell at this earlier point in his work on the specifically temporal dimensions of the relation of memory to past, present and future. His concern with Augustine's interpretation of the *temporality* of *memoria*, however,

86 *Ibid.*, § 16, pp. 118–119.

87 *Ibid.*, §8, pp. 96–99; Heidegger, "Augustinus und der Neuplatonismus," *Phänomenologie des religiösen Lebens*, *GA*, vol. 60, p. 187.

lies elsewhere, and must be understood in relation to the vastness of memory in its identification with the interiority of the spirit as self.

In an early section of his analysis in "Augustine and neo-Platonism" (§9), entitled "Astonishment about Memory" ("Das Staunen über die Memoria"), Heidegger evokes the vastness of memory in the Augustinian terms of a "large and infinite sanctuary" (*penetrale amplum et infinitum*). Heidegger notes here that the "treasures" of memory (*thesaurus memoriae*) stored up in this sanctuary, are not comparable to a wealth of "things" the soul possesses, since memory extends in its very infinity far beyond anything that the soul may grasp. If memory is the place where I encounter myself (*ibi et ipse mihi occurro*), this interior space is not indeed a "place," since its infinity is unbounded. The interior treasure of memory opens out to the infinite in rising beyond the confines of personal identity. Heidegger writes in this regard, echoing St. Augustine:

> "Penetrale amplum et infinitum. All of that is mine, but I am unable, myself, to grasp it. The spirit is too narrow to be able to belong to itself. Where might be what, in itself, the spirit is unable to grasp?"[88]

Here we discover the inability of the soul to encompass itself which, indeed, stands at the very heart of Augustine's reflection on memory. And this reflection inspires Heidegger's commentary in these lectures where he draws on early Christian motifs concerning the opacity of the soul, interpreted in terms of the "facticity of life" in which it faces different possibilities of approaching or of fleeing from itself. In this context we find Heidegger's examination of the three modes of *tentatio* through which life is distracted from itself: *concupiscentia carnis*, *concupiscentia occulorum*, *ambitio saeculi*, and also *molestia*, *Bedrängnis* or the feeling of oppression, which brings the facticity of life before the problem of the "I am." Heidegger here adumbrates the later analyses of facticity of *Dasein* in *Being and Time*, where he stipulates that *Dasein* is most often (*zunächst und zumeist*) not itself; in this later context Heidegger explicitly drew on Augustine's *concupiscentia oculorum* evoked in this early course lecture to characterize "curiosity" as an inauthentic mode of existence.[89]

---

88 Heidegger, "Augustinus," p. 182. "[…] 'penetrale amplum et infinitum'. All das gehört zu mir selbst, und ich fasse es nicht selbst. Um sich selbst zu haben, ist der Geist zu eng. Wo soll es sein, was der Geist an sich selbst nicht faßt?" Referring to St. Paul's famous sentence "For surely now we see through a glass darkly, not face to face as yet," Augustine wrote in book X, § 5, pp. 84–85, "yet is there something of man, that the very spirit of man that is in him, knoweth not."

89 Heidegger, *Sein und Zeit*, *GA*, vol. 2, p. 228.

Although Heidegger focuses extensively on Augustine's analyses of the opacity of self-understanding as the mark of life's radical facticity, he is also aware that Augustine's purpose is not to dwell on the facticity of life, but to envision the possibility of *overcoming* that facticity. Memory serves in this quest to guide us, by virtue of its very infinity, beyond the scope of the personal self to the presence within us, in our interiority, of eternal being. It is here, indeed, that we find the trace of the Platonic and neo-Platonic interpretation of memory as *anamnēsis*. For the possibility of surmounting the radical facticity of life depends on the soul's grasp, as memory, of the eternal "presence" of being in a temporal framework initially established by Greek antiquity. Heidegger aims to re-appropriate Augustine's legacy, while stripping it of Platonic and neo-Platonic metaphysical motifs which it had incorporated. And, at the heart of this metaphysical speculation lies Augustine's theory of *memoria* which opens out to eternal being.

In this early Freiburg course lecture, Heidegger does not hesitate to call for a "destruction" (*Destruktion*) of those aspects of Augustine's theology which mobilize ancient Greek speculative ideas in an attempt to resolve the radical problem of the facticity of the self. In a section of the lecture entitled "Toward the destruction of *Confessiones* X" ("Zur Destruktion von *Confessiones* X"), he writes:

> "*Memoria* is not radically conceived in existential terms of fulfillment, but in Greek terms, which in its content falls away [...] what itself is present there, [is] that truth is an unchanging 'asset', in terms of which it exteriorizes and systematizes itself [...]"[90]

When Heidegger later elaborated a clearer understanding of the concept of temporality that would be a central theme of *Being and Time*, he developed an explicit critique of Augustine's seminal idea of time examined in book eleven of the *Confessions*. However much Augustine's conception of the *distentio animi* as the synthetic power of the soul in its capacity to bring together past, present, and future might have anticipated Heidegger's own reflections on the temporal *ekstases* of *Dasein*, by which synthetic temporalizing modes of existence weld time into a unity, Heidegger nonetheless emphasized the distinction between his standpoint and that of Augustine. To the extent that the *distentio animi* presupposes the soul's presence to

90 Heidegger, "Augustinus," pp. 247–248. "Memoria nicht radikal existenziell vollzugshaft, sondern griechisch, gehaltlich abfallend [...] was da selbst vorhanden ist, daß Wahrheit unveränderlich 'Bestand' hat, wohin er sich dann wegwirft und einordnet."

itself, opening out to an infinite and eternal presence, Augustine's speculative concepts, from Heidegger's perspective, confined his analysis within the horizon of time as a succession of present moments: "nothing else but a stretching out in length."[91] This is why the sole reference in *Being and Time* to Augustine's reflection on time compares it to the theories of Aristotle and Hegel as examples of the theoretical approach to time as ordinary or "vulgar" time which, in reducing it to an infinitely extendable series in the framework of world-time, overlooks the finitude of *Dasein*'s temporal existence. According to Heidegger's well-known interpretation in *Being and Time*, this idea of time as an infinitely extendable presence neglects the authentic *temporal* priority as Heidegger interprets it: the priority not of the present but of the future, anticipating the futurity of Dasein's being-toward-death as the temporal horizon of authentic choice. It is thus in this perspective, and in essential accord with his critique of neo-Platonism in the earlier 1921 Freiburg lectures, that Heidegger interprets the traditional idea of eternity as presence which perdures. Although Augustine's *memoria* is no longer mentioned in this context, it is clear that in *Being and Time* the theological notion of eternity and of eternal truth, which the Augustinian *memoria* revealed in the interiority of the soul, must be radically deconstructed. As Heidegger writes in *Being and Time*:

> "The affirmation of 'eternal truths' as also the conflation of the phenomenally founded 'ideality' of *Dasein* with an idealized absolute subject belong to the age-old vestiges of Christian theology which have not been radically eliminated within the philosophical problematic."[92]

II

Although Heidegger explicitly enunciated his critique of the Augustinian theory of time in *Being and Time*, his preoccupation with the theme of memory, both in Augustine's thought and more generally, faded into the background. From the first sentence of this work we are reminded that Heidegger's primary ontological question concerns not "memory," but forgetting: "The so-called question [the question of Being] has today fallen

91 St. Augustine, *Confessions*, book XI, ch. XXVI, p. 268–269; Heidegger, *Sein und Zeit*, *GA*, vol. 2, pp. 563–64.

92 Heidegger, *Sein und Zeit*, *GA*, vol. 2, pp. 303–304; "Die Behauptung 'ewiger Wahrheiten,' ebenso wie die Vermengung der phänomenal gegründeten 'Idealität' des Daseins mit einem idealisierten absoluten Subjekt gehören zu den längst noch nicht radikal ausgetriebenen Resten von christlicher Theologie innerhalb der philosophischen Problematik."

into forgetfulness."[93] And, under the aegis of the *Seinsfrage*, of ontology, memory is subordinated to forgetfulness, to *Seinsvergessenheit*, as *Being and Time*'s immediate focus. Memory, indeed, can assume ontological significance only to the extent that it recalls what has fallen into forgetfulness. In one of the rare passages in which Heidegger evokes the topic of memory, *Erinnerung*, he subordinates it to forgetfulness in stipulating that "memory is possible only on the ground of forgetting and not the other way around."[94] Forgetting, according to Heidegger's interpretation, prefigures *Dasein*'s everyday existence in the world. Forgetfulness envelops the everyday preoccupations of *Dasein* through which it continually neglects the finite character of its existence as being-toward-death. It is thus on the ground of this ontological forgetfulness of finitude, which is characteristic of inauthentic existence, that Heidegger introduces his brief examination of memory in *Being and Time*. Here the rootedness of memory in the facticity of existence recapitulates the central theme of the 1921 Freiburg course lecture "Augustine and neo-Platonism."

In this context it is particularly significant that Heidegger's analysis of *Dasein*'s authentic mode of existence centers not on memory (*Erinnerung*), but on repetition (*Wiederholung*), which is designated as the authentic existential counterpart to forgetfulness.[95] The term *Wiederholung* might at a first glance seem to shift the theme of authentic retrieval from the Augustinian *memoria* to that of Kierkegaard's "repetition," in terms of which the Danish philosopher explicitly attempted to reformulate the traditional Greek theory of memory as "reminiscence." According to Kierkegaard's interpretation, whereas reminiscence in this sense recalls the past, repetition is oriented toward the future: "repetition is forward oriented remembrance."[96] At the same time, however, Kierkegaard related the temporal dimension of repetition to a "now" which, from Heidegger's perspective, remained within the horizon of world-time. As he stipulated in the 1927 course lectures, *Fundamental Problems of Phenomenology* (*Grundprobleme der Phänomenologie*), which were presented in the same year as the publication of *Being and Time*: "Kierkegaard [...] identifies the moment (*Augenblick*) with the now (*Jetzt*) according to the vulgar understanding of time. From this standpoint he constructs the paradoxical

93 *Ibid.*, p. 3; "Die genannte Frage ist heute in Vergessenheit gekommen [...]."
94 *Ibid.*, p. 449; "[...] die Erinnerung [ist] nur auf dem Grunde des Vergessens [möglich] und nicht umgekehrt."
95 *Ibid.*, p. 463.
96 Søren Kierkegaard, *Die Wiederholung, Die Krise*, *Werke*, vol. II, trans. L. Richter (Reinbeck bei Hamburg: Rowohlt, 1961), p. 7.

relation between now and eternity."[97] If repetition, *Wiederholung*, for Heidegger, is oriented toward the future, it is not in view of any eternal or infinitely extendable now, but of decision in light of *Dasein*'s finite being-toward-death. And it is this emphasis on the finite dimension of repetition which leads him to elaborate this concept in its essential distinction from both the Augustinian *memoria* and Kierkegaard's repetition. Heidegger was already aiming to reconstruct the metaphysical foundations of memory which became a primary focus of his work during the years immediately following the publication of *Being and Time*.

III

In *Being and Time* Heidegger described his philosophical project as "fundamental ontology," whereas he tended to reserve the term "metaphysics" to characterize the metaphysical tradition he sought to overcome. During the years following the publication of *Being and Time*, however, he sought to elaborate a new interpretation of metaphysics, in light of fundamental ontological analysis, which he depicted as a "metaphysics of finite *Dasein*."[98] At the same time, this reappropriation of the topic of metaphysics also coincided with a renewed concern for the phenomenon of memory. Most significantly, he refers in this context not only to memory as "Erinnerung," but as reminiscence or "Wiedererinnerung," which had traditionally been the German term chosen to translate the Platonic *anamnēsis*. "Wiedererinnerung" is the German word that Schleiermacher chose in his early nineteenth century translation of Plato's *Phaedon*.[99] And, following

97 Heidegger, *Grundprobleme der Phänomenologie* (1927), *GA*, vol. 24, p. 408; "Kierkegaard [...] identifiziert den Augenblick mit dem Jetzt der vulgär verstandenen Zeit. Von hier aus konstruiert er die paradoxen Verhältnisse des Jetzt zur Ewigkeit."

98 This point has been analyzed by François Jaran in his insightful book *La métaphysique du Dasein: Heidegger et la possibilité de la métaphysique* (1927–1930) (Bucharest: Zeta Books, 2010).

99 Plato, *Phaedon*, trans. F. Schleiermacher, *Werke in 8 Bänden*, vol. 3 (Darmstadt: Wissenschaftliche Buchgesellschaft, 1977). It is of particular interest to note that Schleiermacher did not uniformly translate *anamnēsis* with "Wiedererinnerung" but tended, for example in his translation of the *Meno*, to employ the word "Erinnerung." The passage in the *Phaedon* (72b) in which "Wiedererinnerung" appears refers to reminiscence as proof of meaning that preexists in us and thus supports the metaphysical argument concerning the immortality of the soul: "Und eben das auch, sprach Kebes einfallend, nach jenem Statz, o Sokrates, wenn er richtig ist, den du oft vorzutragen pflegtest, daß unser Lernen nichts anderes ist als Wiedererinnerung (*anamnēsis*), und daß wir deshalb notwendig in einer früheren Zeit gelernt haben müßten, wessen wir uns wiedererinnern, und daß dies unmöglich wäre, wenn unsere Seele nicht schon war, ehe sie in diese menschliche Gestalt kam; so daß auch hiernach die Seele etwas Unsterbliches sein muß [...]."

Schleiermacher, Hegel also employed this term "Wiedererinnerung" to translate the Greek *anamnēsis* in his *Lectures on the History of Philosophy*.[100] In harmony with the perspective of fundamental ontology elaborated in *Being and Time*, Heidegger, however, redefined the concept of "Wiedererinnerung" by stripping it of its essential trait for the Platonic and neo-Platonic tradition: its temporal reference to eternity. In so doing, he referred it directly to the finite temporality of *Dasein*. As he wrote in a particularly evocative passage of the 1928 course lecture, *The Metaphysical Foundations of Logic from Leibniz Onward* (*Metaphysische Anfangsgründe der Logik im Ausgang von Leibniz*):

> "In conceiving of Being, we grasp nothing new, but rather something that is fundamentally comprehended, that is, something the understanding of which involves our existence as we relate to what we term beings. This reminiscence (*Wiedererinnerung*) concerns being and hence reveals a primordial time-relatedness of being: it is conceived as always already there and yet always once again returning. This is not the vulgar remembrance of ontic occurrences, of beings, but it is *metaphysical remembrance* (*Erinnerung*), in which that primordial time-relatedness of being announces itself. It is in this metaphysical remembrance that humans (*der Mensch*) understand themselves in their authentic essence: as beings who understand being and who, on the ground of this understanding, relate to beings."[101]

This passage clarifies the interpretation of finite memory, anchored in the facticity of *Dasein*, which brings to full articulation the critical motif of his destruction of traditional expressions of the metaphysics of memory, particularly in their Platonic and neo-Platonic forms, while retrieving the

100 G. W. F. Hegel, *Vorlesungen über die Geschichte der Philosophie*, vol. 2, *Werke*, vol. 19 (Frankfurt am Main: Suhrkamp, 1971), p. 43. Hegel wrote in his depiction of Plato's philosophy: "Was wir zu lernen scheinen, ist nichts anderes als *Wiedererinnerung*. Und es ist ein Gegenstand auf den Platon oft zurückkommt; vorzüglich behandelt er diese Frage im *Menon*."

101 Heidegger, *Metaphysische Anfangsgründe der Logik im Ausgang von Leibniz* (1928), *GA*, vol. 26, p. 186; "Sein erfassend erfassen wir nichts Neues, sondern ein im Grunde Bekanntes, d.h. solches, in dessen Verstehen wir immer schon existieren, indem wir uns zu dem verhalten, was wir jetzt das Seiende nennen. Diese Wiedererinnerung betrifft das Sein und offenbart demnach eine ursprüngliche Zeitbezogenheit des Seins: immer schon da und doch immer nur im Wiederzurückkommen darauf erfaßt. Das ist nicht die vulgäre Erinnerung an ontisch Geschehenes, an Seiendes, sondern die *metaphysische Erinnerung*, in der sich jene ursprüngliche Zeitbezogenheit von Sein bekundet. In dieser metaphysische Erinnerung versteht sich der Mensch in seinem eigentlichen Wesen: als das Seiende, das Sein versteht und auf dem Grunde dieses Verstehens sich zu Seiendem verhält." See also in this context the description of "Wiedererinnerung" in relation to the finitude of *Dasein* at the end of *Kant und das Problem der Metaphysik.*, *GA*, vol. 3, p. 233. Here Heidegger stipulates that the "fundamental-ontological basic act of the metaphysics of Dasein as the foundation of metaphysics is a reminiscence." ("Der fundamentalontologische Grundakt der Metaphysik des Daseins als der Grundlegung der Metaphysik ist [...] eine 'Wiedererinnerung'").

theme of remembrance which in *Being and Time* had been overshadowed by the ontological motif of repetition.

To conclude this brief interpretation of Heidegger's reflection on memory, I will indicate what seems to me to be the problematic character of Heidegger's metaphysical concept of memory which he himself abandoned in the years following the reversal or *Kehre* in his thinking beginning in the mid-1930s. From my perspective, Heidegger's understanding of memory, in spite of the importance of his insight, unduly restricts it to the finite facticity of *Dasein*. Where the metaphysical tradition he brought into question evacuated the finite temporality of memory in favor of the temporal permanence of eternal being recalled by the Platonic *anamnēsis*, Heidegger focused exclusively on the opposite tendency: he oriented all authentic possibilities of remembrance in terms of the mortality of singular *Dasein*. Here Heidegger's reflection inverts the fundamental presupposition of the tradition to which he responds, as he substitutes radically singular contingency for unchanging eternal being as the metaphysical basis of remembrance. Yet, when we place in question the metaphysical foundations of the Platonic tradition, we must ask whether finitude understood in terms of the *mortality* of existence, raised to the status of a metaphysical principle, constitutes an adequate basis for understanding the essential expressions of finitude as such. As I interpret it, collective remembrance draws on communal expressions of finitude that are not simply derived from the singularity of being-toward-death, but arise from autonomous configurations of a shared memory, conveyed by symbols which, at their own level of contingent movement or "historicity," manifest a perdurability that neither participates in the eternity of metaphysical being nor is derivable from the finite memory of singular *Dasein*.[102] This topic however, which calls for deeper investigation of the articulations of communal finitude, takes us beyond the framework of Heidegger's mode of investigation.

---

102 See in this regard my interpretation of memory in *Collective Memory and the Historical Past* (Chicago and London: University of Chicago Press, 2016).

Chapter 3

Saint Paul, Spinoza, and the Ethical-political Implications of Heidegger's Thought

The exegesis of St. Paul's "Epistle to the Romans" I, 20 played a singular role in the theology of the Protestant Reformation inaugurated by Martin Luther. In the twentieth century, the young Martin Heidegger examined this verse in philosophical perspective and his interpretation provides a revealing indication of the broader orientation of his thought in the period leading up to and including *Being and Time* (1927). In "Romans," I, 20 Paul wrote:

> "[...] for since the creation of the world God's invisible qualities—His eternal power and divine nature—have been clearly seen, being understood from what has been made."

In this chapter, I will take this verse as a prism through which to examine Luther's interpretation of the epistles of Paul at an early stage of the Protestant Reformation and to set in relief by way of this examination the ethico-political implications of the young Martin Heidegger's twentieth century reception of this interpretation. Luther presented his exegesis of Paul's "Romans" I, 20 in the celebrated Heidelberg "Disputatio" of 1518, which Heidegger interpreted in his course lectures of 1920–21 at the University of Freiburg im Breisgau, entitled "Augustine and neo-Platonism" ("Augustinus und der Neuplatonismus").[103]

In what follows, my analysis will only be indirectly concerned with the question of the long reception of "Romans" I, 20 over the course of the history of religious ideas and philosophy; my principal aim will be to analyze Heidegger's interpretation of Luther's exegesis of Paul's verse as a

103 Martin Luther, "De Lege et Fide conclusiones xxviii cum resolutionibus (Heidelberger Disputation)," in *Werke. Kritische Gesamtausgabe* (Weimar: Böhlau, 1883), vol. 1, pp. 353–55; English translation, Martin Luther, "Theses for the Heidelberg Disputation, 1518" in *Martin Luther: Selections from his Writings*, ed. John Dillenberger, (New York: Anchor Books, 1962), pp. 500–03; Martin Heidegger, "Augustinus und der Neuplatonismus," in *Phänomenologie des religiösen Lebens*, *GA*, vol. 60; English translation, "Augustine and neo-Platonism," in *The Phenomenology of Religious Life*, trans. Matthias Fritsch and Jennifer Anna Gosetti-Ferencei (Bloomington and Indianapolis: Indiana University Press, 2004). On Heidegger's interpretation of Luther's theses in the "Heidelberg Disputatio" see the classic analysis of this theme in Otto Pöggeler, *Der Denkweg Martin Heideggers* (Pfullingen: Neske, 1990), pp. 36–45.

means of setting in relief what I take to be the philosophical significance of a number of the assumptions he drew from it and developed in the fundamental ontology of *Being and Time*.

In view of elaborating what I take to be the philosophical significance of Heidegger's interpretation of Luther's exegesis of Paul, I will contrast it with another possibility of interpretation of Paul's verse that radically contradicted Luther's understanding of it: Spinoza's commentary on "Romans" I, 20, presented in chapter four of his *Theological-Political Treatise* on the topic of divine law. Martin Heidegger, indeed, never explicitly referred to Spinoza's theological interpretation in the *Theological-Political Treatise*. If, nine years after the publication of *Being and Time*, in his course lectures on Schelling, Heidegger evoked Spinoza's philosophy in light of the reception of his geometrical method and ethics in the framework of eighteenth century Germany philosophy,[104] he never alluded to Spinoza's critique of the position represented by Lutheran orthodoxy, nor to the seminal influence of Spinoza's philosophy of religion on nineteenth century German liberal theology. Be this as it may, Heidegger, as I will have occasion to note in what follows, took the presuppositions of liberal Protestant theology of his period sharply to task in the course lectures "Augustine and neo-Platonism." In the framework of my analysis, I will draw on the theological presuppositions Spinoza mobilized in his analysis of "Romans" I, 20 to set in relief the implications of Heidegger's mode of philosophical analysis. I aim to illustrate that even if Heidegger accorded a more peripheral role to theological themes in the years after his early Freiburg lectures during the period of composition of *Being and Time* when he increasingly concentrated on ontological questions, the fundamental ontology elaborated in this work was nourished by presuppositions drawn from his earlier theological reflection. These presuppositions, as I will argue, appear in their clearest relief when they are elucidated in terms of interpretative possibilities that they radically exclude. In pursuing this method of analysis, my aim will be to set in critical perspective Heidegger's conception of the ontological level of analysis in *Being and Time* by exploring the implications of this conception which—in radical, if never explicitly analyzed, contradiction with the philosophy of Spinoza—deprives *ethics* of any fundamental role.

104 Martin Heidegger, *Schelling: Vom Wesen der menschlichen Freiheit, (1809) (1936)*, *GA*, vol. 42, ed. Ingrid Schüssler (Frankfurt am Main: Klostermann, 1988), pp. 56–60.

I

I will take as my starting point Luther's exegesis of Paul which Heidegger later examined in his course lectures of 1920–21, "Augustine and neo-Platonism." Luther presented this exegesis in the Heidelberg "Disputatio" of 1518, collected under the title "De lege et fide conclusiones XXVIII, cum resolutionibus," which contain forty conclusions, of which twenty-eight are on theological and twelve on philosophical themes. In his course lectures, Heidegger discussed the nineteenth, the twenty-first, and twenty-second of Luther's philosophical theses, and he alluded without commentary to the twentieth philosophical thesis. All of the theses relate to "Romans," I, 20:

> "[…] For since the creation of the world God's invisible qualities—His eternal power and divine nature—have been clearly seen, being understood from what has been made."

In his commentary, Heidegger cited Luther's theses as follows:

> 19) "The one who beholds what is invisible of God, through the perception of what is made, is not rightly called a theologian." ("Non ille theologus dicitur, qui invisibilia Dei per ea quae facta sunt, conspicit");
>
> 20) "Rather the one deserves to be called a theologian who grasps the visible and manifest things of God through the passion and the cross." ("Sed qui visibilia Dei, et posteriora per passionem et crucem conspecta intelligit");
>
> 21) "The theologian of glory calls evil good and good evil. A theologian of the cross calls the thing what it actually is." ("Theologus gloriae, dicit malum bonum, et bonum malum. Theologus crucis, dicit id quod res est");
>
> 22) "That wisdom which beholds the invisible things of God as perceived from works completely puffs up, blinds, and hardens man." ("Sapientia illa, quae invisibilia Dei ex operibus intellecta conspicit, omnino inflat, excaecat et indurat").[105]

Heidegger's interpretation of Luther highlighted the Reformer's critique of the traditional ways in which Christian theology had relied on Paul's verse to justify the employment of ancient Greek metaphysics to assert the possibility of grasping the super-sensuous order of divine truth. St. Augustine, as Heidegger emphasized in his lecture, relied in this way on Platonic and neo-Platonic conceptual structures in interpreting Paul's verse to

105 Martin Luther, "De lege et fide conclusiones XXVIII, cum resolutionibus" (Heidelberger Disputation), *Werke*, vol. 1, p. 354; Eng. trans. "Theses for the Heidelberg Disputation," p. 500–503, translation modified; Heidegger, "Augustinus und der Neuplatonismus," *Phänomenologie des religiösen Lebens*, *GA*, vol. 60, pp. 281–82.

confirm the possibility of a "(Platonic) rise from the sensuous to the supersensuous world."[106]

In an earlier lecture series in Freiburg, Heidegger also evoked Luther's opposition to the Aristotelian sources of Christian speculation about God, but in this brief commentary on the reception of Paul's verse, Heidegger did not mention the Aristotelian sources of the later Scholastic reception of Paul's verse which was the primary target of Luther's attack.[107] Under the influence of Aristotle's system, and his confidence in the metaphysical power of human reason to grasp the eternal order of ultimate truth, the Scholastics affirmed the possibility of attesting God's existence on the basis of natural reason without recourse to the doctrines of faith and revelation. To cite only one example, St. Thomas Aquinas's interpretation of "Romans" I, 20 well illustrates this position and also the significance of the critique that Luther directed against it in *De lege et fide conclusiones*. In a key passage of the *Summa contra gentiles*, St. Thomas cited the words of the Apostle "God's invisible qualities—his eternal power and divine nature—have been clearly seen, being understood from what has been made," in order to refute the opinion of those who assume that "God's existence is only known through faith and cannot be demonstrated" ("Deum esse sola fide tenetur, et demonstrari non potest"). Against this assumption, St. Thomas taught, on the basis of Aristotle's authority, the capacity of reason to reach beyond the natural sensuous world.[108] And it is precisely such a capacity, as we have seen, that Luther

---

106 Heidegger, "Augustinus und der Neuplatonismus," p. 281. As Heidegger realized (for example in "Augustinus und der Neuplatonismus," p. 281), the topic of Augustine's reception of neo-Platonism is complex. A closer look at his doctrine illustrates that aspects of his theology, where he insists on God's inscrutable will, are difficult to reconcile with neo-Platonic assertions of the certitude of metaphysical knowledge of supersensuous truth. Although in his discussion of Augustine, Heidegger did not mention Augustine's commentary on Paul's "Romans," I, 20, Augustine's interpretation in many ways anticipated Luther's doctrine. In referring to Paul's verse, "His 'invisible attributes' are now seen, 'being understood by the things that are made,'" he admonished that "we must rely more on the eyes of faith, whereby we believe, than on the eyes of the body, whereby we see the beauty of the material universe." Saint Augustine, *The City of God*, Books 17–22, trans. Gerald G. Walsh, S.J. and Daniel J. Honan, in *Writings of Saint Augustine*, vol. 8 (Washington, D.C.: The Catholic University of America Press, 2008), p. 504.

107 Martin Heidegger, "Einleitung in die Phänomenologie der Religion," *Phänomenologie des religiösen Lebens, GA*, vol. 60, p. 97.

108 St. Thomas Aquinas, *Summa contra gentiles. De veritate catholicae fidei*, I, 12 (Naples, Tipographia Virgiliana, 1846), p. 7; Eng. trans. *On the Truth of the Catholic Faith. Summa contra gentiles*, trans. Anton C. Pegis, Book I, ch. 12 (Garden City, NY: Douleday, 1955), pp. 83–85.

placed in question in the philosophical theses of the Heidelberg "Disputatio."

Since the invisible domain of the divine cannot be grasped through works in the created world, theology, as Heidegger interpreted it, cannot take its purpose to be the metaphysical contemplation of these works. His exegesis of "Romans" I, 20 retrieved Luther's seminal critique of ancient Greek metaphysical speculation that, over the centuries, had been imported into Christian dogma.

II

Although he did not directly mention the names of the principle theologians of the Protestant Reformation, Spinoza presented an interpretation of St. Paul in his *Theological-Political Treatise* that stood in radical contradiction to the theology of faith that had inspired it. In this work, Spinoza designated Paul as the apostle of a "universal religion" who, following Christ, played a particularly important theological role. Where the young Luther, on the basis of Paul's epistles, emphasized in *De lege et fide conclusiones* God's utter transcendence of the world, which could neither be comprehended by reason, nor influenced by good works, Spinoza invoked Paul against precisely this assertion. Where Luther in *De lege et fide conclusiones* qualified as the true theologian the one who beholds the invisible realm of God, not on the basis of created things, but only of the cross and the passion, Spinoza, at the end of chapter four of the *Theological-Political Treatise*, invoked "Romans" I, 20 in order to refute this thesis. He thus interpreted "Romans" I, 20 as follows (according to the version of the Epistle rendered by Tremellius from the Syriac text):

> "For from the foundations of the world, God's hidden things are visible in his creatures through the understanding, and his power and divinity, which are to eternity; so they are without escape. By this he indicates clearly enough that everyone, by the natural light, clearly understands God's power and eternal divinity, from which he can know and deduce what he ought to pursue and what he ought to flee. Hence he concludes that no one has any escape and none can be excused by their ignorance, as they certainly could be, if he were speaking of the supernatural light, and of the fleshly passion of Christ and his resurrection […]"[109]

In this way, Spinoza invoked no less an authority than the Apostle Paul to support his critique of religion founded on supernatural revelation. By

109 Benedict Spinoza, *Theological-Political Treatise*, ch. 4, in *Collected Works of Spinoza*, vol. 2, trans. Edwin Curley (Princeton and Oxford: Princeton University Press, 2016), p. 137.

assimilating God's eternal order to nature, and teaching that humans, in the limits of human intelligence, are capable of attaining a clear and distinct idea of this order,[110] the conception of universal Christianity that Spinoza taught clearly reached beyond the boundaries of traditional Christian doctrine, whether Protestant or Catholic. And Spinoza invoked the Apostle Paul once again in chapter four of the *Theological-Political Treatise* when he contested the privilege Christianity traditionally accorded to faith, while identifying the ultimate vocation of humanity with the knowledge of God, and piety with the fulfillment of virtuous works. Where Paul's declarations might seem to contradict Spinoza's teaching, such as "Romans" III, 28, according to which justification before God depends not on works or obedience to the law, but on faith alone, Spinoza simply replied that "faith" in such cases signifies nothing more than "full consent of the heart."[111] Since humans, like all natural creatures, express God's eternal power, faith cannot be separated from a human excellence which depends on "God's internal aid."[112] In this perspective, the vocation of human beings is to attain, through true knowledge accompanied by virtuous works, consciousness of the divine power working within them, which is the source of beatitude. In this manner Spinoza's ontology embraced at the same time a specific theological and ethical orientation.

Spinoza's teaching in the *Theological-Political Treatise* nonetheless raises an important question in regard to his method of interpreting the Bible. What, indeed, authorized Spinoza to interpret Paul's gospel in contravening its intrinsic supernaturalism, thus attributing to it a sense that hardly seems to correspond to what it explicitly stated? Fully cognizant of this difference between his interpretation and the explicit content of Paul's text, Spinoza appealed in chapter four of the *Theological-Political Treatise* to his well-known distinction between the transparent and the hidden aspects of the Bible, which he applied to the words of the Apostle. From this standpoint, Paul communicated a transparent message in "Romans" I, 20, in which he "clearly" evoked the human capacity, on the basis of reason alone, to grasp the true source of virtue and the way leading to salvation in the created world. Nonetheless, when Paul made use of supernatural images to convey this message, such as Christ's passion or divine grace, he deployed a veiled message, addressed to the multitude of believers who, since they were incapable of comprehending truth on the basis of rational

110 *Ibid.*, p. 128.
111 *Ibid.*, p. 134.
112 *Ibid.*, p. 137.

argument, could be convinced only by such images, constituting the sole manner of communicating to them the *ethical* significance of the sacred doctrine.

From the preface to the *Theological-Political Treatise* onward, Spinoza highlighted the importance of this devaluation of faith in the supernatural, including miracles and the mysteries they involve: since faith in divine supernatural intervention, or what Spinoza termed "God's external aid,"[113] can find no justification in the rational order of nature, the images which are employed to inspire faith in the miraculous cannot be explained by virtue of universally valid, rational principles. Therefore, such faith is all the more easily subjected to the will of a particular sect, which considers it to be its own privileged domain and degrades it to the level of a weapon that is wielded against any other particular sect it seeks to subject to its authority and control. Since supernatural faith is subject to no rational explanation and finds no necessary justification in terms of ethical works in the world, it all the more readily falls prey to superstition capable of hiding the arbitrary basis of its claims which, in Spinoza's words, "consists in nothing now but credulity and prejudices."[114]

III

Heidegger rarely evoked the name of Spinoza in his writings and, at first sight, this might seem surprising in view of his extensive analyses of the other great sources of modern metaphysics, Descartes and Leibniz. This absence is to my mind highly significant, and it is even more revealing than other omissions in Heidegger's voluminous analyses of modern philosophers, for example the paucity of his elucidations of the sources of modern empiricism, Locke and Hume. Much like Locke and Hume, whose respective orientations, according to Heidegger's rare references to them, were mere offshoots of Descartes's fundamental position,[115] Heidegger also challenged the originality of Spinoza in his works after *Being and Time*. This came to clear expression, for example, in Heidegger's course, *Schelling. The Essence of Human Freedom* presented in 1936. In this context, in which Heidegger examined Spinoza in the perspective of his

113 *Ibid.*, pp. 113–14, 137.

114 *Ibid.*, p. 70.

115 In the second volume of *Nietzsche*, Heidegger thus wrote that Locke and Hume, as Nietzsche recognized, were simply "coarsenings (*Vergröberungen*) of Descartes' fundamental position." Martin Heidegger, *Nietzsche*, *GA*, vol. 6, 2, ed. Brigitte Schillbach (Frankfurt am Main: Klostermann, 1997), p. 180.

reception in Germany in the late eighteenth and early nineteenth centuries, he considered Spinoza to be a nothing more than a reiteration of medieval scholasticism, "which he built into his system in a singularly uncritical manner," and extended farther on the basis of elements borrowed from Descartes and Giordano Bruno.[116]

The paucity of reflection in Heidegger's works on Spinoza's thought and, where brief reference to Spinoza is made, his tendency to denigrate the originality of Spinoza's philosophical contribution, expresses more to my mind than simple animosity toward Spinoza as a single philosopher. As I interpret it, it reflects a more general tendency of Heidegger's ontology that sheds light on the ethical-political implications of his thought. These implications, and the deeper incompatibility of his thought with Spinoza's ethical-political position, may be placed in clearer focus if we now consider a further ramification of his interpretation of St. Paul's epistles and of Luther's commentary on them which bears on the orientation of Heidegger's philosophical analysis in *Being and Time*.

I noted at the beginning of this chapter the inspiration that the young Heidegger found in Luther, notably in his exegesis of "Romans" I, 20, which served as a point of orientation for his early phenomenology at the beginning of the 1920s. In referring to Luther's criticism of ancient Greek metaphysics, Heidegger highlighted the futility of metaphysical speculation which, independently of faith alone, attempts to grasp the creator through a comprehension of created works. In his early courses at the University of Freiburg between 1919 and 1921, Heidegger's reference to Luther's critique was closely affiliated with a further motif, which Luther's theology had placed in a new perspective: the faith of the original Christian community (*Urchristentum*), inspired by St. Paul, which had animated Christianity before its adaptation, by means of metaphysics, to a cultural and dogmatic vocation. In this perspective, the emphasis on faith by the original Christian community involved the eschatological anticipation of the end of the world and the resolute negation of the worldly order. In his Freiburg course of 1919–20, *The Fundamental Problems of Phenomenology*, Heidegger described this eschatological "negation of the world" (*Weltverneinung*) in the following terms:

116 Martin Heidegger, *Schelling: Vom Wesen der menschlichen Freiheit (1809)*, *GA* vol. 42, ed. Ingrid Schüssler (Frankfurt am Main: Klostermann, 1988), p. 60.

> "What is found in the life of the original Christian community (*christliche Urgemeinde*) signified a radical transformation of the orientation of life, which is most often associated with the negation of the world (*Weltverneinung*)."[117]

Heidegger elaborated on this statement in his commentary on the eschatological tendency inaugurated by Paul's epistles in the context of original Christianity and its call for the negation of the world.[118] *Weltverneinung* in this sense was the earliest Christian expression of an affirmation of faith that underlines the ephemerality of a world awaiting the final judgment of Christ and emphasizes the futility of life that seeks to secure itself through works in this world.

Heidegger's interest in St. Paul and in the eschatological concerns of the first Christian community that inspired Luther brought him close to neo-orthodox or dialectical theology in this period just after World War I. Following his appointment to the University of Marburg in 1923, he engaged in collaboration with one of the main proponents of dialectic theology, the young Rudolf Bultmann.[119] When his lecture "Phenomenology and Theology," initially presented in Marburg in 1927, was published in later years, Heidegger dedicated it to Rudolf Bultmann, and evoked once again in the preface the faith of the original Christian community: "the negation of the world in the expectation of its end."[120]

Heidegger's affinity with dialectical theology was reinforced by the hostility he shared with Bultmann and his associates, fueled by both theological and philosophical considerations, toward the current of liberal theology that predominated among the Protestant orientations in the German universities up until World War I. Following Spinoza's endorsement of critical-historical methods that questioned the supernatural assumptions of faith, the eighteenth century Enlightenment, and the rise at the end of the nineteenth century of the empirical and scientific spirit in the German universities, liberal theology had attenuated the emphasis of Lutheran orthodoxy on the theology of faith; by the end of the nineteenth century the accent in Protestant theology had shifted toward studies of the history of Christian dogma (Adolf von Harnack), of the cultural contribution of

---

117 Heidegger, *Grundprobleme der Phänomenologie (1919–1920)*, *GA* 58, pp. 61–62.

118 Heidegger, "Einleitung in die Phänomenologie der Religion," *GA*, vol. 60, pp. 98–105.

119 In a letter he addressed to Karl Löwith on August 19, 1921, Heidegger indeed wrote: "It belongs to my facticity—stated briefly—that I am a Christian theologian"; Martin Heidegger, Karl Löwith, *Briefwechsel, 1919–1973*, p. 53.

120 Heidegger referred in this context to the renewal of interest in the original Christian community by Franz Overbeck who inspired the movement of dialectical theology of the 1920s; Martin Heidegger, *Phänomenologie und Theologie*, in *Wegmarken*, *GA*, vol. 9, pp. 45–46.

Christianity (Ernst Troeltsch), or of its influence on philosophy (Wilhelm Dilthey). Liberal theology thus focused on the role of Christianity in the world of historical culture.[121] This accommodation of theology to the concerns of the historical world came to light above all through the emphasis by liberal theologians on critical-historical methods of biblical interpretation, which had initially been developed by the secular sciences, and through their tendency to underscore the role of Christianity in promoting ethical and cultural values. It was here above all that liberal Protestant theology showed a clear affinity with the theological orientation inaugurated by Spinoza.[122] And, in view of Spinoza's rejection of all forms of supernaturalism in favor of a pantheistic identification of God with Nature, it is this affinity that the young Rudolf Bultmann placed in evidence in a critique of liberal theology he wrote in 1924, in which he accused liberal theology of "historical pantheism" analogous to a pantheism of nature.[123]

In the introduction to *Being and Time*, Heidegger alluded to the intense theological debate of his period and he evoked the quest among contemporary university disciplines to search for more adequate foundations for their research. He cited as an example of this quest the renewal of investigation among contemporary theologians of a more primordial understanding of the meaning of faith. In light of Luther's inspiration, this theological current had begun to understand that,

> "The 'foundation' upon which its system of dogma rests has not arisen from an inquiry in which faith is primary, and that conceptually this 'foundation' not only is inadequate for the problematic of theology, but conceals and distorts it."[124]

---

121 In his Freiburg course lectures in 1921, Heidegger singled out Adolf von Harnack, Ernst Troeltsch, and Wilhelm Dilthey for critique due to their respective interpretations of the role of St. Augustine in adapting Christianity to a cultural task in the historical world. See Martin Heidegger, "Augustinus und der Neuplatonismus," in *Phänomenologie des religiösen Lebens, GA*, vol. 60, pp. 159–64. I have dealt with this theme in greater detail in Jeffrey Andrew Barash, *Martin Heidegger and the Problem of Historical Meaning* (New York: Fordham University Press, 2003), pp. 132–156.

122 At the dawn of the nineteenth century, Schleiermacher's theology attested a new attitude of Protestantism toward Spinoza. In his discourses on religion, *Ueber die Religion: Reden an die Gebildeten unter ihren Verächtern*, Schleiermacher referred to the "repudiated, saintly Spinoza (*heiliger, verstossener Spinoza*)," p. 54. For Hans-Georg Gadamer, and justly so, "Spinoza and Moses Mendelssohn stood at the most advanced line of the spiritual debates that led up to the epoch of liberalism"; Hans-Georg Gadamer, "Philosophie und Religion des Judentums," *Gesammelte Werke*, vol. 4, *Neuere Philosophie 2, Probleme – Gestalten* (Tübingen: Mohr, 1987), p. 69.

123 Rudolf Bultmann, "Die liberale Theologie und die jüngste theologische Bewegung," in *Glauben und Verstehen*, vol. 1 (Tübingen: Mohr/Siebeck, 1966), pp. 5–6.

124 Heidegger, *Sein und Zeit, GA*, vol. 2, pp. 13–14; Eng. trans. p. 30.

This allusion to Luther's inspiration in *Being and Time* brings us back to the central questions that concern us in this chapter. What *philosophical* significance might be accorded to theological doctrine stemming from St. Paul and Luther, and reaffirmed by contemporary neo-orthodox theology, which emphasized the primary role of faith as opposed to a theology of works that underscored the cultural and ethical contribution of Christianity in the context of the historical world? And what does the *contrast* between the theology of faith that inspired Heidegger in Luther's exegesis of Paul and Spinoza's resolute emphasis on a theology of works indicate concerning the ethical-political implications of Heidegger's ontology in *Being and Time*?

Amid the many references to Paul, Luther, and Kierkegaard in *Being and Time*, the theological topic that bore a striking affinity to Heidegger's philosophical analyses lies in his conception of the "world," designated in terms of *Dasein*'s being-in-the-world. As Heidegger explained at different points in *Being and Time*, being-in-the-world does not signify a realm or region in which Dasein is found, but it designates an ontological structure that constitutes the being of Dasein. Whether Dasein exists inauthentically, concealing from itself the burden of its mortal finitude, or authentically, where it resolutely chooses its way of being in the face of its finite existence, in every case its existence presupposes being-in-the-*world*. At the same time, if the world for Heidegger designates the ontological structure of Dasein that its existence presupposes at all times, it is also *toward* the world that Dasein falls in its inauthentic flight from death. On one hand, Dasein's finite temporality universally underlies its way of being-in-the-world; on the other hand, the singular mark of its inauthentic temporality lies in its tendency to dissimulate its radical finitude by interpreting it in the guise of the perdurability of world time (*Weltzeit*) and of world history (*Weltgeschichte*), extending infinitely beyond its singular being-toward-death. The "world" in Heidegger's vocabulary assumes a double significance as the universal mode of being of Dasein that its existence always presupposes and, more particularly, as a mode by virtue of which its inauthentic tendency to fall into its everyday worldly preoccupations comes to the fore.

In the second part of *Being and Time*, Heidegger brought to expression a striking affinity between the earlier theological inspiration of his thought and his philosophical analysis when he addressed the topic of *Dasein*'s temporality. In this context, *Dasein*'s turn away from worldly preoccupations, engaging an authentic grasp of the singularity of its being-toward-death, holds out the possibility of the "nothing of the world" (*Nichts der Welt*). In the quest for authenticity conceived in terms of the "nothing of the world," the echo of the Christian world negation would seem to resonate most clearly in Heidegger's fundamental ontology.[125] And yet this affinity between Christian eschatological motifs and Heidegger's philosophy should by no means be overstated. He himself was careful to remind his readers of the essential difference between the ontic level of analysis engaged by theology, as by ethics or politics, and the finite ontology all ontic analysis presupposes.

Two years after the publication of *Being and Time*, Heidegger, in the lecture "On the Essence of Ground" ("Vom Wesen des Grundes," 1929), examined the concept of world in St. Paul and St. Augustine in a manner which directly evoked the parallel between the Christian sources and his own concept of "being-in-the-world." In this context, Heidegger alluded to the "new ontic understanding of existence that irrupted in Christianity," bringing forth a new conception of the world. For St. Paul, as Heidegger wrote, whose epistles exemplified this new conception,

> "World means not only and not primarily the state of the 'cosmic,' but the state and situation of *the human being*, the kind of stance he takes *toward* the cosmos, his esteem for things. *Kosmos* means being human in the manner of a way of thinking that has turned away from God."[126]

St. Augustine, as Heidegger continued, extended this Pauline conception of world in terms of the double meaning he accorded to it: first, in the neutral terms of the *ens creatum*, created being, and second, in the sense of *amare mundum*, the love of worldly things that is "equivalent to not knowing God."[127] Heidegger's own conception of authentic existence as *Dasein*'s turning away from the world to choose a way of being in light of its ownmost finite existence bears a striking affinity to the Christian turning away from the world, from the *amare mundum* which is the precondition for faith in the invisible realm of the deity. And yet in this context once again Heidegger underscored the essential difference between theological and ontological levels of investigation of the concept of world.[128]

125 *Ibid.*, pp. 367, 449–457; Eng. trans., pp. 320–21, 389–96.

126 Martin Heidegger, "Vom Wesen des Grundes," in *Wegmarken*, *GA*, vol. 9, p. 143; "On the Essence of Ground," trans. William McNeill, in *Pathmarks*, ed. William McNeill (Cambridge, UK: Cambridge University Press, 1998), p. 112.

127 *Ibid.*, pp. 144–45; Eng. trans. p. 113.

128 *Ibid*, pp. 143–44, 154; Eng. trans. pp. 112–13, 120.

Heidegger's manner of separating the "ontic" concerns of theology, ethics, and politics from what he took to be the fundamental level of ontological analysis is particularly significant in revealing the deep disparity that distinguishes fundamental ontology from the theological sources that initially inspired it. True to the separation of ontological from ontic levels of investigation, Heidegger's elucidation of *Dasein*'s inauthentic tendency to fall into the world (*verfallen*), adamantly avoided any contamination at this ontological level of interpretation by ontic considerations, and most specifically by judgments of a theological or an ethical-political order. In *Being and Time* this aim to avoid contamination of the fundamental level of ontology by ontic themes had particularly important implications, which are made abundantly clear, above all in the chapter on the "existential structure of the authentic potentiality for being" in relation to the ontological analysis of *conscience* (*Gewissen*). Far from proposing a theological or ethical interpretation of conscience guided by divine sanction, such as in St. Paul's "Epistle to the Romans" II, 14–16, the voice of conscience in the ontological sense recalls *Dasein* to its ownmost self, which is radically singularized (*vereinzelt*); this recall to its ownmost self brings *Dasein* before the possibility of its death, a death which at once "engenders no relations (*unbezüglich*) is not to be outstripped (*unüberholbar*), and is certain (*gewiss*)."[129] And it is through being-toward-death which "engenders no relations" that the voice of conscience, in its uncanniness (*Unheimlichkeit*), sets *Dasein* before the possibility of the "nothing of the world" (*nichts der Welt*).[130]

If this interpretation of *Dasein* might seem to indicate a subterranean trace of the theological tendency in *Being and Time*, for which the return to the self in light of the nothing of the world constitutes, if not an act of faith, at least a precondition for *Dasein*'s authentic existence, Heidegger's ontological position distinguished itself not only from the ethical intention of a theology of works, but explicitly severed all ties with the illumination of faith that stood at the heart of Paul's and Luther's inspiration. And yet, if Heidegger resolutely distinguished fundamental ontology from ontic concerns and accentuated the disparity of his philosophy from the theology of faith that initially inspired it, is his assumption that the touchstone of authenticity lies in the call of conscience that sets Dasein before the possibility of death which "creates no relations," and of the "nothing of the world," not from the outset charged with implications of an ethical-

129 *Sein und Zeit*, *GA*, vol. 2, p. 351; Eng. trans., p. 309.
130 *Ibid.*, pp. 366–67; Eng. trans., pp. 320–21.

political order? Here Heidegger's incomprehension of Spinoza's philosophy signals what is to my mind a profound blind spot characteristic of his thought more generally: his inability to discern that the claim to separate ethical-political considerations from ontology *itself* engages a decision of a specifically ethical order. Indeed, where ontological judgment arises from confrontation with the possible "nothing of the world," and the affairs of this world impose no limits on its reach, how is the danger of purely arbitrary basis of decision to be avoided? In such an ontological perspective, what is to prevent the possibility, so clearly identified by Spinoza, that "credulity and prejudice" penetrate to the heart of our fundamental beliefs, a possibility which only appears more likely once the constraints traditionally imposed by faith have disappeared?

Chapter 4

The Question of Race in Heidegger's Thought

The question concerning the relation of Heidegger's thought to the ideology of the Nazi regime has been a topic of intense debate ever since his engagement as rector of the University of Freiburg im Breisgau in 1933–34. Although this engagement was limited to a period of eight months, the publication in recent years of a large number of his course lectures dating from the Nazi period in Germany and of his *Black Notebooks* (*Schwarze Hefte*) clearly demonstrates that his complicity with the Nazi ideology extended well beyond the period of his official function.[131] In this chapter I will focus on Heidegger's relation to Nazism by setting in relief his interpretation of a central aspect of the Nazi ideology: the concept of race. The Nazis, as is well known, based their politics of domination and exclusion, and subsequently of extermination, on assumptions concerning the hierarchy of human races, postulating their innate superiority or inferiority both in terms of physical characteristics and intellectual and moral aptitudes. This hierarchy justified in their eyes a policy of racial selection and hygiene that aimed to inhibit the propagation of what they took to be inferior racial characteristics. What then was Heidegger's attitude toward this central aspect of the Nazi doctrine? What philosophical interpretation did he propose regarding the biological or racial status of human beings?

I

During the years after its creation in 1919, the Weimar Republic in Germany witnessed a marked radicalization of political life between the ideological positions of the extreme left and the extreme right. The organizations of the extreme right were characterized by pan-German ideologies that were already present before World War I which in large measure

131 Over the past decades there has been a marked tendency either to reduce Heidegger's thought to an ideological expression of Nazism or, on the contrary, to disregard the role of this ideology in its interpretation. In regard to the first tendency, see Victor Farias, *Heidegger et le nazisme* (Paris: Verdier, 1987) and more recently Emmanuel Faye, *L'Introduction du nazisme dans la philosophie. Autour des séminaires inédits de 1933–1935* (Paris: Albin Michel, 2005); regarding those who tend to minimize the relation between Heidegger's thought and his political engagement, see for example the preface of François Fédier to *Heidegger à plus forte raison* (Paris: Fayard, 2007), ed. François Fédier, as well as the accompanying chapters of this book.

promoted the doctrine of the superiority of the Arian race. This doctrine, which was already noticeable in the works of certain intellectuals during the decades prior to the war, became increasingly influential in the work undertaken in medicine and biology in a number of universities during the post-war years. A new focus on research themes elaborated in the ideological perspective of eugenics and racial hygiene emerged in large departments and research centers, most notably at the Universities of Munich, Berlin, or Freiburg im Breisgau, where Martin Heidegger studied and taught in the period following World War I, and where he was promoted to a full professorship in 1928.

We may best set in relief Heidegger's position in regard to the role of biology and of race for the determination of human beings, both before and after 1933, by recalling the outlines of the theory of the Arian or Nordic race that were influential in the intellectual movements of his times and in the scientific disciplines of his university. In the period between the two world wars, Freiburg was not only an important center of research that nourished the ideology of the superiority of the Arian race, but it was the place of origin of doctrines that configured the political mythology at the center of the Nazi *Weltanschauung*. Freiburg, indeed, was the town where the writer Ludwig Schemann resided, the translator into German and interpreter of the primary source of the ideology of Arian racial superiority, Arthur de Gobineau's *Essay on the Inequality of the Human Races* (*Essai sur l'inégalité des races humaines*, 1853, 1855, German translation, 1893–1902). In 1894 Schemann founded the Gobineau Society which popularized Gobineau's speculations in Germany, while adapting them to the ideology of the Arian or Nordic race.[132] In the area of scientific research during the final decades of the nineteenth century, the University of Freiburg became an important center of development and propagation for theories that applied the concepts of natural selection and survival of the fittest to the domain of human social organization which was adapted to the political mythology of Arian racial superiority. At the University of Freiburg,

132 Beside the speculations of Gobineau, Schemann based his ideology of the superiority of the Arian race on the doctrines of the French biologist Georges Vacher de Lapouge. The two men became close friends and Vacher de Lapouge, who joined the Gobineau Society, visited Schemann in Freiburg on numerous occasions. The speculations of Vacher de Lapouge furnished one of the principal sources of the notorious racial theories of the raciologist Hans F. K. Günther, who played an important role in the elaboration the Nazi racial ideology. On this topic see Benoît Massin, "L'anthropologie raciale comme fondement de la science politique. Vacher de Lapouge et l'échec de l''anthroposociologie' en France," in Claude Blanckaert, ed., *Les Politiques de l'anthropologie: discours et pratiques en France (1860–1940)* (Paris: L'Harmattan, 2003), p. 273.

the biologist August Weismann, director of the zoological institute, decisively modified the Darwinian theory of heredity in a way that had important consequences for the theory of racial degeneration at the basis of the call for eugenic selection. Where Darwin taught that biologically inherited characteristics are subject to accidental mutation, Weismann transformed this doctrine by postulating the transmission of a core of non-modifiable traits that he situated in what he termed germ-plasma (*Keimplasma*). According to this hypothesis, the germ-plasma that determines the long-term human biological makeup is in no way subject to influence by use, exercise, or external environmental factors, but maintains its continuity over the course of generations. Only interbreeding can bring about changes in the cellular combination and configuration of the germ-plasma, and it is here that the influence of these modifications on differences in group and individual variability determine human biological aptitude in the struggle for survival.[133] From this conclusion that variability is essentially dependent on interbreeding through transmission of germ-plasma over the course of generations, it was a small step to the ideas elaborated by Weismann's students according to which favorable or unfavorable interbreeding leads either to the biological improvement of inferior races, or to the degeneration of superior races. It is this hypothesis that led to the conclusion that measures of "social hygiene" had to be taken to safeguard the superior Nordic race.[134]

The germ-plasma hypothesis had a strong influence on the theoretical orientation of a young anatomist at the University of Freiburg, Eugen Fischer, whose ideas, while assuming the guise of scientific plausibility, provided perhaps more than any other contemporary theory the vehicle for race mythology.[135] Since the publication of the book of Victor Farias, *Heidegger and Nazism (Heidegger et le nazisme*, 1987), it is widely known that Martin Heidegger was not only the colleague of Eugen Fischer at Freiburg during the 1920s, but that the philosopher and the eugenicist maintained a personal

---

133 August Weismann, *Über die Vererbung. Ein Vortrag* (Jena: Gustav Fischer, 1883), p. 3–59; August Weismann, *Aufsätze über Vererbung und verwandte biologische Fragen* (Jena: Gustav Fischer, 1892), p. 639–672; August Weismann, "Germinal Selection," *The Evolution Theory*, vol. 2, trans. J. Arthur Thomson and Margaret R. Thomson (London: Edward Arnold, 1904), pp. 113–158.

134 Peter Weingart, Jürgen Kroll, and Kurt Bayertz, *Rasse, Blut und Gene. Geschichte der Eugenik und Rassenhygiene in Deutschland* (Frankfurt am Main: Suhrkamp, 1992), p. 81–88, 321–326; Benoît Massin, "Vacher de Lapouge et l'échec de l'anthroposociologie," in Claude Blanckaert, ed., *Les Politiques de l'anthropologie: discours et pratiques en France (1860–1940)*, pp. 309–311.

135 Concerning the influence of Weismann on the ideas of Eugen Fischer, see Peter Weingart, Jürgen Kroll, and Kurt Bayertz, *Rasse, Blut und Gene*, p. 192.

relationship, above all after 1933. They continued to remain in close contact well after the fall of the Nazi regime and the end of World War II.[136] Nonetheless, beyond the circumstance of their personal acquaintance, did the hypotheses of Eugen Fischer or, more generally, the political myth of Arian racial superiority have an impact on Heidegger's philosophy? Let us examine Fischer's orientation more closely in relation to that of Heidegger.

Prior to the outbreak of World War I, Eugen Fischer was known in Germany as a pioneer of racial eugenics. His research concerned racial intermixture and he elaborated a theory to account for what he took to be its danger. Fischer taught anatomy at the University of Freiburg beginning in 1900, where he was appointed to a position of professor after 1918. His first work was published in 1913 on the racial intermixture between white and black populations in South Africa. In it he concluded, on the basis of assumptions that were bereft of scientific foundation, that the offspring of such racial intermixing were both intellectually and morally superior to the black population, and inferior to the white population.[137] Fischer's conclusions were widely discussed in the fields of biological and medical research. During the period of the Weimar Republic, when in 1927 the social-democratic government decided to create an important institute for the study of biology and eugenics, the Kaiser-Wilhelm Institute for Anthropology, the Theory of Biological Legacy and Eugenics (Kaiser-Wilhelm-Institut für Anthropologie, menschliche Erblehre und Eugenik), Eugen Fischer was appointed to serve as its director. He promised at this time to pursue research on human races on a "purely scientific basis," "without political bias,"[138] yet his theories were animated throughout by extra-scientific value judgments, void of empirical basis, concerning the natural superiority of the white race in comparison to the black race.[139]

Eugen Fischer served as the mentor to a generation of raciologists, including the most notorious among them during the Nazi period, Hans F. K. Günther (referred to by his colleagues as "Rassen-Günther"). After 1933, during the period of the Nazi regime, his influence grew markedly and lent a scientific aura to the ideology of racial hygiene and the practice of sterilization.

---

136 Victor Farias, *Heidegger et le nazisme*, p. 79; see also in this regard Hugo Ott, *Martin Heidegger. Unterwegs zu seiner Biographie* (Frankfurt am Main: Campus, 1988), pp. 155f; 281f.

137 Eugen Fischer, *Die Rehobother Bastards und das Bastardierungsproblem beim Menschen: anthropologische und ethnographische Studien am Rehobother Bastardvolk in Deutsch-Südwest-Afrika* (Jena: Fischer, 1913), pp. 296–305.

138 Peter Weingart, Jürgen Kroll, and Kurt Bayertz, *Rasse, Blut und Gene*, pp. 239–246.

139 *Ibid.*

II

In his writings prior to Hitler's accession to power in Germany in 1933, Heidegger accorded a very limited role to biological considerations. His major work of this period, *Being and Time* (*Sein und Zeit*, 1927), concerns human finitude (*Dasein*) and the fundamental question that finite existence brings to the fore: "what does it mean to be?" Through the choice of a way of being, *Dasein* decides *who* it essentially is, independently of biological makeup and racial characteristics. At the beginning of *Being and Time* (§ 10), Heidegger specified that ontological analysis concerning the question of being must be carefully distinguished from all "ontic" investigations undertaken by the different scientific disciplines such as anthropology, psychology, and biology. At a later point in *Being and Time* (§ 57), in the passages where Heidegger related the question concerning "who" *Dasein* is to its finite temporal existence, he stated once again that ontological analysis must be carefully distinguished from biological factors.[140] The ontological question concerning "who" *Dasein* is admits indeed of a response only through the voice of conscience (*Stimme des Gewissens*), which brings each singular *Dasein* to face its finitude as being-toward-death. Any attempt to account for the phenomenon of conscience in terms of biological factors simply explains it away, since it posits conscience as a thing among other things at hand in the world. Conscience, however, far from being a worldly object, is called forth from its ontological foundation not as a thing in the world, but through *Dasein*'s grasp of nothingness: the possibility of its own non-being.[141]

In the years following the publication of *Being and Time* Heidegger pursued his investigation of the relation of biology to philosophical ontology in his course lectures at the University of Freiburg, *The Fundamental Concepts of Metaphysics. World, Finitude, Solitude* (*Die Grundbegriffe der Metaphysik. Welt, Endlichkeit, Einsamkeit*, 1929–30). It is noteworthy that Heidegger, in the sections of these lectures that aim to define biological organisms and delineate the specific difference between humans and animals, did not examine the theme of race (*Rasse*, *Geschlecht*, *Art*). Although he referred to different theories of the organism and mentioned the concept of biological heredity and adaptation, he did not enter into a

140 Martin Heidegger, *Sein und Zeit*, *GA*, vol. 2, p. 366; English trans. *Being and Time*, p. 320.

141 Martin Heidegger, *Sein und Zeit*, *GA*, vol. 2. p. 355–364; Eng. trans., pp. 311–319.

detailed discussion of the theory of Darwin, nor of the modifications made in this theory by biologists like Weismann or Fischer.

Heidegger's investigation of the concept of the biological organism in these lectures focused above all on theories of what he characterized as the leading contemporary biologists, Wilhelm Roux and Jacob Johann von Uexküll, who sought to define the organism by comparing it with the functional capacity of tools and mechanisms. Thus Wilhelm Roux identified the organism with a "complex of instruments" (*ein Komplex von Werkzeugen*) where, in a different perspective, Jacob Johann von Uexküll characterized the machine as an "imperfect organism" (*unvollkommener Organismus*).[142] Against the kind of comparison proposed by Roux and Uexküll, Heidegger sought to establish a radical distinction between the capacity of the organism and the "serviceability" (*Dienlichkeit*) of the instrument or machine. He referred to one of the principal aspects of the theory that Uexküll elaborated in his book, *The Environment and the Inner World of Animals*, (*Umwelt und Innenwelt der Thiere*, 1909, 1921). Heidegger acknowledged with Uexküll the central role of the environment (*Umwelt*) for the development of organisms and he agreed with Uexküll's critique of the Darwinian theory of adaptation due to what he took to be the English biologist's failure to adequately take into consideration the dynamic relation between the morphological development of animals and their environmental niche.[143] Precisely this consideration of the environing world, for Heidegger, permits us to complement Uexküll's biological insight through what he took to be a more fundamental concept of the environing "world." In this manner, Heidegger sought to apply the concept of *Dasein*'s being-in-the-world he developed in *Being and Time* to attain what he took to be a more radical demarcation between humans and other animals. In extrapolating from the existential analytic of *Being and Time*, Heidegger distinguished the environment of the organism and of the animal described by biology and zoology from finite human being-in-the-world. The animal, for Heidegger, which is limited to the patterns of behavior corresponding to a given environment, is "poor in world" (*Weltarm*). The environing world that provides the habitat for animal life is nothing but a place for the deployment of its capacities. By contrast, humans are "world-forming" (*weltbildend*), by virtue of their ability to

142 Martin Heidegger, *Die Grundbegriffe der Metaphysik. Welt, Endlichkeit, Einsamkeit*, *GA*, vol. 29–30, pp. 312–15; English trans. *The Fundamental Concepts of Metaphysics. World, Finitude, Solitude*, trans. William McNeill and Nicholas Walker (Bloomington and Indianapolis: Indiana University Press), pp. 213–15.

143 Heidegger, *Die Grundbegriffe*, p. 384; Eng. trans., pp. 263–64.

configure an image (*Bild*) of the world as a whole.[144] In the framework of his philosophical orientation Heidegger radicalized the distinction between humans and non-human animals and, without engaging in a detailed discussion of Darwin's biological theories, he challenged the Darwinian assumption that the concept of adaptation and of survival of the fittest might be uniformly applied to all natural organisms. In this perspective, the application of the same model of explanation to humans and other animals, as well as to natural organisms more generally, overlooks the unique and irreducible distinction between the way in which *Dasein* configures its world and the modes of relation of non-human animals and organisms to their natural environment.[145]

In regard to Heidegger's extrapolation from the philosophy of *Being and Time* to encompass biological themes, it is above all significant that he defended a concept of biological adaptation, in the wake of the theories of Jacob von Uexküll, that accorded an essential role to *environmental* factors for the determination of animal organisms. This orientation was generally incompatible with the ideology of the Arian race which tended to de-emphasize the role of the environment in favor of race as the principal determining factor for humans and non-human animals. Indeed the principal raciologists of the Nazi period in Germany explicitly rejected such forms of "environmentalism."[146] If Heidegger manifested little interest in the topic of race, his conception of fundamental ontology in its independence from biological factors, underlying his radical distinction of *Dasein*'s world-making from animal adaptation to an environment, clearly distinguished his philosophical position not only from the biologism of ideological currents that emphasized what they took to be the superiority of the

144 Heidegger, *Grundbegriffe*, pp. 284–396; Eng. trans., pp. 192–273.

145 Martin Heidegger, *Grundbegriffe*, pp. 402–03; Eng. trans., pp. 277–78.

146 Hence the Nazi raciologist Hans F. K. Günther rejected "theories of the environment which identify everywhere development, determination, dependence where [the turning-point of our period], in opposition to all of these negative intuitions, places in evidence the essence itself, the a-historical being of things." For Günther, this essence resides in the racial principle. See in this regard Hans F. K. Günther, *Rassenkunde des deutschen Volkes* (Munich: Lehmann, 1922, 1933), p. 3. Whatever divergences might have existed between Uexküll's theory and the hardline Nazi ideologues, Uexküll did not hesitate to express his confidence in Hitler's leadership capacities in the updated edition of his book *Staatsbiologie* (*Biology of the State*, first edition, 1920), published in 1933. Nonetheless, he at the same time clarified his theoretical position in this work on the subject of race in ways which clearly contradicted the Nazi doctrine. Hence, for example, he stressed the positive aspects of racial diversity in a state and contested the idea that such diversity might in itself lead to racial infirmity; see Jacob von Uexküll, *Staatsbiologie. Anatomie – Physiologie – Pathologie des Staates* (Hamburg: Hanseatische Verlagsanstalt, 1933), pp. 73–76.

Arian race, but also from apologists of this ideology in the scientific disciplines.

Whatever Heidegger's indifference to the topic of biological race, he did not refrain even before 1933 from expressing his negative appraisal of Jews, as witnessed in 1916 in a letter he sent to his wife Elfride in which he complained of a growing "Jewification (*Verjüdung*) of our culture and of our universities." During the years that followed, Heidegger repeated this assertion in other private letters and in evaluations for university commissions.[147] In regard to his political convictions in the years before Hitler's accession to power, Heidegger wrote in a letter addressed in 1932 to his colleague and friend from the period of their collaboration at the University of Marburg in the 1920s, Rudolf Bultmann, that he could only deny a rumor that was circulating according to which he had already joined the Nazi party. "I am not a member of this party," he wrote, "and I never will be, any more than I have been a member of any other party of whatever sort."[148] Nonetheless, Heidegger declared in this same letter written shortly before Hitler's accession to power in January, 1933 that he agreed with many points of the Nazi party platform, even if he had certain reservations concerning its "cultural" program.

III

After accepting the position of rector of the University of Freiburg, Heidegger joined the Nazi Party in May, 1933. He proceeded to insure the political conformity (*Gleichschaltung*) of the university in accord with the requirements of the Nazi regime. He did not hesitate in his official speeches and writings to adapt his philosophical terminology to the Nazi ideology. He quickly abandoned his completely isolated former mentor, Edmund Husserl, and he himself later qualified this act as "human failing" (*menschliches Versagen*).[149]

---

147 Heidegger, *"Mein liebes Seelchen!" Briefe Martin Heideggers an seine Frau Elfride, 1915–70*, ed. Gertrud Heidegger (Munich: Deutsche Verlagsanstalt, 2005), p. 51; see also in this regard, Karl Jaspers, *Notizen zu Heidegger* (Munich: Piper, 1978), p. 257 and Ulrich Sieg, "Die Verjüdung des deutschen Geistes," *Die Zeit*, 52, 22 December, 1989, p. 50, and Claudia Schorcht, *Philosophie an den bayerischen Universitäten, 1933–45* (Erlangen: Fischer, 1990), p. 161.

148 Martin Heidegger, letter to Rudolf Bultmann, 16 December, 1932, Rudolf Bultmann, Martin Heidegger, *Briefwechsel, 1925–1975*, ed. Andreas Grossmann and Christof Landmesser (Frankfurt am Main/Tübingen: Klostermann/Mohr Siebeck, 2009), p. 191.

149 Martin Heidegger, "Spiegel-Gespräch mit Martin Heidegger (23.09.1966)," *Reden und andere Zeugnisse eines Lebensweges: 1910–1976*, *GA*, vol. 16, p. 663.

In the spring of 1934 Heidegger resigned his rectorship and, although he took a certain distance from the ideological platform of the Nazi Party, his course lectures and writings in this period, as noted at the outset of this chapter, illustrate his complicity with the political orientation of the Nazi regime.[150] Heidegger's Freiburg course lectures reveal his enthusiastic reaction to Hitler's rise to power and, to take only one example, he hailed in his course of the summer semester 1933, *The Fundamental Question of Philosophy* (*Die Grundfrage der Philosophie*), the "greatness of the historical moment" (*Grösse des geschichtlichen Augenblicks*) when the German people as a group "find their leadership" (*findet seine Führung*).[151] These and other passages in his course lectures of this period leave little doubt regarding his active participation in the Nazi "revolution" and his adhesion to a number of its general principles even after his initial enthusiasm cooled. One also finds in his writings of this period references to the central concept of the Nazi ideology, that of "race." This raises the question that is of central importance for our present investigation: what is the function of the concept of race in Heidegger's writings of the 1930s and 1940s and what might his interpretation of race reveal about the relation of his thought to the political mythology disseminated by the Nazi ideology?[152]

Both his course lectures of the 1930s and 1940s and the *Black Notebooks* dating from the same period illustrate that in spite of Heidegger's occasional references to the concept of race following Hitler's rise to power, he never accorded to it a central role in his reflection. In his course lectures of 1933–34 "On the Essence of Truth" ("Vom Wesen der Wahrheit"), Heidegger was careful to distinguish his own concept of race (*Rasse, Stamm, Geschlecht, Art*) from what he characterized as "liberal biology." By the term "liberal biology" he designated above all Darwinian principles, involving the theories of adaptation stemming from the

150 Among the many examples that might be cited, his well-known remarks in his work *Introduction to Metaphysics* (*Einführung in die Metaphysik*, 1935, second edition 1953) concerning the "inner truth and greatness" (*die innere Wahrheit und die Grösse*) of Nazism may be understood in this sense; Martin Heidegger, *Einführung in die Metaphysik*, *GA*, vol. 40, p. 208. In regard to Heidegger's willingness to adapt his philosophical terminology to the Nazi ideology, see above all the documents published in the volume, Martin Heidegger, *Reden und andere Zeugnisse eines Lebensweges: 1910–1976*, *GA*, vol. 16.

151 Martin Heidegger, "Die Grundfrage der Philosophie," *Sein und Wahrheit*, *GA*, vol. 36–37, ed. Hartmut Tietjen (Frankfurt am Main: Klostermann, 2001), p. 3.

152 In the opinion of Emmanuel Faye, for example: "By way of the words "being," "essence," "truth of being" [...] Heidegger found a vehicle for the principles themselves of Nazism," Emmanuel Faye, *L'Introduction du nazisme dans la philosophie*, p. 218.

assumptions of late nineteenth century English liberalism and positivism. In this vein, an indication of Heidegger's attitude toward race came to light during the early years of the Nazi regime in his critique of the novelist, literary critic, and Nazi apologist Guido Kolbenheyer (1878–1962), who interpreted the political developments of the contemporary period from the standpoint of the ideology of the Arian (or Nordic) race.[153] In the notes he prepared for his commentary on Kolbenheyer's speech, Heidegger expressed his admiration for Kolbenheyer's literary production, and lauded above all his novel *Paracelsus* which, following its publication in the period between 1917 and 1926, won wide acclaim in Nazi Germany for the *völkische* themes it advocated. In his talk in Freiburg, however, as Heidegger continued, Kolbenheyer attempted to buttress his political ideology by means of presuppositions drawn from Darwinian biology and theories of "plasma and cell structure." Here Heidegger engaged his sharp critique. Kolbenheyer's orientation, in insisting that such biological factors were the determining forces of human existence, overlooked for Heidegger what he took to be the *historical* essence of a people (*Volk*). This historicity is fundamentally determined by "choices of a given will to being (*Seinwollen*) and a destiny (*Schicksal*)"; by a freedom (*Freiheit*) that cannot adequately be accounted for in terms of functional, biologically-determined capacities.[154] The biological concept of race, if it is one among other characteristics, is by no means the unique source of the historical existence of a people.[155]

Heidegger's manner of interpreting the concept of race (*Rasse*, *Geschlecht*) in his writings of the Nazi period obliges us to establish certain nuances in referring to his adhesion to the Nazi ideology. None of Heidegger's statements in other course lectures and writings of the period between 1933 and 1945 lead us to suppose that the doctrine of the biological transmission of racial characteristics and, on the basis of these

---

153 Heidegger referred above all to a speech Kolbenheyer presented at the University of Freiburg in January 1934, "The Value for Life and Vital Effects of Poetry for a People" ("Lebenswert und Lebenswirkung der Dichtkunst in einem Volke"). This speech concerned what Kolbenheyer took to be the role of poetry in the "struggle for vital adaptation" (*Anpassungskampf des Lebens*) of a people. See Guido Kolbenheyer, *Werke* vol. 8, *Aufsätze, Vorträge und Reden* (Munich: Langen/Müller, 1941), pp. 63–86 and Martin Heidegger, "Vom Wesen der Wahrheit," *Sein und Wahrheit*, *GA*, vol. 36–37, pp. 209–215.

154 Ibid., p. 210.

155 This point has been insightfully analyzed by Robert Bernasconi, "Heidegger's alleged challenge to the Nazi concepts of race," in *Appropriating Heidegger*, ed. James E. Faulconer and Mark A Wrathall (Cambridge, UK/New York: Cambridge University Press, 2000), pp. 50–67.

characteristics, of a hierarchy of human races, played a role in Heidegger's orientation during the period of Nazi rule. This leads us to the more difficult question concerning the precise ideological scope of Heidegger's writings in this period in comparison with the ruminations of the more extreme Nazi apologists such as Eugen Fischer and Hans F. K. Günther or Alfred Bäumler and Alfred Rosenberg.

To identify more precisely the ideological scope of Heidegger's writings during the Third Reich and its points of convergence with the political mythology of the Nazi regime, it is important to interpret his critique of biological theories of race typical of the Nazi ideology in the framework of the broad change in his philosophical orientation during the years following his resignation from the rectorship of the University of Freiburg. This period was marked by the turn in this thinking, the so-called "Kehre," which led to a shift from the exploration in *Being and Time* of the ways in which the modes of being of *Dasein* confer sense on what it means "to be," to a more direct focus on Being in its distinction from human beings. Being in this later sense denotes the hidden ground of the "history of Being" (*Seinsgeschichte*) that comes to the fore over the different epochs of human history. Independently of any human effort or human will, the history of Being evokes transformations in different historical epochs of the fundamental conceptions of truth and of the language that conveys it. Such changes in truth and language signal basic changes in human ways of being, and thus in humanity itself. Corresponding to this direct focus on a history of Being which he situated at the ground of human historicity, Heidegger abandoned the earlier activism of *Being and Time*, which placed the accent on decision of a way of being in the face of nothingness and death, to embrace an attitude of attentive disengagement from the will to historical mastery that he came to see as the central feature of the contemporary quest for planetary technological control.

In the period of the *Kehre*, Heidegger's critique of biological racism was animated by his interpretation of its place in this larger history of Being. In the Nazi ideology, biological racism had as its consequence measures of racial hygiene in view of breeding (*Züchtung*) racially pure Arians and the creation of a German master race. From Heidegger's standpoint in the late 1930s, this outlook corresponded to the concept of truth that rose to predominance during the ultimate stage of metaphysics bringing to the fore the conviction that humanity is capable of mastering its destiny by technical means. In this ultimate phase of metaphysics, called forth by Being, Heidegger qualified the quest to nurture and breed humanity in his texts composed between 1938 and 1940, "The History of Being" ("*Die Geschichte des Seins*") and "Koinón" as "a necessary measure toward which modern times tend at their culminating point" (*eine notwendige Massnahme, zu der das Ende der Neuzeit drängt*).[156] By characterizing this tendency as a necessary phase of modernity, Heidegger clearly did not seek to propagate it; rather he employed it to identify what he took to be the ultimate point of modern forgetfulness of Being as the unthought ground of human interpretation of truth and of its metamorphoses. In this function, contemporary racial assumptions mark the final unfurling of the steady deepening of the forgetfulness of Being set in motion by the epoch-making philosophies of Descartes and Leibniz, who posed subjectivity and the representations of the subject, founded in the absolute will of the transcendent God, as the ground and certitude of truth. In its further articulations elaborated by German Idealism, absolute subjectivity came to self-realization as the absolute ground of truth and the later biological conception of race and racial breeding provided a still more unbridled perspective on the absolute predominance of the subject in its pure power to posit itself as the self-engendering ground of truth. Heidegger supplemented his account of this modern movement of truth in the seventh "Consideration" (*Überlegung*) of the *Black Notebooks* (1938–39) in a passage entitled "History" ("Geschichte"):

> "What emerges and itself propels and sustains in this unfolding of the unconditioned subjectivism of the racial people (*Rassenvolk*) and the racial conflict (*Rassenkampf*) is in any case *not* a creative departure of a *changing* humankind, but the power of downward impulsion of forces in present humans, tending toward their self-establishment in terms of the presently given."[157]

IV

To set in relief the relation of Heidegger's writings to the racial ideology of the Nazi regime, the critique of Heidegger's political engagement by the philosopher Karl Jaspers, who frequented Heidegger well before 1933

156 Martin Heidegger, *Die Geschichte des Seyns. 1. Die Geschichte des Seyns (1938/40). 2. Koinón. Aus der Geschichte des Seyns (1939/40)*, *GA*, vol. 69, ed. Peter Trawny (Frankfurt am Main: Klostermann, 1998), pp. 70–71, 183, 223.

157 "Was in dieser Entfaltung des unbedingten Subjektivismus des Rassenvolkes und des Rassenkampfes heraufkommt und eigentlich treibt und trägt, ist allerdings auch *kein schöpferischer* Aufbruch des *sich verwandelnden* Menschen, sondern die Macht eines Druckes niederziehender Mächte im vorhandenen, auf sein Vorhandenes sich einrichtenden Menschen"; Martin Heidegger, *Überlegungen, VII–XI (Schwarze Hefte 1938/39)*. *GA*, vol. 95, p. 41. See also Heidegger, *Die Geschichte des Seyns, GA, vol. 69*, p. 182–183.

and found himself in a perilous situation following the advent of Hitler's dictatorship, is particularly instructive. Jaspers's critique, written in the early 1960s and published posthumously in 1978, touched on Heidegger's resignation from the rectorship in 1934 and his attitude toward Nazism in later years:

> "In what way did it come to an end in 1934? There are no documents. In any case there is no struggle against National Socialism; not insight (*Einsicht*), but his objective political uselessness. After initially using him, they treated him like a marionette that they then threw into a corner."[158]

Jaspers took Heidegger to task for his lack of "insight" (*Einsicht*), and this critique seems to me to touch the heart of the matter. This lack of insight becomes most clearly evident in the broad lines of historical interpretation Heidegger drew to portray an overarching continuity (*Zusammenhang*) linking together the different epochs of modernity that culminate in the Nazi ideology of Arian racial superiority that called for racial breeding to nurture it. This ideology, according to Heidegger's categories of interpretation, brought to the fore not something radically unique, but the unavoidable fulfillment of earlier tendencies at work in the philosophical itinerary of the modern period. Seen in this perspective, Nazi racial doctrines set the modern conception of absolute subjectivity on a wholly new basis that was freed from its earlier dependence on transcendent foundations or spiritual purpose and identified with the biology of racial self-production. Here the very lines of continuity he established betray above all a refusal to acknowledge what was truly *unprecedented* in the Nazi racial ideology, animating a political mythology that led to the extermination of vast European populations.

Heidegger himself did not directly advocate genocide and, as we have seen, did not adopt the biological categories in terms of which it was justified by its perpetrators. Nonetheless, in the period after 1938 and before the genocide, marked by radical discrimination against the Jews and other populations judged to be inferior, Heidegger's ruminations on the history of Being hardly brought him to question the historical categories employed by the Nazi ideology. Where he questioned the legitimacy of its

158 "Wodurch das Ende 1934? Keine Dokumente. Jedenfalls kein Kampf gegen N.S., nicht Einsicht, sondern objektive Unbrauchbarkeit in der Politik. Er war wie ein Hampelmann gewesen, den man nun in die Ecke warf, als man ihn für den Anfang verwendet hatte." Karl Jaspers, *Notizen zu Heidegger*, p. 236. On Heidegger and Nazism see also the insightful analysis of Dieter Thomä, "Heidegger und der Nationalsozialismus. In der Dunkelkammer der Seinsgeschichte," in Dieter Thomä, ed., *Heidegger Handbuch. Leben-Werk-Wirkung* (Stuttgart: Metzler, 2003), p. 141–61.

"racial" basis, he directly re-asserted similar radical prejudices which he set on a "metaphysical" basis. As he stated in "Consideration" fourteen of the *Black Notebooks*:

> "The question of the role of world-Jewry is not a racial, but a metaphysical question concerning the kind of human that, in complete independence, is capable of undertaking as its world-historical 'task' the uprooting of all beings from Being."[159]

In conformity with this bias concerning the world-historical role of the Jews, Heidegger's ideological position, if it admitted critical reservations concerning the present Nazi masters, could at the same time affirm the Nazi orientation itself "on the basis of thought" (*aus denkerischen Gründen*).[160] And this, then, brings us to the decisive point: as expressed in sections of the *Black Notebooks* composed at the beginning of World War II, Heidegger's ideological position was principally animated by his firm conviction concerning the privileged world-historical mission of the Germans who, as he saw it, were uniquely capable as a people (*Volk*) of taking up and bearing a foundational role in regard to the essence of truth (*Gründerschaft des Wesens der Wahrheit er-trägt*). This supreme historical mission hardly required justification in terms of biological racism for it was conferred by the call of Being.[161]

159 "Die Frage nach der Rolle des Weltjudentums ist keine rassische, sondern die metaphysische Frage nach der Art von Menschentümlichkeit, die schlechthin ungebunden die Entwurzelung alles Seienden aus dem Sein als weltgeschichtliche 'Aufgabe' übernehmen kann," Heidegger, "Überlegung" XIV, *Schwarze Hefte*, *GA*, vol. 96, p. 243.

160 Heidegger, "Überlegung" XI, *Schwarze Hefte*, *GA*, vol. 95, § 27, p. 408.

161 See in this regard the details of Heidegger's political mythology as elaborated notably in Martin Heidegger, "Überlegung" XII, *Schwarze Hefte*, *GA*, vol. 96, § 27, p. 48, to which I will return in the following chapters.

Chapter 5

And What can Catastrophes Do? The Second World War in Heidegger's Interpretation of the History of Being

Following the intervention of the United States in World War II on December seventh 1941, Martin Heidegger made the following statement in his course lectures at the University of Freiburg im Breisgau, *Friedrich Hölderlins Hymne "Der Ister,"* in the summer semester of 1942:

> "We know today that the Anglo-Saxon world of Americanism has resolved to annihilate Europe, that is the homeland (*Heimat*), the origin of the West (*Anfang des Abendländischen*). The originary is indestructible. America's entry into this planetary war is not its entry into history; rather it is already the ultimate American act of American historylessness (*Geschichtslosigkeit*) and self-devastation (*Selbstverwüstung*)."[162]

In the context of Heidegger's *Gesamtausgabe*, such statements are particularly disconcerting. However far one might stretch revisionist interpretations of World War II, Heidegger's account of what he described as American aggressivity against Europe and American "historylessness" presents a wholly uncritical view of the Nazi war effort in a period when, following an aggressive war of conquest, German troops occupied much of Europe.

It is true that during the years of Nazi rule in Germany Heidegger at times stated his disaccord with the Nazi ideology in works that for the most part remained unpublished until decades later, like *Contributions to Philosophy: Of the Event* (*Beiträge zur Philosophie. Vom Ereignis*, 1936–39) or the *Black Notebooks* (*Schwarze Hefte*). In *Contributions to Philosophy*, for example, he ridiculed the typical Nazi equation of Judaism with Bolshevism,[163] but this by no means prevented him from expressing a complicity with the Nazi war effort or, as illustrated by the *Black Notebooks*, from voicing opinions concerning what he took to be the destructive role of "world Jewry" in what was undoubtedly the darkest period of Jewish history. Heidegger's course lectures of the war years and the *Black*

---

162 Martin Heidegger, *Hölderlins Hymne "Der Ister," GA*, vol. 53, ed. Walter Biemel (Frankfurt am Main: Klostermann, 1984), p. 68; English translation, *Hölderlin's Hymn "The Ister."* trans. William McNeill and Julia Davis (Bloomington and Indianapolis: Indiana University Press, 1996), p. 54–55; translation modified.

163 Martin Heidegger, *Beiträge zur Philosophie. (Vom Ereignis)*, *GA*. vol. 65, ed. Friedrich-Wilhelm von Herrmann (Frankfurt am Main: Klostermann, 1989), p. 54; English trans. *Contributions to Philosophy: (From Enowning)*, 1999, p. 38.

Notebooks illustrate that his affirmation of central aspects of Nazi politics extended well beyond the period of his resignation from his official function as rector of the University of Freiburg in 1934, when he eagerly bent the language of the *Daseinsanalyse* of *Being and Time* to the Nazi ideology.[164]

My purpose in this chapter will not be to rehash the much discussed question concerning the relation between Heidegger's philosophy and the Nazi ideology. I will focus rather on the conception of historical understanding that informed his interpretation of history more generally. In this regard, his manner of depicting World War II raises the following question: What might the conception of historical thought governing his interpretation of the devastating events of his period reveal in regard to his broader depiction of the course of world history and, indeed, of the transformations of fundamental conceptions of truth since antiquity that he identified as the history of Being? In answering this question, I will highlight above all the political implications of Heidegger's conception of historical understanding that come to light with particular clarity in his interpretation of what he took to be the place of the Second World War in the history of metaphysics. Let us begin by setting in relief the broad lines of his conception of historical understanding and then relate this to his manner of depicting World War II.

I

In accounting for the entry of the United States into World War II, Heidegger claimed, as noted in the above quote, that America threatened to annihilate Europe due to its "a-historical" way of being, or what he termed American "historylessness" (*Geschichtslosigkeit*). What, however, did Heidegger mean by this reference to American historylessness and what does it reveal in regard to his own conception of history and historical understanding?

In making this statement, Heidegger clearly did not intend to repeat the idea that commonly circulates in Europe according to which the United States, as a "young" country, lacks the historical experience of older civilizations and the longstanding historical knowledge in which their

164 Heidegger's comments on what he took to be the destructive role of "world-Judiasm" can be found in the *Black Notebooks*, cf. *Überlegungen XII–XV (Schwarze Hefte, 1939–41)*, *GA*, vol. 96, pp. 46, 243; on Heidegger's complicity with the Nazi regime during his rectorship in 1933–34 see his official speeches and other documents in Martin Heidegger, *Reden und andere Zeugnisse eines Lebensweges*, 1910–1976. *GA*, vol. 16.

identities are rooted. On the contrary, beginning with *Being and Time* Heidegger sharply criticized the modern emphasis on historical knowledge where it was fueled by the assumption that the meaning of the past resides in its status as an acquisition that has been accumulated over time, providing an over-arching continuity (*Zusammenhang*) in which the possibilities of present comprehension are anchored. Such presumptions situate the meaning of history in its objective perdurability and availability to all who retrieve it in each successive present.

Against this assumption, Heidegger stipulated in *Being and Time* that the historicity of finite human beings (*Dasein*) does not primarily depend on the acquisition of historical knowledge, nor on the transmission of historical traditions by means of this knowledge. As he wrote in the section of this work entitled "Temporality and Historicity": "It is not because historical epochs are indifferent to historical knowledge (*unhistorisch*) that they are as such unhistorical (*ungeschichtlich*)."[165] Beyond the mere acquisition of historical knowledge that one commonly believes to be in and of itself endowed with a generally available significance, Heidegger underscored the primary role of the historian's *approach* to the historical past—the ways in which the historian's quest for meaning in history enables specific possibilities of comprehension. In light of the historian's own finite modes of temporal and historical existence, this quest engages a decision concerning what is significant in the past and worthy of retrieval for future possibilities of existence.

As has often been noted, and as we have seen in previous chapters, Heidegger's thought in the decade following *Being and Time* from the mid-1930s onward, changed its focus. This reorientation in Heidegger's thought, the so-called turn or *Kehre*, led him to shift his emphasis from the manner in which the ways of being of finite *Dasein* call forth an understanding of being toward an elucidation of what he designated as *Seinsgeschichte*, the history of Being. In this later period, he devoted closer attention to epochal metamorphoses in language and truth that Being calls forth over the long course of its history. According to Heidegger's well-known description in this later period of his thought, *Seinsgeschichte* elicits a deepening forgetfulness of an original sense of Being and of truth which, at the heart of ancient Greek thought, discerned Being as the sovereign hidden ground of all that humans can conceive. Being unveils truth, drawing it from the opacity of its obscure depths. The history of Being

165 "Unhistorische Zeitalter sind als solche nicht auch schon ungeschichtlich"; Martin Heidegger, *Sein und Zeit*, p. 523; *Being and Time*, p. 448, translation modified.

describes the deepening forgetfulness of this originary intimation over the course of centuries. Plato inaugurated this metaphysical forgetfulness through his identification of truth with the idea deployed by the human intellect and Descartes accentuated it in its modern form by identifying truth with the certitude of the cogito's representations, assured by the absolute Divine subject. The gradual eclipse over the modern period of all transcendent foundations in God or in the inscrutable noumenal realm, and then its identification with the absolute Hegelian subject, gave way to the reduction of Being and truth to what can be made an object of human representation and fashioned by the human will. According to Heidegger's well-known conception, this ushered in the era of technology leading to the ultimate stage of the history of Being. Truth is identified with what can be represented by the natural or historical sciences.

In the framework of Heidegger's orientation in the late 1930s and the period of World War II, he extended and further elaborated the critique proposed in *Being and Time* of the ideal of historical knowledge pursued in the historical disciplines (*Historie*). As in *Being and Time*, he stipulated that conventional forms of historical knowledge, far from guides for understanding the past, tend to obscure what is essential in it. In works such as *Contributions to Philosophy* of the late 1930s, he went so far as to claim that history as a scientific discipline (*Historie*) "never attains history itself (*Geschichte*)."[166] Far from affording insight into what is essential in the past, historical reckoning in the technological epoch serves as a tool through which the meaning of the past is leveled down to exclude all that cannot be made an object of human representation.

Heidegger directed his critique of historical science against what he took to be an anthropocentric paradigm that had become predominant over the course of the previous century. In the rare instances in his later works where he singled out specific currents of thought for critique, he took to task Wilhelm Dilthey's attempt to provide an anthropological foundation for historical science.[167] He also rebuked the theory of the human sciences of Max Weber, who was for him a typical expression of nineteenth century scientific ideals that sought to comprehend human society in terms of

166 Martin Heidegger, *Beiträge*, p. 479; *Contributions to Philosophy*, p. 337.

167 Martin Heidegger, "Die Zeit des Weltbildes," *Holzwege*, *GA*, vol. 5, pp. 99–100; Martin Heidegger, *Anmerkungen I–V (Schwarze Hefte 1942–48)*, *GA*, vol. 97, ed. Peter Trawny (Frankfurt am Main: Klostermann, 2015), pp. 171–72; Martin Heidegger, *Beiträge*, pp. 74, 218; *Contributions to Philosophy*, pp. 51, 152.

principles of rational accord and mutual interest.[168] Max Weber, as Heidegger also noted, was closely affiliated with the neo-Kantian school which sought a scientific basis for history as a discipline. The central assumption of this discipline, that Max Weber voiced with particular clarity, lay in the conviction that the attempt to provide a faithful representation of past actions and events, however limited it might be by the historian's own singular perspective, is capable of gleaning a measure of historical truth that clearly distinguishes it from willful distortion. Even where it proves unsettling for the present, the attempt to faithfully reconstruct the factual reality of the past is a source of insight capable of guiding future action.[169] From Heidegger's perspective, the quest of the contemporary historical disciplines to provide a "true" and impartial account of the past could only prove illusory, since it overlooks the tacit accord of their fundamental assumptions with the designs of the technological epoch in which they come to predominance.

From the total perspective projected by Heidegger's interpretation of the history of Being, the historical disciplines (*Historie*), whose methods limit them to psychological, sociological, political, or other forms of human representation, are wholly unable to attain an intimation of the extra-human ground of truth and of its historical metamorphoses. Historical explanations, which rest on psychological, sociological, or political representations, turn a blind eye to their own historical significance, called forth in the contemporary history of Being. In the contemporary epoch, the historical disciplines assume the paradoxical role of promoting "historylessness" that their own manner of representation is unable to discern. [170]

If, as Heidegger conceived of it, "historylessness" favored by the historical disciplines has become a principle vehicle of the technical epoch, this is due to its promotion of a specific experience of historical time which is entirely preoccupied by the *present*. It overlays all representations of the past with the veneer of currency that no longer discerns the singular difference of the past from all that does not conform to current

168 Martin Heidegger, *Zu Ernst Jünger*, *GA*, vol. 90, ed. Peter Trawny (Frankfurt am Main: Klostermann, 2004), p. 118.

169 Max Weber, "Der Sinn der 'Wertfreiheit' der soziologischen und ökonomischen Wissenschaften," in *Verstehende Soziologie und Werturteilsfreiheit. Schriften und Reden, 1908–17*, *Gesamtausgabe*, section. 1, vol. 12, ed. Johannes Weiss and Sabine Frommer (Tübingen: Mohr/Siebeck, 2018), pp. 445–512; Max Weber, "Wissenschaft als Beruf," *Wissenschaft als Beruf 1917/1919, Politik als Beruf, 1919, Gesamtausgabe*, section 1, vol. 17, ed., Wolfgang J. Mommsen, Wolfgang Schluchter, and Birgitt Morgenbrod (Tübingen: Mohr/Siebeck, 1992), pp. 71–112.

170 Heidegger, *Beiträge*, p. 493; *Contributions to Philosophy*, p. 347.

preoccupations.[171] Turning a blind eye to what cannot be assimilated to a timely relevance, historical reckoning, in company with the technical aim of natural science—the "technical-historical consciousness" (*technisch-historisches Bewusstsein*)—excludes the untimely and radically anachronistic dimension of the past. It has no sense for the "originary" (*das Anfängliche*) that resides in a reminiscence of the question of Being inaugurated in ancient Greek thought.[172]

As a metaphysical attitude, the sense of time promoted by the historical disciplines is not confined to the intellectual sphere of the universities; on a more primary level it reveals itself to be a generalized tendency of organization and planning in the broadest sectors of contemporary life. In *Contributions to Philosophy*, Heidegger specified that this profusion of historical reckoning had become so pervasive that it was no longer possible to detect the extent to which its hidden forms had gained control over the modes themselves of human being (*das menschliche Sein*).[173]

This consideration leads us to a clearer understanding of Heidegger's interpretation of "historylessness" in the movement of *Seinsgeschichte*. If several years before the outbreak of World War II, Heidegger employed the term "historylessness" in *Contributions to Philosophy* to describe contemporary historical science and he later applied this same concept to "Americanism" on the occasion of the entry of the United States into this war, this was because "historylessness" for him directly concerned the sense of the past that prevailed *both* in Europe and America. The "historylessness" he attributed to America was only the extreme form of a tendency which, in the contemporary technological epoch, reigned on a global scale.

If Heidegger insists that the pervasive metaphysical attitude promoted by the historical disciplines, characterized by its manner of assimilating the past to the order of current preoccupations, has come to permeate human sensibilities more generally, this is nowhere better attested for him than the increasing convergence of academic history with journalism.[174] Here too there is a remarkable contrast between Heidegger's attitude toward journalism and the position of Max Weber who, in the years following World War I, extended his ideal of historical scholarship to champion journalism's investigative role. In the years just after World War I, when

171 Heidegger, *Beiträge*, pp. 151–152; *Contributions to Philosophy*, pp. 104–05.

172 Martin Heidegger, *Grundbegriffe* (1941), *GA*, vol. 51, ed. Petra Jäger (Frankfurt am Main: Klostermann, 1991), pp. 7–8.

173 Heidegger, *Beiträge*, pp. 492–93; *Contributions to Philosophy*, p. 347.

174 Heidegger, *Beiträge*, p. 153; *Contributions to Philosophy*, p. 106.

Weber aimed to assure the political stability of the Weimar Republic, he insisted on the central role of journalism as a means of denouncing corruption and assuring the existence of an informed public opinion, which to his mind was instrumental in shaping the political destiny of a people.[175] Heidegger, however, admitted no such function for investigative reporting. He nowhere acknowledged a distinction between reporting that seeks to present, from different points of view, as complete an account of events as possible, and propaganda that distorts accounts of factual events for the purpose of mass manipulation. Heidegger's radical refusal to accord any significance to such distinctions arose from his conviction that the role of mass journalistic reporting, as the mode of historical representation favored by the technological epoch, was not limited to the public dissemination of information; as a ubiquitous mode of organization of human efforts (*treiben*) pervading all spheres of human comprehension, Heidegger considered that it exercised an epoch-making force that is left unquestioned. In this unquestioned way of everyday patterning of human representation, historylessness reinforces its grip.[176] In its ultimate form, historical reckoning in the guise of journalism, radio, and cinema displays its clear affinity with Americanism. In its extreme American stage it is marked by the utter decline of knowledge (*Verfall des Wissens*). As he stated in his course lectures of the summer of 1941, *Grundbegriffe*:

> "It may be permitted to ask if people of today, whose 'culture' ('Bildung') is often drawn only from 'tables' and 'curves', 'illustrated newspapers,' 'radio bulletins,' and 'film theatres,' if these purely American people spun about in a whirlwind, know at all and are capable of knowing what it means to 'read'."[177]

In the 1942 course lectures *Hölderlins Hymne "Der Ister,"* Heidegger extended this interpretation to encompass an analysis of what he took to be the political ramifications of the contemporary predominance of historylessness. In these lectures he set in relief the function of the political in the ultimate stage of the history of Being by contrasting it with the interpretation of the political in Greek antiquity, where it was intimately tied for Heidegger to the originary Greek grasp of truth out of the unconcealment of Being. In this ancient Greek context, the political pertained to order and

---

175 Max Weber, "Parlament und Regierung im neugeordneten Deutschland" (1917), in *Gesammelte politische Schriften* (Munich: Drei Masken Verlag, 1921), pp. 171–72; Max Weber, "Politik als Beruf", in *Gesamtausgabe*, section 1, vol. 17, pp. 191–96.

176 Martin Heidegger, *Überlegungen, VII–XI (Schwarze Hefte 1938/39), GA*, vol. 95, pp. 64, 119.

177 Martin Heidegger, *Grundbegriffe*, pp. 13–14.

disorder, to what is allowed and forbidden in the polis, to what is fitting and unfitting, to a being at home (*Heimischsein*) in the midst of beings as a totality. The polis is concerned with:

> "The turning to the gods, the kind of festivals and the possibility for celebration, the relationship of master and servant (*Herr und Knecht*), of suffering and battle, of honor and fame [...] Out of the relationship between these relationships and from out of the grounds of their unity, there prevails what is called the polis."[178]

Being at home in the polis in the face of the gods and of the uncanny intimation of Being marked for the originary phase of Greek antiquity the primordial capacity of its historical existence.[179]

By contrast, in the modern period of desacralization, and of an incomprehension of historical truth commanded by the utter forgetfulness of Being, politics is reduced to what can be assimilated to human representations and to the quest for mastery of beings in their totality. It is placed in the service of the devastating force, the "machination" (*Machenschaft*), that presides over the technical epoch. In this ultimate stage of the history of Being, the political is deployed in the sphere of historical representation to promote what is taken to be the "self-certitude of historical consciousness" (*Selbstgewisssein des historischen Bewusstseins*) in its will to technological mastery. The political in its contemporary guise promotes the will to historical self-certitude through organization and planning of the state, which claims a total reach for the political.[180]

Heidegger's evocation of the political in his course lectures presented at the height of World War II raises the question concerning the political implications of his vision of the advent of the historical consciousness in the epoch of technology. If the historical mutations of language and truth and the self-comprehension of human beings in given historical epochs depends upon the call of Being and not on collective human action, what is the concrete political significance of the contemporary rise of the *Machenschaft*, promoted by historical science and journalism, for the organization of human co-existence in a common world? I will turn in the second part of this chapter to an elucidation of this question in relation to Heidegger's interpretation of what is often taken to be the most politically fateful event in the period of Heidegger's later lectures and writings: the catastrophe of World War II.

---

178 Heidegger, *Hölderlins "Der Ister,"* p. 101; English translation, p. 82; translation modified.
179 Ibid., pp. 101–02; English trans., pp. 82–83.
180 Ibid., pp. 117–18; English trans., p. 94.

II

In the years that followed the German defeat in World War II, a wide variety of attempts were made to comprehend the catastrophe that had occurred. In the immediate aftermath of the war of aggression and the genocide perpetrated by the Nazi regime, Karl Jaspers, in his book, *The Question of German Guilt* (*Die Schuldfrage*, 1946) raised the question of German moral responsibility for the catastrophic consequences of the war.[181] The historian Friedrich Meinecke, after trying to come to grips with the historical outcome of the war in his book *The German Catastrophe* (*Die deutsche Katastrophe: Betrachtungen und Erinnerungen*, 1946), admonished the Germans to turn toward the heritage of the past bequeathed by German Idealism and the humanism of Goethe's Weimar.[182] While Heidegger showed little interest in such works, he too devoted a singular effort to interpreting World War II and its place in the history of Being, notably in dialogue with Ernst Jünger.

Well before the war, during the years between 1934 and 1940, Heidegger became interested in Jünger's writings, above all in Jünger's book *The Worker* (*Der Arbeiter*, 1932). In the years of the Hitler dictatorship and of World War II, Heidegger wrote a series of detailed notes on Jünger's *The Worker* and he presented a seminar on this book in Freiburg during the first months of the war in January, 1940. These reflections on Jünger were subsequently published as a volume of Heidegger's collected works.[183]

In *The Worker*, Jünger presented an historical interpretation of the legacy of the Enlightenment and of the French Revolution that had overthrown the political and religious order of the *ancien régime*. The demise of the old order was followed in the nineteenth century by the rise to predominance of the liberal conception of political institutions, which presupposed that the political order is amenable to ongoing historical improvement through rational organization. After inspiring the reorganization of European social and political life, by the late nineteenth century this conviction began to show its weaknesses. The deepening void left by the enervation of religious beliefs contributed to the devaluation of all supreme values—the dire situation that Nietzsche had diagnosed as nihilism. The industrial and technological development of this period paved the way to

181 Karl Jaspers, *Die Schuldfrage* (Heidelberg: L. Schneider, 1946).

182 Friedrich Meinecke, *Die deutsche Katastrophe: Betrachtungen und Erinnerungen* (Wiesbaden: E. Brockhaus, 1946).

183 Martin Heidegger, *Zu Ernst Jünger*, *GA*, vol. 90.

the era of the "total mobilization" (*total Mobilmachung*) of World War I, which signaled a fundamental transformation of humanity. In this context, the quest for individual freedom incarnated in the liberal ethos and the system of parliamentary democracy proved unable to fulfill the requisites of an age in which a wholly new guise of humanity, the "worker," rose to predominance as the prime mover in society. The advent of the worker called for mass organization on a wholly unprecedented scale and the creation of a radically different set of political principles to meet the requirements of collective action in a new age. In Jünger's opinion, traditional "bourgeois" freedoms, such as liberty of opinion and of the press, which had been the central pillars of the parliamentary system assured by constitutional guarantees, were no longer adequate in the present situation. To his mind, the contemporary reality called for new forms executive decision that were best assured by "authoritative" (*autoritative*) forms of government.[184]

In the aftermath of World War II, Jünger contributed the essay, "Over the Line" ("Über die Linie"), to the volume published in 1950 in honor of Heidegger's sixtieth birthday. In this essay he surveyed the catastrophe the war had wrought and reaffirmed his faith in the historical resilience of German scientific, literary, and religious traditions, which held out the hope in the midst of the contemporary predicament that nihilism might be vanquished. In dissipating illusions of the past, and in loosening the hold of ideologies, the catastrophe of World War II, indeed, revealed its positive side.[185] The catastrophe of World War II, as he wrote,

> "has made clear to many and even to the broad masses (*den grossen Massen*) a lack (*Mangel*) that they had never previously perceived. That is the productive force of pain, und such initial moves toward healing are of special value for care and protection."[186]

In the years after the war, Heidegger presented a very different conception of the historical significance of this dark event. In lectures presented in 1951–52 under the title "What is Called Thinking?", Heidegger insisted that the world wars, in spite of their horror, had decided nothing. They had no influence on the "essential destiny (*Wesensgeschick*) of humans on this earth." Yet, as Heidegger continued, what is undecided may

184 Ernst Jünger, *Der Arbeiter*, *Werke*, vol. 6, *Essays* II (Stuttgart: Klett, 1960), pp. 283–297, 309.

185 Ernst Jünger, "Über die Linie," *Werke*, vol. 5, *Essais* I, *Betrachtungen zur Zeit* (Stuttgart: Klett, 1960), pp. 275–80.

186 Ibid., p. 275.

> "prepare a decision where it is not once again forced into short-winded and inconsequential political-social and moral categories, in this way preventing the attainment of an appropriate discerning (*Besinnung*)."[187]

Several years later, Heidegger responded directly to Jünger in the essay "On the Question of Being" ("Zur Seinsfrage," 1955), which was originally included in a *Festschrift* in honor of Jünger's sixtieth birthday. In this essay he placed in doubt the idea that a revitalization of religious and intellectual traditions of the past might play a role in surmounting the catastrophes of the twentieth century and he sharply contested the idea that signs had become visible in the aftermath of the war indicating that nihilism might be overcome. Catastrophes, indeed, had no influence on the march toward nihilism in the contemporary epoch of history of Being. As he stated in this essay:

> "What can catastrophes do? The two world wars have neither stopped the course of nihilism, nor have they changed its course." [188]

True to his conception of the history of Being, Heidegger sought less to deny the violent impact of World War II than to denounce the presumption that historical representations based on sociological, psychological, or political factors might provide adequate standards to account for it. Such representations of the war, far from capable of discerning its inner truth, correspond only to the illusory quest of the machination to assimilate all Being to what can be made an object of human representation and control. It is this quest, as Heidegger explained in his essay on Ernst Jünger, that lies at the root of the total mobilization of human beings and of resources on a planetary scale that is designated as a world war. Indeed, the search for scientific understanding, which is for Heidegger either tacitly or openly oriented by the will to technical organization and mastery, belongs to the same configuration constituted by modern technology as the wars it aims to comprehend. In the perspective of historical science, as Heidegger exclaimed in an essay of the late 1930s, "The Overcoming of Metaphysics" (1936–46), one readily presumes that "leaders" (*Führer*) acting in accord with a "blind, self-seeking fury," obstinately initiate world-historical events. In fact, they themselves are only the necessary results of contemporary errancy (*Irrnis*) that calls for

187 Martin Heidegger, *Was heisst Denken?*, *GA*, vol. 8, ed. Paola-Ludovika Coriando (Frankfurt am Main: Klostermann, 2002), p. 71.

188 Martin Heidegger, "Zur Seinsfrage," in *Wegmarken*, *GA*, vol. 9, p. 394. As Heidegger explained in the later edition of this essay in *Wegmarken*, its original title in the Jünger *Festschrift* was "Über 'Die Linie'." Regarding the debate on nihiliism between Heidegger and Ernst Jünger, see especially Günter Figal, "Der metaphysische Charakter der Moderne. Ernst Jüngers Schrift *Über die Linie* (1950) und Martin Heideggers Kritik Über 'Die Linie' (1955)" in Günter Figal, *Zu Heidegger: Antworten und Fragen* (Frankfurt am Main: Klostermann, 2009), pp. 205–221.

the "ordering and securing of beings by the leaders (*Führer*)."[189] Far from human choices, the world wars of the twentieth century must be attributed to an abandonment of Being (*Seinsverlassenheit*).

In the framework of Heidegger's works published in the decades after the end of World War II, such statements are clearly ambiguous. Heidegger's historical interpretation, which radically downplayed the role of human decisions in orienting the course of history, and even denied the significance of the "blind, self-seeking fury" of leaders initiating them, sets the practical implications of his statements in a questionable light. Indeed, his stance in attributing the most sinister of historical events to the call of Being bringing forth contemporary errancy might well be seen, in a situation of unprecedented ethico-political bankruptcy and disarray, as an attempt at exculpation from responsibility for the Nazi war and the genocide. Such statements may well appear to be an attempt to excuse the consequences of the Nazi reign and Heidegger's own political complicity with it.

The publication of Heidegger's *Black Notebooks*, marking the completion of his collected works, permits us to set Heidegger's political attitude during the events of the Nazi period up to the end of World War II in clearer relief. They illustrate above all the *political* implications of his radical critique of the historical disciplines and of journalism in the epoch of technology. If, indeed, Heidegger considered that historical science and its journalistic expression, in the guise of the machination, pervaded the technological era on a planetary scale, he unabashedly associated its radical articulation with the politics of popular sovereignty and democratic organization.

Heidegger's negative assessment of democracy came most clearly to light in his conception of the specifically political role of journalism. Here again his attitude stands in sharp contrast with the ideals of Max Weber. Where Max Weber emphasized the essential role of journalism for maintaining a well-informed public opinion necessary for democratic institutions, Heidegger excluded from the outset any possibility that the democratic expression of the will of the people might play a role in orienting a nation's history. Democratic forms of government only reinforce what he took to be the illusion that peoples were the initiators of the historical movement of the societies they presumed to govern. As Heidegger wrote in regard to journalism and its relation to democracy in the *Black Notebooks*:

> "Journalism—it belongs to technology (*Technik*). It is the technical organization of the necessary illusions of the public realm, according to which the 'people' (*Volk*), that is the mass (*die Masse*), imagines that it determines and rules itself."

189 Martin Heidegger, "Überwindung der Metaphysik," *Vorträge und Aufsätze*, *GA*, vol. 7, ed. Friedrich-Wilhelm von Herrmann (Frankfurt am Main: Klostermann, 2000), pp. 91–92.

> "'Democracy' is the code name for the planetary swindle. It is so deceitful that it is not valid at all to understand it as the 'rule of the mob' from below (*Pöbelherrschaft vom unten*), since even this is a mere appearance, in the framework of the imperialism of the dictatorship of the bureaucrats (*Funktionäre*) of the unleashed will to will as the unconditioned machination (*unbedingte Machenschaft*)."[190]

This statement brings us to the key issue that Heidegger's political assumptions raise. If, indeed, all human societies in the epoch of the planetary domination of technology participate in the same errancy and the same forgetfulness of Being; if the Bolshevik dictatorship and, as he became convinced during the later years of Nazi rule, the Nazi regime itself had succumbed to an errancy that had enveloped all of human history, was there any possible reason to prefer any *one* political form of government to another? If modern depictions of history which attribute its causes to sociological, political, economic, and other humanly representable factors are illusions; if even such cataclysmic events as World War II had no decisive impact on its fundamental orientation, are not all forms of government equally deaf to the call of Being?

Heidegger's *Black Notebooks* respond to this question in illustrating that his vehement rejection of democratic forms of government was correlated with a resounding preference for dictatorial rule. If he was willing to acknowledge that neither the democratically organized people, nor the dictator exercise power in any fundamental sense, he nonetheless singled out democratic ideals for reproof, since to his mind democratic principles of organization weaken the capacity of peoples to discern (*besinnen*) what stands beyond the realm of their own representations and productions; their apparent power, their great wealth, their inherited culture can only obstruct the transition toward modernity's culmination. For those who content themselves with democracy, the leaders who open the way to the culmination of modernity (*Vollendung der Neuzeit*) can only be qualified as "dictators"; they are rejected on the basis of moral considerations.[191] For Heidegger, however, this kind of judgment completely misconstrues the greatness of these leaders, for only they "are able to sense the hidden necessity of the machination of Being and are able to avoid being derailed." (*dass sie die verborgene Notwendigkeit der Machenschaft des Seins erspüren und durch keine Verführung sich aus der Bahn drängen lassen*).[192] Democracy's act of obstruction (*Sperre*) cannot prevail in hindering the movement of the history of Being.

---

190 Heidegger, *Anmerkungen I–V (Schwarze Hefte 1942–48)*, *GA*, vol. 97, p. 146.

191 Heidegger, *Überlegungen, VII–XI (Schwarze Hefte 1938/39)*, *GA*, vol. 95, pp. 405–406; Heidegger, *Die Geschichte des Seyns*, *GA*, vol. 69, pp. 189–90.

192 Heidegger, *Überlegungen, VII–XI (Schwarze Hefte 1938/39)*, *GA*, vol. 95, p. 404.

If, following the disillusionment with the Nazi regime that led to his resignation from the rectorship of the University of Freiburg in 1934, Heidegger no longer endorsed its politics, his favorable assessment of dictatorship is nonetheless entirely consonant with the political convictions he expressed well after the period of his disillusionment with Nazi rule. He was convinced, as he wrote in *Introduction to Metaphysics* republished in 1953, that the Nazi officials themselves had not understood the "inner greatness" of their movement.[193] As noted in the *Black Notebooks*, he rejected on this score the ideology of the Nazi regime, exemplified by the "myth of the twentieth century" elaborated by the Nazi ideologue Alfred Rosenberg, due to its illusory identification of the human essence with the body and its biological characteristics. This identification did nothing more, according to Heidegger, than establish on another basis the errancy set in motion by Descartes and the identification of human being with self-reflexive subjectivity in its capacity to represent true Being. The predominant Nazi myth was in this sense the ultimate fulfillment of early modern "a-mythical, rational subjectivism and liberalism." The consequence of the early modern freeing of human subjectivity was the unleashing of an ever more unlimited quest for power which, over the course of centuries, would erupt in the world wars of the twentieth century.[194]

In the final analysis, Heidegger's political assumptions bring to the fore a broad vision of the continuity of history as a unity, in which the most apparently incompatible articulations are all reconciled as moments in a cohesive, over-arching process. In its total scope, it is a vision that allows of no possible refutation on the basis of historical experience or of argumentation that does not accept the premises on which Heidegger's history of Being is based. Be this as it may, Heidegger's vision allows to my mind of one particularly compelling counter-argument. This counter-argument concerns the practical implications of the fatalism it warrants. Where the fatalism dictated by his vision of Being ultimately denies any principle of human responsibility, it runs the risk of becoming a self-fulfilling prophecy.[195] To the extent that it is capable of inspiring belief, it only renders more probable the political consequences that follow from its predictions.

193 Martin Heidegger, *Einführung in die Metaphysik*, p. 208.

194 *Heidegger, Überlegungen, VII–XI (Schwarze Hefte 1938/39), GA*, vol. 95, pp. 412–413.

195 This point has been perceptively made by Hans Jonas: "Fatalismus wäre die eine Todsünde des Augenblicks. Berliner Ansprache (Juni 1992)," in *Fatalismus wäre Todsünde. Gespräche über Ethik und Mitverantwortung im dritten Jahrtausend*, ed. Dietrich Böhler (Münster: LIT Verlag, 2005), pp. 53–56.

Chapter 6

Politics and Mythology in Martin Heidegger's History of Being

In the different periods of his interpretation of the history of Being from the 1930s onward, Heidegger identified what he took to be the central significance of myth in the articulation of this history. In his references to myth, he primarily identified it with a narrative concerning the gods, corresponding to the ancient Greek meaning of this term as *muthos*. Hence, when Heidegger examined the concept of myth in interpreting the first chorus of Sophocles's *Antigone* in his 1935 course *Introduction to Metaphysics*, he depicted it as an originary narrative relating to the gods set in relief by authentic historical understanding.[196] Seven years later in his course *Parmenides*, presented in the winter of 1942–43 at the University of Freiburg im Breisgau, Heidegger further pursued this interpretation. He remarked that he confined use of the word "mythos" to its original Greek meaning, since only the ancient Greeks comprehended myth on the basis of its primordial relation to truth as *alētheia*. *Muthos*, he explained, "is what opens, unveils, and allows to see; there is myth only among the Greeks, for whom the essence of language is rooted in truth as *alētheia* [...], thus designating a primordial relation to the hidden, the obscured."[197]

In this chapter I will focus less directly on the significance Heidegger attributed to myth in this primordial sense than on another meaning he accorded to this term in a work of the period 1939–41, *Ponderings* XII in the *Black Notebooks*. In this context, Heidegger shifted his use of the term myth to deal with the *contemporary* epoch. He referred to what he took to be the myth that predominates in the epoch of the culmination of metaphysics defined by the planetary domination of technology. In the passage of the *Black Notebooks* dealing with contemporary myth, he placed the word myth in quotation marks.[198] In this context, he interpreted it in a

196 Martin Heidegger, *Einführung in die Metaphysik* (1935), *GA*, vol. 40, pp. 164–167.

197 Martin Heidegger, *Parmenides* (1942–43), *GA*, vol. 54, ed. Manfred Frings (Frankfurt am Main: Klostermann, 1992), p. 89.

198 Martin Heidegger, *Überlegung* XII, § 35, in *Überlegungen* XII–XV (*Schwarze Hefte*, 1939–41), *GA*, vol. 96, p. 54; English translation, *Ponderings*, XII–XV. *Black Notebooks, 1939–41*, trans. Richard Rojcewicz (Bloomington, IN: Indiana University Press, 2014), p. 42. Heidegger does not seem to have made a distinction between the terms "Mythos" and "Mythus" which are both current in German. If Heidegger used the term

highly revealing manner, for he characterized its role at the culmination of the history of Being in opposition to his allusions to ancient Greek myth at the primordial origin of the history of Being. He wrote:

> "The 'reporting' ('Reportage') of machination in 'picture' and 'sound' is the global 'myth' (*Mythus*) of the consummating phase of modernity. The world of the most remote German farmstead is no longer determined by the mystery of the rhythm of the year, i.e. by 'nature' in which the earth still holds sway, but rather by the illustrated newspaper with its presentation of underclothed ballerinas and film actresses, of prize-fighters and race-car drivers, and other 'heroes' of the day. Here it is no longer merely a matter of the destruction of 'morality' and of 'propriety', but of a metaphysical process, the devastation of every possibility of Being that is reduced to the products of makeable, producible, and representable beings."[199]

In this passage Heidegger portrayed contemporary "myth"—in quotation marks—as a vehicle of dissemination of what he termed the "machination"—the *Machenschaft*—in the era of predominance of technology. As we have seen in previous chapters, the seminal term *Machenschaft* appeared in many of Heidegger's writings and course lectures of this period, beginning in the 1930s, notably in *Contributions to Philosophy* (*Beiträge zur Philosophie*), *Discernment* (*Besinnung*), *Parmenides*, and *Essays and Conferences* (*Vorträge und Aufsätze*). If it is often rendered as "machination," this translation does not adequately convey its different connotations in German. *Machenschaft* signifies at once *machen* (doing) and *herstellen* (producing); it also recalls the "*Macher,*" the able self-promoter, who may be engaged in collusion and intrigue. If we compare with one another the primordial Greek myth and the "myth"—in quotation marks—unfurled by the *Machenschaft* in the era of the planetary domination of technology, it becomes clear that their significations stand in an inverse relationship: where the primordial myth unveils the truth of Being, drawing truth out of its hidden depths, the contemporary myth, at the culminating point of a long history, obscures truth in portraying it in terms of what can be produced, represented, or felt by the human subject in the guise of lived experience (*Erlebnis*). Where the primordial myth names the sacred and, as

---

"Mythos" in designating the primordial myth of ancient Greece, while he employed the word "Mythus" in the above passage found in "Überlegungen" XII of the *Black Notebooks,* he nonetheless erroneously referred in another passage of the *Black Notebooks* to the title of the book of the Nazi ideologue Alfred Rosenberg, *Der Mythus des XX. Jahrhunderts* as the "Mythos" des XX. Jahrhunderts." See *Überlegung* XI, § 58, in *Überlegungen* VII–XI (*Schwarze Hefte* 1938–39), *GA* 95, p. 412.

199 Martin Heidegger, *Überlegung* XII, *GA*, vol. 96, p. 54; *Ponderings XII–XV*, pp. 42–43; translation modified.

Heidegger noted in *Parmenides*, refers to the divinity,[200] the myth disseminated by the *Machenschaft* through reporting in "sound" and "image," casts a spell (*Behexung*). The *Machenschaft*, as Heidegger commented in a suggestive passage in *Contributions to Philosophy*, expends its efforts toward the re-enchantment of power (*Verzauberung der Macht*), which at the same time engages a disenchantment of beings (*Entzauberung des Seienden*).[201]

Contemporary myth in this way extends and reinforces the power of the *Machenschaft*. And this brings us to the heart of the matter: How are we to understand this *mythology* animated by the *Machenschaft* that casts its spell by means of reporting in sound and image, leading through the production, representation, and lived experience of beings to the "devastation of every possibility of Being"? In examining Heidegger's portrayal of this mythology more closely, I aim to underscore the central problem at the very core of his interpretation of the history of Being that he to my mind sidestepped and left *unthought*.

I

In order to more closely characterize contemporary myth we must pursue Heidegger's conception of the *Machenschaft* that infuses and propels it. Heidegger situated the advent of the *Machenschaft* in the framework of a long history initiated at the beginning of the metaphysical tradition above all by Plato. Following the emergence of ancient metaphysics, as he explains in *Contributions to Philosophy*, the emergence of the *Machenschaft* was prepared by the great transformation brought by belief in the Judeo-Christian creator God, characterized by His infinite power to *make* the world—the *ens creatum*.[202] Over the course of centuries, the onslaught of the machination is achieved once this power is resolutely transferred from the divine to the human agent and the objects of human representation and production are identified with the sole source of truth. At this stage, the machination eradicates (*ausrotten*) all genuine questions by setting beyond its purview whatever cannot be technologically produced and represented, and communicated in the public sphere (*Öffentlichkeit*) to stimulate lived experience through sound and image.[203]

---

200 Martin Heidegger, *Parmenides* (1942–43), *GA*, vol. 54, pp. 165–66.

201 Martin Heidegger, *Beiträge zur Philosophie (Vom Ereignis)* (1936–38), *GA* 65, pp. 107, 124; *Contributions to Philosophy*, pp. 75, 86–87.

202 Ibid., pp. 126–128; *Contributions to Philosophy*, pp. 88–90.

203 Ibid., p. 110; *Contributions to Philosophy*, p. 77.

In this final phase of Western metaphysics, the *Machenschaft* exercizes a "total" grip, which contaminates *all* of human culture, whether in the domain of science, religion, economics, politics, or art. Nothing escapes from its hold: without revealing its veritable character, it continually reinforces its power and disseminates the myth that assures its domination on a planetary scale. Only the thought of Being (*Seinsdenken*) may announce the dawn of another beginning.

What is most striking in Heidegger's manner of describing the total grip of the machination on human culture is above all its massive and monolithic character, which admits of no nuances or distinctions. This total, monolithic character of the *Machenschaft* and of the myth it propels comes to light with singular clarity in Heidegger's conception of historical understanding in the framework of the history of Being. In the articulation of this history, Heidegger's refusal to acknowledge nuances that distinguish different cultural endeavors in the era of technological domination reduces all forms of historical reflection in the contemporary context, aside from his own *Seinsdenken*, to so many expressions of the *Machenschaft* and assimilates them to the myth it propagates. It is here, as I shall argue, that the equivalence Heidegger establishes between the pursuits of the different historical disciplines and the contemporary myth of the *Machenschaft* permits us to place the unthought dimension of his monolithic interpretation most clearly in evidence.

In his examination of the historiography of the nineteenth century, Heidegger willingly acknowledged important distinctions which he interpreted in *Contributions to Philosophy* and in *Parmenides*. In these works he made a distinction between the "historian" (*Historiker*) and the "historical thinker" (*Geschichtsdenker*). In contrast to the historian, the historical thinker does not attempt to explain history, nor to calculate its effects, but to place in evidence its unique and inexplicable character.[204] In *Parmenides*, Heidegger qualified the historian Jacob Burckhardt as a *Geschichtsdenker*, who illustrated in an original manner the "atrocity and cruelty, the unhappiness that characterized the Greek *polis*." At the same time, he was able to depict the "rise and fall of humans in the essential place of their emergence."[205] However, even Burckhardt, in his work *Griechische Kulturgeschichte*, was unable to grasp the true sources of Greek understanding when he anachronistically applied the term "culture," which was of Latin origin, to characterize ancient Greek history.

---

204 Ibid., p. 154.
205 Heidegger, *Parmenides*, *GA*, vol. 54, pp. 133–34.

In the final analysis, Burckhardt's historical thought remained for Heidegger a phenomenon of the nineteenth century. According to *Contributions to Philosophy*, the difference between the historical thinker, exemplified by Burckhardt, and the mere historian disappeared in the twentieth century. In the contemporary world, for Heidegger,

> "History as a discipline (*Historie*) [...] corresponds to an intensification of its activity as scientific journalism. It manifests the quality of reporting, of a presentation of the whole of events [...] which places historical discernment (*geschichtliche Besinnung*) into a situation of utter confusion."[206]

With the planetary domination of technology, different forms of historical reflection converge. The branches of the historical discipline, without distinction or nuance, are adapted to the role of "reporting" (*Reportage*). This reduction of disciplinary history to "reporting" complements the function of "reporting" in sound and image, as specified earlier in the passage drawn from the *Black Notebooks*, in which "reporting" reveals itself to be the vehicle of contemporary myth. This monolithic judgment Heidegger made in regard to the contemporary historical disciplines was not a simple expression of hyperbole or of rhetorical embellishment. Indeed, his indifference to any distinction between the pursuits of the historical disciplines and contemporary myth is further reinforced in other sections of the *Black Notebooks*. In a short passage in this work, Heidegger lumped together what he took to be different forms of historical interpretation practiced in disciplines of theology, political science, economics, intellectual history (*geisteshistorisch*), or racial studies (*die rassischen*): each of these modes of historical interpretation was for him "as superficial as the others."[207] Here Heidegger clearly refused to acknowledge any fundamental distinction between economic, political, and intellectual history, and the so-called "racial science" of his period. Without nuance, he reduced all distinctions between them to the same level. It cannot therefore in any way be surprising to learn in the same passage that the historical disciplines (*Historie*) are nothing but a heap of propaganda and stupefaction (*Propaganda und Betäubung*).[208]

The absence of nuances and distinctions in Heidegger's judgment of the contemporary historical disciplines is attested at many points in his

---

206 Heidegger, *Beiträge zur Philosophie, GA*, vol. 65, p. 154; *Contributions to Philosophy*, p. 107; translation modified.

207 Heidegger, "Überlegung" XII, § 34, in *Überlegungen XII–XV (Schwarze Hefte, 1939–41), GA* 96, pp. 51–52; *Ponderings XII–XIV*, pp. 40–41.

208 Ibid.

works in this period, but a further example will suffice to pinpoint its implications for Heidegger's concept of historical thought. This example concerns Heidegger's position in regard to the historical speculation of Oswald Spengler in his book *The Decline of the West*, which was published in the aftermath of World War I. In his early Freiburg course lectures in the years after the war, Heidegger continually attacked Spengler's methodology in this work. Heidegger directed his attack against Spengler's historical determinism, according to which human history develops in accord with rigid laws, analogous to those of biology and botany.[209] In his later course *Parmenides* Heidegger reiterated his attack on Spengler stating that Spengler "debases history from the very start (*die Geschichte im Voraus herabwürdigt*) to the level of a biological process and makes of it a greenhouse of cultures that flourish and decline like plants."[210] Nevertheless, in spite of this sharp criticism in his course lectures, Heidegger modified his evaluation of Spengler in the *Black Notebooks*. In this framework, he insisted on the *importance* of Spengler's book which had the courage to "confront historical science in a serious manner" (*mit der Historie ernstzumachen*).[211] In this example, one might well raise the question concerning the seriousness Spengler's historical reflection. One might above all wonder how Spengler's historical determinism presented a serious challenge to the historiography of his period, above all in view of his position at the beginning of this book, according to which he advocated:

> "Physiognomical tact, decision of the blood [...], innate scrutiny turned toward persons and situations, toward the event (*Ereignis*), the necessary, in the place of mere scientific criticism and knowledge of data."[212]

It would reach beyond the framework of the present chapter to provide a detailed examination of Spengler's historical method and to enter into the debate concerning the difference between historical reflection based on verifiable documentary research that is scrutinized in terms of divergent possibilities of interpretation from different points of view and speculation

---

209 Heidegger, *Phänomenologie des religiösen Lebens, GA* 60, pp. 31–45.

210 Heidegger, *Parmenides, GA*, 54, p. 168.

211 Heidegger, *Anmerkungen I–V (Schwarze Hefte, 1942–48), GA* 97, p. 159.

212 Oswald Spengler, *Der Untergang des Abendlandes*, vol. 2, *Welthistorische Perspektiven* (Munich: Beck, 1922), p. 56. As Ernst Troeltsch wrote in a contemporary review published in 1922, Spengler's biologism and racial theory showed marked ideological tendencies in view of "the romantic cynicism and new conservatism of belief in the blood." Ernst Troeltsch, "Welthistorische Perspektiven," in *Aufsätze zur Geistesgeschichte und Religionssoziologie, Gesammelte Schriften*, vol. 4, (Tübingen: Mohr [Paul Siebeck]), 1925, p. 690.

on the basis of unverifiable hypotheses that situate biological or racial factors at the source of human historical development. It suffices for the present analysis to note that Heidegger's judgment *does not accord any importance* to such a distinction. To his mind, any distinction of this kind is meaningless: the *Machenschaft* and the myth it propels configure all contemporary historical thinking in view of attaining a re-enchantment of power imposed by technology leading to the disenchantment of beings.

II

The idea that the process of rationalization and technological development leads to the disenchantment of the world (*Entzauberung der Welt*) was closely associated in the years after World War I with the writings of Max Weber, the sociologist who forged this concept. In a review of Karl Jaspers's *Psychology of World Views* (1919–21) that Heidegger wrote at an early point in his teaching career at the University of Freiburg im Breisgau, and which was published posthumously, Heidegger directed a strong critique against Weber's sociological method which Jaspers had lauded in his book.[213] Eleven years later, in 1932, Karl Jaspers published a book on Max Weber in a period of growing radicalization of the political situation in Germany a year before the Nazi rise to power. In dealing in this book with Weber's conceptions of philosophy, politics, and science, Jaspers examined Weber's conception of the rationalization of all sectors of human life leading to the "disenchantment of the world." Disenchantment for Weber, as Jaspers recalled, is the heavy price that humanity has paid for rationalization and the rise of technology it accompanied, which dissipated belief in the intervention of hidden magical forces. As Jaspers noted, Weber defended the disenchantment that rationalization had brought in its wake, and he lauded above all the scientific method that he took to be its crowning acquisition.[214] He distinguished the limited goals of empirical science and historical research from prophecy and from any claim to reach a total vision of history. Following the publication of his book on Weber, Jaspers sent Heidegger a copy, and Heidegger, in a letter to Jaspers dated 8 December 1932, admonished that to his mind there could be no question of renewing Weber's orientation in the post-World War I context. He

213 Martin Heidegger, "Anmerkungen zu Karl Jaspers *Psychologie der Weltanschauungen,*" *Wegmarken, GA* 9, pp. 40–41.

214 Karl Jaspers, *Max Weber. Politiker, Forscher, Philosoph* (Bremen: Storm, 1946), pp. 39–43. As Jaspers noted in the preface to this book, it is an exact reproduction of the 1932 edition.

succinctly summed up his attitude in remarking that "Max Weber will to the end always remain foreign to me."[215] Later, during the years of the Hitler regime, Heidegger briefly alluded to Weber in his *Remarks on Ernst Jünger* that were posthumously published in the framework of his collected works. In this context he qualified the social theory of Max Weber as the scientific ideal corresponding to the "liberalism" and the "bourgeois ideology of the nineteenth century."[216]

Beyond Heidegger's derisive comments on Weber, he did not to my knowledge relate the conception of "disenchantment" or "disenchantment of beings" to Weber's thought. Nonetheless, a brief reference to Weber's conception of disenchantment will serve to delineate the radical difference that distinguishes their respective interpretations of this concept and to further highlight what is to my mind the unthought and particularly problematic aspect of Heidegger's ruminations on the myth of the *Machenschaft*.

In his theoretical works, Weber freely acknowledged the difficulty raised by rationalization and the resulting disenchantment of the world, for rationalization brought with it the disappearance from the public world (*Öffentlichkeit*), not only of superstition and credulity, but of what were considered to be the most sublime aspects of human existence. And Weber well understood that the vacuum left by this disappearance prepared the ground for a quest for re-enchantment and a rebirth of myth. Yet the danger that Weber forecast was situated in a completely different area than that later identified by Heidegger. The disenchantment of the world led above all for Weber to a weakening of religious convictions inherited from the Judeo-Christian tradition and at the same time to the collapse of the rationalism of ethical life that this tradition had established. The quest for re-enchantment and for new forms of myth could thus open the way to what this tradition had long opposed: the resurrection of the old demons of archaic mythology, which were the vestiges of a past that had never been entirely vanquished. As Weber described this situation in a famous passage of *Science as a vocation* (*Wissenschaft als Beruf*, 1919): "a plethora of ancient gods, in a disenchanted form and in the guise of anonymous powers, rise from their graves and attempt to dominate human beliefs."[217]

215 Martin Heidegger, Karl Jaspers *Briefwechsel, 1920–1963*, ed. Walter Biemel and Hans Saner (Frankfurt am Main: Klostermann/Munich/Zurich: Piper, 1990), p. 148.

216 Martin Heidegger, *Zu Ernst Jünger*, *GA*, vol. 90, ed. Peter Trawny (Frankfurt am Main: Klostermann, 2004), p. 118; Heidegger, "Winke, Überlegungen (II) und Anweisungen," *Überlegungen II–VI (Schwarze Hefte 1931–1938)*, *GA*, vol. 94, p. 50.

217 Max Weber, "Wissenschaft als Beruf," in *Wissenschaft als Beruf 1917/1919, Politik als Beruf, 1919, Gesamtausgabe*, section 1, vol. 17, p. 101.

When Heidegger evoked archaic myths, he did so, as we have seen, in a radically different way, since he discerned above all their Greek origin, at the moment for him when myth revealed a pristine truth. Over the course of a long history, it is only in the period of technical rationalization that he detected the power of modern myth to cast a spell on a planetary scale. And if the weakening of the Judeo-Christian tradition favors the emergence of new forms of myth, it is not to open a way to the return of the repressed demons of old but, as I have illustrated, to reinforce on the anthropocentric basis of modern technology the Judeo-Christian doctrine of the creation of beings by an omnipotent providential will. Far from providing a force to repress the ancient demons and to restrain their occult power, the Judeo-Christian heritage, on the contrary, prepared the emergence of the modern myth propelled by the *Machenschaft*.

As a counterpart to the modern myth of the *Machenschaft*, Heidegger did not hesitate in the *Black Notebooks* to conjure up potent mythical motifs drawn from archaic Germanic sources, which he nowhere characterized as myths. In this context, far from dreading the occult power of pagan myths bequeathed by an archaic past, he found in these myths a source of future hope and the inspiration of a heritage (*Überlieferung*) that according to him no historical discipline is capable of grasping: "hidden Germanity (*verborgene Deutschheit*) in its harmony with Being." According to Heidegger:

> "Once again—and how often will it be—the German essence is thrown far back into an uncanny concealment; it still lacks the clarity and courage to dominate from out of the calm conferred by the supreme struggle in Being itself, which is the preserved origin of the final god."[218]

Heidegger's assumption that the national heritage could provide a path to salvation, if it was a timely belief shared by many of his compatriots in the Hitler period, reveals above all the fragility of any quest for "rationalization" which, beyond the simple will to technological mastery, seeks to dissipate the power of old demons and archaic superstitions, and the prejudices of blood and soil. Here Heidegger's indifference to nuances that separate different forms of rationalization and distinguish them from the illusions of racial doctrines, which are all for him equally relative to the contemporary epoch, and his eagerness to assimilate all of them indifferently

218 "Wieder ist—und wie oft noch wird—das deutsche Wesen weit zurückgeworfen in eine unheimliche Verborgenheit; noch fehlt ihm die Helle und der Mut zur Herrschaft aus der Stille der Verschenkung höchsten Kampfes im Seyn selbst, das der aufbewahrte Ursprung des letzten Gottes ist"; Heidegger, *Überlegungen XII–XV (Schwarze Hefte 1939–1941)*, *GA*, vol., 96, pp. 32, 48, 55; *Ponderings XII–XV*, pp. 26, 38, 43.

to the myth of the *Machenschaft*, raises earnest questions concerning the sweeping vision he proposed of the history of Being. In claiming to grasp this history, his depiction of the emergence of the contemporary myth of the machination arrogates to itself *alone* the capacity to reach beyond the confines of the period in which it is rooted and to discern a truth that machination cannot appropriate. In the final analysis, however, his appeal to myth in the framework of *Seinsgeschichte* cannot but leave unthought the ways in which his monolithic vision of history might itself bring to expression a catastrophic political mythology of our times.

Part II

Politics, Myth, and History: Aspects of the Critical Reception of Heidegger's Thought

Chapter 7

Politics and the Public World: Martin Heidegger in the Critical Perspective of Hannah Arendt

In a speech presented to the "American Society of Political Scientists" in 1954, entitled "Concern with Politics in Recent European Philosophical Thought," Hannah Arendt referred to an aspect of Martin Heidegger's work which was, in her eyes, especially pertinent to her own philosophical endeavors. As she explained:

> "It lies in the nature of philosophy to deal with man in the singular, whereas politics could not even be conceived of if men did not exist in the plural. Or to put it another way: the experiences of the philosopher—insofar as he is a philosopher—are with solitude, while for man—insofar as he is political—solitude is an essential but nevertheless marginal experience. It may be—but I shall only hint at this—that Heidegger's concept of 'world,' which in many respects stands at the center of his philosophy, constitutes a step out of this difficulty. At any rate, because Heidegger defines human existence as being-in-the-world, he insists on giving philosophic significance to structures of everyday life that are completely incomprehensible if man is not primarily understood as being together with others."[219]

Hannah Arendt underlines here Heidegger's interpretation of human existence as being-in-the-world, in other words the characterization of human existence as inherence in a common world pre-structured by a network of relations to things and to other people. If Arendt emphasizes this Heideggerian interpretation, it is because it seems to her to present the possibility of a preliminary overcoming of what she designates as the traditional isolation of the philosopher from the common world of human affairs. And, in her own writings, Hannah Arendt sought to surmount precisely this traditional isolation on the basis of political theory. She intended, above all, to place in question a tradition which to her mind has not sufficiently recognized the philosophical implications of political interaction in the context of a public world.

In spite of the importance she accords to Heidegger's interpretation of being-in-the-world, reflection on what she took to be this traditional relation between philosophy and politics led her to criticize Heidegger's thought. This criticism concerned not only Heidegger's official support of

219 Hannah Arendt, "Concern with Politics in Recent European Philosophical Thought," *Essays in Understanding (1930–54)*, ed. Jerome Kohn, (New York: Harcourt Brace and Co., 1994), p. 443.

the Nazi regime as rector of the University of Freiburg im Breisgau from May, 1933, until February, 1934, but above all the absence of specifically *political* reflection in *Being and Time*, in spite of Heidegger's claim, in the framework of his analysis of being-in-the-world, to account for human existence in a *public* world. For Hannah Arendt, Heidegger's neglect of the political dimension of human existence in *Being and Time*, far from designating a simple omission in his thinking, represents one of its salient characteristics.[220] The absence of specifically political reflection in Heidegger's work signified for Arendt a depreciation of political experience which, at the very least, bore an *indirect* relation to Heidegger's engagement in favor of the Nazis.

It is not my intention in this chapter to focus on Heidegger's political activity during the Third Reich. By means of Hannah Arendt's critique of Heidegger's account of the public world, I seek rather to place Arendt's own conception of the public world in sharper relief and to determine its role in her theory of politics. I will attempt to demonstrate that Arendt, far from proposing her theory of politics as a mere supplement to the Heideggerian interpretation of being-in-the-world, places the political dimension of the public world at a more radical level of investigation: from her point of view, indeed, without a basis in political reflection the fundamental philosophical problem of *truth* cannot legitimately be addressed. If the very words "public world" take on a meaning in Arendt's thought that sharply differs from Heidegger's understanding of this theme, I will attempt to illustrate that this difference, beyond a simple terminological distinction, provides an important indication for comprehending the originality of her approach to the question of truth.

I

In the preface to *Men in Dark Times* Hannah Arendt evokes the specific aspect of Heidegger's interpretation of the world that stands at the heart of her own critical reflection. In this preface, Arendt quotes Heidegger's assertion in *Being and Time*, "Die Öffentlichkeit verdunkelt alles" ("The public obscures everything"). Without indicating her own intervention, however, Arendt reformulates Heidegger's phrase—it is not clear whether

220 *Ibid.*, p. 5; Hannah Arendt, "What is Existential Philosophy?" (1946), translated by Robert and Rita Kimber, *Essays in Understanding (1930–54)*, pp. 163–187; Hannah Arendt, "Martin Heidegger at Eighty," *New York Review of Books* vol. 17, 6, 21 October, 1971, pp. 50–54, reprinted in Michael Murray, ed., *Heidegger and Modern Philosophy* (New Haven: Yale University Press, 1978), pp. 293–303.

intentionally or inadvertently—in terms of a paradox. She writes: "Das Licht der Öffentlichkeit verdunkelt alles" ("The light of the public obscures everything").[221] In section 27 of *Being and Time*, nonetheless, Heidegger merely wrote:

> "The public obscures everything, and what has thus been covered up gets passed off as something familiar and accessible to everyone."[222]

Although Heidegger here refers to the "public," and not to the public character of the world, the chapter of *Being and Time* from which this quote is drawn is nevertheless entitled, "Being-in-the-world as Being-with and Being-one's-self. The 'they'"; and the "public" clearly signifies the public character of the world. As Heidegger explains in the course of this chapter, the darkening arises essentially from publicness as a structure of being-in-the-world.

What proves to be especially pertinent for Hannah Arendt's interpretation is the specific way in which Heidegger relates publicness and the darkening which it engenders to the phenomenon of the world. As readers of *Being and Time* recognize, Heidegger by no means conceived the phenomenon of "worldhood" (*Weltlichkeit*) as an external cosmos with which humans interact. Worldhood for Heidegger designates the way of being of *Dasein* itself, as the necessary precondition for any possible meaningful relation to things and to other *Dasein*. The priority of worldhood as an ontological structure of human existence expresses itself in the direct interpretability of the everyday environing and common world (*alltägliche Um- und Mitwelt*), to which *Dasein* most immediately relates and on which all comprehension of singular ontic circumstances is founded. In the context of this everyday world *Dasein* never encounters objects or individuals in the abstract, but things or other *Dasein* already engaged in a complex web of meaningful relations.

In *Being and Time* Heidegger relates this priority of the world as a meaningful structure existing before any encounter with isolated individuals or singular objects to the common accessibility and openness of the everyday world, characterized above all by its continuity and its permanence: it is the everyday structure of the world which, as a way of being of *Dasein*, exists for everyone at all times. This continual openness of the everyday world constitutes an anonymous field of action, wholly

221 Hannah Arendt, "Preface," *Men in Dark Times* (Harmondsworth: Penguin, 1973), p. 9.

222 Martin Heidegger, *Sein und Zeit*, *GA*, vol. 2, p. 170; English trans., *Being and Time*, p. 165; translation modified.

indifferent to *Dasein* in its fundamental singularity—the field of action of the "they" (*das Man*)—and it is this anonymous everyday field of action which Heidegger terms the "public world" (*öffentliche Welt*).

According to Heidegger, tools, ordinary objects and, in a broader sense, pathways and streets, nature and the environing world as well as *Dasein* itself, existing in a web of everyday relations, may constantly be interpreted in a public light.[223] Whereas tools and ordinary objects wear out or are overtaken by progress and streets fall into disrepair, nature and the environing world continually change while death claims human individuals. What, however, reveals itself to be the ontological kernel of the unity and continuity of the world plays a particularly important role, as we will later see, in Heidegger's interpretation of truth: the world in its public, everyday dimension, accessible to everyone at each moment, which always precedes the ontic life of each individual and continues after his or her death. This durability of the public world embodies for Heidegger the anonymity of human relations, founded on total indifference to *Dasein*'s singularity, whose essential feature resides in its mortality.[224] It is this durability of the public world which comes to expression for Heidegger in the temporal permanence of the "they" ("the 'they' never dies");[225] this permanence, at the source of the inauthentic interpretation of existence, provides *Dasein*, through the sheer durability of an anonymous, public mode of existence, with the possibility of dissimulating the finitude of its own mortal existence.

With the qualification of the public world in terms of permanence and durability, we encounter the theme of the *temporal* foundation of *Dasein*, which will prove particularly important to our present investigation. As we will see, Heidegger's analysis of the temporal structures of the public world in *Being and Time* constitute the focus of Hannah Arendt's critical reflections concerning Heidegger's interpretation of the "public" world.

In the second section of *Being and Time*, entitled "*Dasein* and Temporality," Heidegger grounds the public interpretability of the world in

223 *Ibid.*, p. 95; Eng. trans., p. 100.

224 *Ibid.*, p. 561, Eng. trans. p. 477. I refer to *Dasein*'s radical singularity in accord with Heidegger's own statements in *Being and Time*: "When it [*Dasein*] stands before itself in this way [before the possibility of its own death], all its relations to any other *Dasein* have been undone" (*Sein und Zeit, GA*, vol. 2, p. 333; Eng. trans., p. 294); "The non-relational character of death [...] singularizes (*vereinzelt*) *Dasein* unto itself" (*Sein und Zeit, GA* 2, p. 349; Eng. trans., p. 308).

225 *Ibid.*, p. 561; Eng. trans., p. 477.

what he terms "public time." If in everyday existence *Dasein* utilizes tools or encounters other *Dasein* in the common, everyday world, such modes of being-in-the-world necessarily depend upon the possibility of a public interpretation of *time*. Indeed, the durability of the everyday world, open to everyone at each moment, presupposes for Heidegger the possibility of general access to a common measurable time. Heidegger states in *Being and Time*:

> "Thus when time is measured, it is made public in such a way that it is encountered on each occasion and at any time for everyone as 'now and now and now.'"[226]

Heidegger designates this measurable time, which has "each time been rendered public" and which can be infinitely extended, as "world time" (*Weltzeit*). Given the domination of the public interpretation of time in its ordinary, everyday dimension, it is by no means accidental, for Heidegger, that this interpretation has also determined the Western idea of time at the theoretical level, from Aristotle to Kant and Hegel—and up to the present.

If for Heidegger "the public obscures everything," this is because the public world overshadows original time by means of the domination of public time. Precisely when it interprets itself in light of the durability of public time, *Dasein* is able to dissimulate the finitude of its own temporal existence and thus to unburden care arising from mortal being which is "in each case my own." This dissimulation or "looking away from finitude" (*Wegsehen von der Endlichkeit*) is at the same time the source of the idea of temporal infinity: by means of this refusal to confront finitude, "the forgetful 'representation' of the 'infinity' of public time can be strengthened."[227]

What concerns us in Heidegger's analysis is less the theme of temporality *per se* than its relation to the interpretation of truth. And, most important in this regard is Heidegger's argument that the universal validity (*Allgemeingültigkeit*) of the criteria of truth arises from the generality of a public world accessible to everyone at each moment and, consequently, from the neglect of finite time in favor of public time.

According to *Being and Time*, the criteria of truth presupposed by the Western metaphysical tradition only serve to reinforce the everyday domination of the public interpretation of the world and of world time. This is the tradition stemming from the Platonic identification of ideas with immutability and eternity and from the Aristotelian doctrine of

226 *Ibid*., p. 551; Eng. trans., p. 470.
227 *Ibid*., p. 560; Eng. trans., p. 477.

substance as "ousia" or permanent presence. In positing the atemporal permanence of being, it is precisely the temporal finitude of *Dasein* that these criteria either set aside or hold to be merely secondary. It is by no means accidental for Heidegger if, on the basis of this domination of the public interpretation of the world and of time, modern scientific theories of truth have adopted the criteria of "universality," even after having abandoned all claims to metaphysical validity. The very fact that "objective" scientific truth is also "universal"—that is to say, uniformly accessible to everyone at all times—is for Heidegger the clearest testimony to the domination of the public interpretation of the world and of time. The laying bare of this tendency to dissimulate truth rooted in finitude provides the occasion for reflection on the idea of scientific theory, which concerns, above all, historical science, whose object is *Dasein* itself. In this regard, Heidegger writes in *Being and Time*:

> "In no science are the 'universal validity' of standards and the claims to 'universality' which the 'they' and its common sense demand less possible as criteria of 'truth' than in authentic historical inquiry."[228]

I set aside in this context the question, which Heidegger himself barely examines, concerning how, in the light of the finitude of *Dasein*, authentic science might be envisioned. Although granting that even such authentic science, rooted in Dasein's being-in-the-world, can never entirely extract itself from the inauthentic dimension of existence, our question concerns the direct relation designated by Heidegger between the criteria of universal validity and inauthenticity. Must this claim to truth, valid for everyone at all times, necessarily be equated with the modes of comprehension dominated by the 'they,' rooted in inauthentic temporal existence? It is precisely this question that I will now examine in the perspective of Hannah Arendt's thinking.

II

As the starting point for the second part of this analysis, let us return once again to the quotation taken from Hannah Arendt's book *Men in Dark Times* which I evoked at the beginning of this chapter. Here is the entire passage in the context of which Hannah Arendt presented her paraphrase of Heidegger's sentence "The public obscures everything":

---

228 *Ibid.*, p. 522; Eng. trans., p. 447; translation modified.

> "In his [Heidegger's] description of human existence, everything that is real or authentic is assaulted by the overwhelming power of 'mere talk' that irresistibly arises out of the public realm, determining every aspect of everyday existence, anticipating and annihilating the sense or the nonsense of everything the future may bring. There is no escape, according to Heidegger, from the 'incomprehensible triviality' of this common everyday world except by withdrawal from it into that solitude which philosophers since Parmenides and Plato have opposed to the political realm. We are here not concerned with the philosophical relevance of Heidegger's analyses (which, in my opinion, is undeniable) nor with the tradition of philosophic thought that stands behind them, but exclusively with certain underlying experiences of the time and their conceptual description. In our context, the point is that the sarcastic, perverse-sounding statement, *Das Licht der Oeffentlichkeit verdunkelt alles* ('The light of the public obscures everything'), went to the very heart of the matter and actually was no more than the most succinct summing-up of existing conditions."[229]

In this passage we immediately notice how Hannah Arendt adapts Heidegger's interpretation of the public world to her own ends. Whereas for Heidegger *Dasein* always exists in a public world, and the facticity of *Dasein* presupposes its rootedness at all times in an everyday public world, Hannah Arendt relates Heidegger's analyses to "certain underlying experiences of the time" rather than to human existence *per se*. Heidegger conceived existence in the public world and its obscuring of truth as a mode of being of *Dasein*. We will see that Hannah Arendt transforms the meaning of Heidegger's thought. But what is the purpose of this apparently insignificant modification of Heidegger's analyses? Might it lead us to the heart of a critical reinterpretation of Heidegger's philosophy?

One might be tempted to underestimate the implications of Arendt's assertions for her own conception of the world. Arendt indeed explains that she does not wish to insist on her own judgment concerning the philosophical relevance of Heidegger's analyses and her statement would seem rather to confirm than to place in question Heidegger's conceptions. Does Arendt not limit the range of Heidegger's analysis to a diagnosis of the period, whereas Heidegger placed the accent on *Dasein*'s mode of being *per se*, beyond any determinate period? To support the correctness of this thesis, one might very well appeal to statements in *Being and Time* itself: according to Heidegger, even if it is impossible to completely sever one's roots in the public, everyday world, the task of *Dasein*'s authentic mode of existence is to resist the type of interpretation this world fosters, and to strive to interpret itself in the light of its finitude. Moreover, the domination of the public world is variable in its intensity, as Heidegger indicates in *Being and Time* when he writes that "the extent to which its

---

229 Hannah Arendt, "Preface," *Men in Dark Times*, pp. 8–9.

[the 'they's'] dominion becomes compelling and explicit may change in the course of history."[230] Nonetheless, the domination of the "they" and the darkening of truth that proceeds from this domination belong to the original constitution of *Dasein* as such, independent of any consideration of its historical context. Yet here too Hannah Arendt would seem to agree when in the preface to *Men in Dark Times* she asserts that "dark times" hardly represent anything truly new or specifically modern.

One could not justifiably try to determine Hannah Arendt's fundamental position in regard to Heidegger on the basis of these isolated remarks, as suggestive as they may be. More decisive for her critique of Heidegger is the distance between them that reveals itself in their respective concepts of the philosophical "tradition." Whereas Heidegger defines this tradition essentially in terms of the tacit question of the finitude of *Dasein*, from Arendt's very different perspective, the theme of the public world provides the touchstone for understanding this tradition ever since Parmenides, Plato, and Aristotle took positions on this topic. For this reason I will examine the critique of Heidegger that Hannah Arendt advances in light of the philosophical tradition that she herself designates as her fundamental target.

Like Heidegger, Hannah Arendt attempts to place the modern scientific tradition in question in relation to what she takes to be the domination of a specific historical form of the philosophical conception truth. However, whereas Heidegger as we have seen defines the tradition in relation to its claim to the temporal permanence and universal validity of the criteria of truth, Arendt's radically different interpretation of this tradition proceeds from a theme specific to her own manner of investigation: for her, the concept of truth since Plato and Aristotle gives testimony above all to the philosopher's hostility to the *polis*, which has traditionally predominated in the West and has given rise to a depreciation of the political realm in comparison to pure thought.[231] In her essay "Tradition and the Modern Age," which originally appeared in German in 1957 in a work entitled *Fragwürdige Traditionsbestände im politischen Denken der Gegenwart* (*Questionable Remains of Tradition in Contemporary Political Thought*), Arendt describes the allegory of the cave in Plato's *Republic* as the starting point of this tradition:

230 Heidegger, *Sein und Zeit, GA*, vol. 2, p. 172; Eng. trans. p. 167.

231 Hannah Arendt, Karl Jaspers, *Briefwechsel* (Munich: Piper, 1985), p. 325; "Tradition and the Modern Age," in *Between Past and Future* (New York: Viking, 1954), p. 17.

> "The beginning was made when, in *The Republic*'s allegory of the cave, Plato described the sphere of human affairs—all that belongs to the living together of men in a common world—in terms of darkness, confusion, and deception which those aspiring to true being must turn away from and abandon if they want to discover the clear sky of eternal ideas."[232]

Following Plato, according to Arendt, Aristotle also accepted this depreciation of the world of human affairs when he accorded a superior role to the "bios theoretikos" in relation to the "bios politikos."

During the years just after the Second World War, when Hannah Arendt began to search for the traces of this philosophical tradition in her contemporary context, she focused her investigation primarily on Heidegger. Her early examination of Heidegger's thought in this light led to a provocative article originally published in 1946 under the title "What is Existential Philosophy?" In this essay, Arendt articulated a sharp critique of Heidegger's tendency to separate the authentic task of philosophy from human affairs in the public world. For her, this tendency gives testimony to the subtle tribute Heidegger pays to the Aristotelian tradition, above all in regard to the privilege this tradition accorded to pure philosophical contemplation.[233] Be this as it may, Hannah Arendt later substantially moderated this critique and, in her 1954 talk entitled "Concern with Politics in Recent European Philosophical Thought," as mentioned earlier, she even went to the point of representing Heidegger's concept of being-in-the-world as a first step toward overcoming this tradition. Nevertheless, Arendt did not refrain in this same talk from criticizing Heidegger's thinking, above all in regard to his interpretation of the public world. In this vein she wrote:

> "Thus, we find the old hostility of the philosopher toward the *polis* in Heidegger's analyses of average everyday life in terms of *das Man* (the "they," or the rule of public opinion, as opposed to the "self"), in which the public realm has the function of hiding reality and preventing even the appearance of truth."[234]

In relation to our present theme, I have emphasized that Heidegger identifies the public world primarily with an inauthentic mode of existence of *Dasein*, which continually serves to hide original truth. And it is precisely the unmitigated character of this interpretation which poses a problem: if

232 "Tradition and the Modern Age," *Between Past and Future*, p. 17.
233 Hannah Arendt, "What is Existential Philosophy?" *Essays in Understanding (1930–54)*, pp. 176–182.
234 H. Arendt, "Concern with Politics in Recent European Philosophical Thought," *Essays in Understanding (1930–54)*, pp. 432–33.

politics can hardly dispense with a foundation in the everyday public world, how can one marshal support on the basis of *Being and Time* for a theory of the political realm that is invested with a dignity beyond mere *inauthenticity*? Granted that Heidegger allows for the possibility in *Being and Time* of an authentic human community, the ontological analysis of this authentic community is nonetheless enunciated in its distinction from a public world which would be capable of serving as an authentic ontological foundation for the political realm. And given that Heidegger's analysis of the public realm hardly accords a space for political existence or for "ontic" political activity grounded in authentic *public* being-in-the-world, it can only be of minor interest for the reconsideration and revaluation of politics in the Western tradition that constitutes Arendt's primary aim. It is thus in terms of this aim that we can comprehend the implications of her interpretation of the public world.

Sharply distinguishing her interpretation from any analysis that would derive the public, everyday character of the world from *Dasein*'s quest to dissimulate its finitude, Arendt's fundamental presupposition approaches the public world from a very different perspective. In her work, the public world is above all portrayed as a symbolic, communicational space—an "interspace"[235]—that, far from arising out of the radical singularity of *Dasein*, finds its source in an original plurality whose essential signification can in no way be reduced to a finite ontology of human existence.

In her book *The Human Condition*, as in her collection of essays *Between Past and Future*, Arendt attempts to demonstrate that the "public" character of the world cannot be grasped on the basis of the mere mortality of isolated human existence. For the durability of the public world does not stem from an inauthentic interpretation of *Dasein* in flight from its own finitude, but on the contrary designates the space itself in which human existence protects and preserves itself. In this sense the public realm designates a common world as the sphere of what Arendt terms the *vita activa*, with its different modes of work, fabrication, and action, the latter of which constitutes the authentic political domain.[236]

From Hannah Arendt's standpoint, the durability of the public world does not originate, as for Heidegger, from a mode of existence character-

---

235 Hannah Arendt, "On Humanity in Dark Times. Thoughts about Lessing," *Men in Dark Times*, p. 21.

236 Hannah Arendt, *The Human Condition* (Chicago: University of Chicago Press, 1958), pp. 7–58.

istic of *Dasein per se*; on the contrary, as the framework of human activity, the world proves to be essentially problematic. Its continuity is precarious, given that as a public "interspace" it is subject to historical *endangerment*. And this historical fragility of the world does not by any means correspond to the ephemerality of mortal *Dasein*. For Arendt, the disappearance of the public world does not necessarily involve the disappearance of the human beings who inhabit this world. In the essay "On Humanity in Dark Times," Arendt describes the possibility of "worldlessness," to which persecuted minorities above all are subject when "the interspace we have called world [...] has simply disappeared."[237] What proves to be particularly problematic for Hannah Arendt is not the fallenness of a *Dasein* that interprets itself in terms of the public world, but rather the threat to the public world itself. For this reason she insists on the importance of sustaining the public realm through human activity.

Provided with Arendt's characterization of the public world, we are now able to reexamine more closely her rendition of Heidegger's sentence: "The light of the public obscures everything." Taken exactly, this darkening does not result, as for Heidegger, from the public dimension of the world as such, but from the *distortion* of this dimension. This darkening describes an historical phenomenon that is increasingly accentuated during the modern period. As Hannah Arendt explains in her 1959 speech, "On Humanity in Dark Times":

> "[...] The public realm has lost the power of illumination which was originally part of its very nature. More and more people in the countries of the Western world, which since the decline of the ancient world has regarded freedom from politics as one of the basic freedoms, make use of this freedom and have retreated from the world and their obligations within it. This withdrawal from the world need not harm an individual; he may even cultivate great talents to the point of genius and so by a detour be useful to the world again. But with each such retreat an almost demonstrable loss to the world takes place; what is lost is the specific and usually irreplaceable in-between which should have formed between this individual and his fellow men."[238]

Here we can appreciate the extent to which Arendt's analysis—in spite of the use of certain topics familiar to Heidegger—distinguishes itself from the basic tendency of his thinking. When Arendt claims that the darkening that overshadows the "public" dimension of the world is only meant to characterize "certain underlying experiences of the time," this is less

---

237 H. Arendt, "On Humanity in Dark Times. Thoughts about Lessing," *Men in Dark Times*, p. 21.

238 *Ibid.*, p. 12.

because it inheres in the temporal and historical structure of *Dasein per se* than by virtue of its link to the historical movement of one specific epoch: that of modernity. If the main current of the Western philosophical tradition has devalued political action in the public realm, the modern darkening of the public world, as Arendt qualifies it, corresponds precisely to the culmination of this tradition in its contemporary, aporetic situation. And the phrase of Heidegger, "the public darkens everything," may indeed prove of particular value in the diagnosis of this situation, even if Heidegger's philosophy itself participates in the modern process of darkening of the public realm. Certainly, in Arendt's opinion, Heidegger's philosophy cannot be considered to be the an ultimate "cause" of this darkening.

It is with this characterization of Hannah Arendt's interpretation of the public world that I return now to our primary question: in what sense do Hannah Arendt's reflections on the public world as a framework of political action involve a specifically *philosophical* investigation concerning truth?

Before directly addressing this question, I should first dissipate a possible misunderstanding. If Arendt relates this philosophical investigation to the political domain, it is not only to advance a claim that philosophers have not sufficiently dealt with politics, in spite of the great number of political writings that belong to our philosophical tradition. The real difficulty concerns the traditional lack of comprehension of the problematic relation between politics and the question of truth. For Arendt, because Heidegger's thought stems from this tradition and plays an important role in its final articulation, it is hardly surprising that the consequences of this tradition for the problem of truth appear in a particularly clear light in her interpretation of the Heideggerian conception of the public world.

In my analysis of Heidegger, I have already had the occasion to recall how the problem of truth relates for him to everyday existence in the public world. If the tradition of Western metaphysics since Plato and Aristotle has generally conceived of truth in terms of eternal, immutable presence, it is because this criterion of truth, for Heidegger, expresses *Dasein*'s everyday tendency to rely upon the durability of the public world as a means of dissimulating its own finitude. And, according to Heidegger, this same "turning away from finitude" comes to expression precisely where the modern sciences—especially the human historical disciplines—presuppose that truth inheres in a permanent and universal standard of objectivity. Even after having abandoned the metaphysical claim to ultimate truth, it is thus this same inauthentic quest for eternity which inspires the "scientific" presupposition of the permanence of the criteria of truth.

The originality of Hannah Arendt's reflections on the problem of truth becomes apparent in her subtle distinction between "immortality" and "eternity." She establishes this distinction between the original ancient Greek conception of temporal perdurability of the public world and the eternity of truth presupposed by contemplative philosophy. In the first instance, Arendt refers to the essentially political signification of the ancient conception of speech and of action which, despite their "material futility, possess an enduring quality of their own because they create their own remembrance" and prove capable therefore of attaining immortal glory.[239] It is at the same time in relation to this capacity to endure that Arendt identifies the specific character of action in so far as it "engages in founding and preserving political bodies," which in turn "creates the condition for remembrance, that is, for history."[240] Conceived in these terms, the temporal significance of immortality consists less in avoiding mortality—which instead characterizes the contemplative thought of eternity—than in creating an earthly dwelling space for human beings in the establishment of a "public world."[241] In the creation of a framework for human plurality, the quest for immortality represents the supreme political activity. It aims at opening a field of action that, in spite of the precariousness and unpredictability typical of human affairs, endows itself with a perdurability capable of extending beyond the short life-span of mortal beings. In this context, Hannah Arendt refers to the foundation of cohesion and of continuity in the public interspace constituted by the "'products' of action and speech" that she terms the "fragile web of human relationships."[242] This web overlays the tangible objects of the public world with a multiplicity of interpretations emanating from different agents. Along with these objects, the web of human relationships constitutes what Arendt terms the "reality" of this world. Far from establishing themselves in terms of fixed structures, the opening to the world depends for Hannah Arendt upon the possibility of convergence of a multiplicity of perspectives in the identification of the same objects of interest.[243] This convergence is founded on what Hannah Arendt terms "common sense": the capacity to fit "into reality as a whole our five strictly individual senses and the strictly particular

239 Hannah Arendt, *The Human Condition*, p. 208.
240 *Ibid.*, pp. 8–9.
241 *Ibid.*, pp. 17–21, 55–56.
242 *Ibid.*, pp. 95, 175–247.
243 *Ibid.*, pp. 57–58, 207–212.

data they perceive."[244] In making accessible a common public world, common sense, according to this usage, makes it possible for our opinions to pass beyond the limits of a particular viewpoint to encompass the viewpoint of others. It permits our opinions to move beyond the horizon of purely personal interests to rise to the level of an "impartial generality."[245] At the same time, with the advent of uniform, socially-conditioned behavior in an increasingly standardized mass society, there is a danger that common sense might atrophy through the loss of its capacity to illuminate a plurality of heterogeneous perspectives at the heart of the public world.[246]

With this notion of "common sense" as an opening to the public world, we reach the precise point where Arendt engages her critique of the traditional presuppositions concerning truth. Indeed if modern criteria of truth as scientific objectivity and universality have become problematic, it is not because, as for Heidegger, the ideal of the permanence of truth tacitly expresses *Dasein*'s continual tendency to avoid its own finitude. If these criteria have become problematic, this is on the contrary because the human sciences have proven increasingly incapable of orienting themselves, on the basis of common sense, in a public world which has become unstable. Far from equivalent to the criteria of universal validity, which for Heidegger express *Dasein*'s quest for eternal, immutable truth, the ability to judge according to the very criteria of objectivity and impartiality risks disappearing, for Arendt, along with the common sense in which they

---

244 *Ibid.*, pp. 208–209.

245 I refer here to the term employed by Hannah Arendt in the essay "Truth and Politics," published in the aftermath of the controversy raised by her book *Eichmann in Jerusalem*; see Hannah Arendt, "Truth and Politics," *Between Past and Future*, p. 242.

246 Hannah Arendt, "The Crisis in Education," *Between Past and Future*, pp. 178–79; Hannah Arendt, "The Crisis in Culture," *Between Past and Future*, pp. 220–21. If this atrophy of common sense is by no means the result of a simple failure of philosophy, it nevertheless first came to expression in philosophical theories which are, for Arendt, symptomatic of what she terms the "alienation from the world." This alienation characterizes for her the relation of modern humans to a world shared in common and it emerged for the first time in theoretical form in Descartes's willingness to entertain the possibility of non-correspondence between the representations of thought and real objects. Hobbes then pushed this problem to its radical extreme. Reason for Descartes as for Hobbes is a "calculation of consequences." This is for Arendt symptomatic of the loss of confidence in the sense thanks to which "the five animal senses are fitted into a world common to all men," underlying the conclusion that "human beings are indeed no more than animals who are able to reason, 'to reckon with consequences.'" See in this regard Hannah Arendt, *The Human Condition*, pp. 273–84. Deepening still further this "alienation from the world" marked by the modern hiatus between consciousness and world, the initial stability of Platonic ideas degenerates into the instability of values which are simply relative, "whose validity is determined not by one or many men but by society as a whole in its ever-changing functional needs"; see Hannah Arendt, "Tradition and the Modern Age," *Between Past and Future*, p. 40.

are grounded. Thus the problem becomes less one of the scientific ideal of universal truth which, like the common world, is supposed to be continually available to everyone, than the capacity to identify—notwithstanding all truth claims of the human sciences—the common aspect of the world which, in permitting us to place ourselves in the perspectives of others, is the source of the very possibility of attaining objective and impartial judgments.[247]

We observe here how for Arendt the political dimension of the public world does not merely represent a theoretical problem for philosophers, but evokes at its very core the original question—and that means the eminently political question—concerning truth. If Hannah Arendt continually returns to this theme in relation to the Greek *polis*, it is by no means due to nostalgia for antiquity, but to lay bare what she designates as the profound disparity between the traditional idea of truth and opinion—"doxa"—grounded in common sense in the framework of the public world. The fact that the criteria of impartiality and of objectivity have become problematic in the human sciences only demonstrates to what extent they have lost their original grip in public affairs. In her essay, "The Concept of History," published in *Between Past and Future*, Arendt devotes a particularly evocative passage to the idea of an original relation in Greek antiquity between the idea of impartiality and objectivity and the public world, a relation which has to her mind become increasingly problematic in the course of modern times. She writes:

> "In this incessant talk the Greeks discovered that the world we have in common is usually regarded from an infinite number of different standpoints, to which correspond the most diverse points of view. In a sheer inexhaustible flow of arguments, as the Sophists presented them to the citizenry of Athens, the Greek learned to exchange his own view-point, his own 'opinion'—the way the world appeared and opened up to him (dokei moi, "it appears to me", from which comes doxa, or 'opinion')—with those of his fellow citizens. Greeks learned to *understand*—not to understand one another as individual persons, but to look upon the same world from one another's standpoint, to see the same in very different and frequently opposing aspects. The speeches in which Thucydides makes articulate the standpoints and interests of the warring parties are still a living testimony to the extraordinary degree of this objectivity [...] What has obscured the modern discussion of objectivity in

247 Later, in her last uncompleted work, *The Life of the Mind*, published in part in 1971, Hannah Arendt noted Heidegger's reference to the term "meaning" (*Sinn*) in evoking the meaning or "sense" of being. Heidegger becomes entangled here for Arendt in the metaphysical fallacy *par excellence*, since he fails to distinguish between "truth" and *Sinn* or "meaning," which might also be translated as "sense" in this passage (New York/London: Harvest/Harcourt-Brace Jovanovich, 1978), p. 15. Since the theme of politics does not occupy a central role in Arendt's examination of truth in this work, it would reach beyond the scope of the present article to discuss it in this later context.

> the historical sciences and prevented its ever touching the fundamental issues involved seems to be the fact that none of the conditions of either Homeric impartiality of Thucydidean objectivity are present in the modern age."[248]

It is at this stage of our analysis that we are able to consider the scope of Hannah Arendt's reflection concerning the Platonic origins of our philosophical tradition. Plato was the founder of this tradition for Arendt because his hostility toward the *polis* led to the devaluation of *doxa,* which comes to expression in a plurality of publicly supported opinions, in favor of the one-dimensional character of an *episteme* held to be eternally valid and shed of all traces of the public world. During the nineteenth century, the critique of metaphysical claims to truth represented an important step toward overcoming this tradition. And it is in this perspective that Heidegger's critique of the traditional criteria of truth and his attempt to remold these criteria in relation to the finitude of *Dasein* constitutes a first step for Arendt toward the overcoming of the traditional idea of absolute, metaphysical truth. And this attempt to overcome the tradition falls prey to its blindness to the implications for the problem of truth of the modern fragility of the common public world.[249] Consequently, Heidegger's interpretation of truth is the clear sign, as Arendt writes in regard to a quote from Walter Benjamin characterizing contemporary philosophy in general, that the "consistence of truth […] has been lost" because truth no

248 Hannah Arendt, "The Concept of History," in *Between Past and Future*, pp. 51–52.

249 See in this regard Hannah Arendt, "Philosophy and Politics" (1954), in *Social Research*, vol. 57, 1, 1990, pp. 73–103. Later Hannah Arendt attempted to clarify this notion of truth in its relation to politics in the essay published in 1967, "Truth and Politics." In this essay she further qualified her idea of truth by introducing Leibniz's distinction between truths of reason, which are necessary and supposedly eternal, and factual truths, which are historical and contingent. Arendt explained that both types of truth are necessarily distinct from politics since, insofar as they require assent, they are unlike the simple opinions that animate political discussion. In its status as "truth," factual truth is not required, any more than rational truth, to present itself as a matter of opinion or an object of political persuasion. Nonetheless, in spite of this radical distinction between truth and politics, the opinion which nourishes politics cannot remain indifferent to truth, above all to factual truth. Arendt specified that precisely the respect for factual truth distinguishes the good opinion, capable of a measure of impartiality, from a bad opinion, which distorts the facts to the point of propagating manipulative lies. While truth in this sense plays a fundamental role in regard to political judgment, the emergence of calculated lies and the fabrication of images by the mass media as a means of controlling mass society represent a particularly grave political danger. It is the danger of a loss of stability endowed by factual truth as a coherent network of interrelations. This loss endangers above all "the sense by which we take our bearings in the real world"; Arendt, "Truth and Politics," *Between Past and Future*, p. 257.

longer possesses those qualities that it "could acquire only through universal recognition of its validity."[250]

In her essay "Tradition and the Modern Age," Hannah Arendt notes that tradition may only reveal its full force once it seems to have been overtaken.[251] If Heidegger's interpretation of truth is to be grasped in the perspective of this tradition, it is because—if we adhere to Arendt's explanation—after renouncing all claims to eternal, absolute truth, he remained incapable of surmounting the traditional separation of philosophical truth from the *polis* to identify truth which might be at the same time "authentic" and rooted in the public world. Here, above all, the question of truth refers to the fundamentally political problem which the public world continually raises.

250 Hannah Arendt, "Walter Benjamin," in *Men in Dark Times*, p. 193.
251 H. Arendt, "Tradition and the Modern Age," in *Between Past and Future*, p. 26.

Chapter 8

In Heidegger's Shadow: Ernst Cassirer, Emmanuel Levinas, and the Question of the Political

In an interview accorded late in his life, Emmanuel Levinas recalled his reaction as a youthful spectator at the famous debate in Davos, Switzerland in 1929 between Ernst Cassirer and Martin Heidegger. Although in subsequent publications Levinas rarely evoked the name of Cassirer, in this interview in 1986, he reminisced about the orientation that Cassirer had elaborated and defended in Davos against Heidegger's trenchant critique. Cassirer, Levinas remarked, was the representative of a "refined humanism." He was, according to Levinas's not entirely favorable comments, a "neo-Kantian, a glorious disciple of Hermann Cohen, the modern interpreter of Kant on the basis of the intelligibility of the sciences [...], in a line of continuity with the rationalism, the aesthetics, and the political ideas of the nineteenth century."[252] Levinas went on to note his remorse in later years—in view of Heidegger's later political allegiance to the Nazi regime a little over three years after this debate—for having preferred, in 1929, Heidegger's philosophy to that of Cassirer.

This chapter will focus on an important but rarely noticed motif in Levinas's political philosophy that, despite his apparent lack of interest in Cassirer's writings, takes on new significance when it is considered in relation to Cassirer's philosophy. I will not dwell upon Levinas's cursory qualification of Cassirer as a "neo-Kantian disciple of Hermann Cohen"—a judgment that hardly does justice to the originality of Cassirer's thought. Closer scrutiny of Cassirer's philosophy would certainly demonstrate that its significance cannot be limited to the continuation of a constellation of typically nineteenth century ideas. Indeed, in 1929 the elder Cassirer manifested a good deal more political discernment than the young Levinas, for the Davos debate illustrated the depth of Cassirer's reservations concerning the ethical-political implications of Heidegger's philosophy. In later years, Levinas came to share similar doubts concerning the implications of Heidegger's ideas—causing him, as noted earlier, to regret his original

252 "Un néo-kantien, glorieux disciple d'Hermann Cohen, interprète moderne de Kant à partir de l'intelligibilité des sciences, [...] dans la continuité du rationalisme, de l'esthétique et des idées politiques du 19ème siècle"; Emmanuel Levinas, François Poiré, *Essai et entretiens* (Paris: Actes Sud, 1996), pp. 80–81.

preference for Heidegger—but not inspiring him to develop an explicit analysis of the political scope of Cassirer's philosophy. Notwithstanding important differences in the respective positions of Cassirer and Levinas, it is worthwhile briefly to identify a principal aspect of Cassirer's political thought that places in relief a still deeper and surprising affinity between their fundamental political orientations. Through an identification of this affinity, I hope to shed light on certain implications of Levinas's own political thought that are not readily evident.

In order to establish a common basis of analysis for two authors of different nationalities and generations and of completely different philosophical temperaments, I shall focus on each philosopher's use of a famous Platonic phrase that has been a source of reflection in a long tradition of commentary reaching back to antiquity: Plato's assertion that "the good" is "beyond essence" or being. At the beginning of the twentieth century, Hermann Cohen analyzed this Platonic phrase in his seminal work *Ethics of Pure Will* (*Ethik des reinen Willens*,1904), which constituted the second volume of his three-volume philosophical work, *System der Philosophie*. Cassirer subsequently evoked this phrase in the second volume of his work, *The Philosophy of Symbolic Forms*, *Mythical Thought* (1925), before reexamining it in more detail in the *Philosophy of Enlightenment* (1932). As is well known, Levinas chose this phrase as the title of his work *Otherwise than Being or Beyond Essence* (*Autrement qu'être. Au-delà de l'essence*, 1978). Of fundamental importance in the respective works of Cassirer and of Levinas is that each of them interpreted this Platonic phrase, "the good beyond essence," in both an ethical and a political sense. Although Levinas never referred to earlier twentieth-century interpretations of this phrase, a consideration of its significance for Plato and also for later twentieth-century interpreters, particularly Cassirer, will highlight the implications of Levinas's thought.

Ethics and Politics: The Platonic Background

Plato employed the suggestive phrase "the good beyond essence" in the sixth book of the *Republic*. In this passage, recording a conversation between Socrates and Glaucon on the relation between the good and intelligible beings, Socrates replied to Glaucon in the following way: "Admit that the objects of knowledge not only receive from the presence of the good their being known, but their very existence and essence is derived from it, though the good itself is not essence but transcends essence (*epekeina tês ousias*) in dignity and power."[253]

That the good should be "otherwise than being" and beyond essence places it at the summit of transcendence of all other intelligible forms to which it imparts its superior dignity. In the context of the Platonic dialogue itself, let us recall Glaucon's reaction to Socrates's strange assertion that the good far exceeds essence in dignity and in power; he responded in a "ludicrous" manner according to Plato: "That the heavens should save us! The exaggeration (*hyperbolē*) could not go farther!" Upon hearing Glaucon's suggestion that he may have exaggerated the matter, Socrates attenuated the radicalism of his remark with the quip: "The fault is yours for compelling me to utter my thoughts about it."[254]

Given Socrates's own ambiguity toward this hyperbole, it is perhaps not surprising that interpretations of it have varied greatly, particularly in the twentieth century. Indeed, it is this hyperbolic quality of Socrates's remark that drew Hermann Cohen's attention in his commentary on this passage in the work *Ethics of Pure Will.* Cohen, indeed, reacted much like Glaucon to this passage, considering it an exaggeration that contradicts its logical sense. For Cohen, such assertions represented nothing more than the outpourings of moral emotion in defense of religious custom. In his words: "'*epekeina tês ousias*'. Ethics is not supported by a preference for such valuations. When an overemphasis of moral feeling leads to an underestimation of logic in relation to ethics, it may be that religious customs triumph; ethics and ethical truth are, however, not supported in this way."[255]

All the more noteworthy in this light is the original interpretation that Cassirer presented of the Platonic good "beyond essence" (*epekeina tês ousias*), due precisely to the affirmative ethical-political connotation he attributed to this notion, thus asserting his independence from his former mentor Hermann Cohen. Let us recall the context in which this reflection was presented.

253 Plato, *The Republic*, 509b (Cambridge, MA: Loeb Classical Library/Harvard University Press, 1980), p. 107; Cf. Emmanuel Levinas, *Totalité et infini. Essai sur l'extériorité* (Paris: Le livre de Poche, 1991/Dordrecht: Kluwer, 1971), pp. iv, 105–06.

254 Plato, *The Republic*, 509b, p. 107.

255 "Die Ethik ist durch solche Vorzugswerte nicht gedient. Wenn im Überschwung des sittlichen Gefühls die Logik gegen die Ethik herabgesetzt wird, so mag die religiöse Sittlichkeit darüber triumphieren; die Ethik und die ethische Wahrheit wird dadurch nicht gefordert"; Hermann Cohen, *Ethik des reinen Willens* (Berlin: Cassirer, 1921), pp. 90, 421.

Cassirer initially evoked the Platonic notion of the "good beyond essence" in his book *Mythical Thought* (*Das Mythische Denken*, 1925) that constituted the second volume of the work, *The Philosophy of Symbolic Forms*. As a central motif of Plato's philosophy according to Cassirer, this notion signified an intrinsic goodness which, far from limited to the ephemeral perspective of mortal individuals in the immanent realm, is the source of an ultimate good transcending this realm in which ephemeral perspectives participate.[256]

On the occasion of the Davos debate with Martin Heidegger in 1929, Cassirer did not evoke the Platonic phrase itself, but the Platonic theme of an absolute ethical and theoretical truth that transcends the finite realm while lending it order and significance. In a preliminary lecture he presented at Davos prior to his direct encounter with Heidegger, Cassirer examined this theme as it was taken up by what he termed the "Platonic-Stoic tradition" in Western thought.[257] In this lecture, which has since become known as the "Heidegger Lecture" ("Heidegger-Vorlesung"), Cassirer contrasted what he termed the "Platonic-Stoic tradition" with Heidegger's philosophy of existence. Cassirer developed his analysis on the basis of what he took to be the theological background to Heidegger's philosophy. He traced Heidegger's emphasis in *Being and Time* on the fundamental role of finite existence in its singularity to what he interpreted to be an analogous position in the thought of Pascal and above all in the theology of Martin Luther. Cassirer termed Luther's position one of "religious individualism," which the reformer defended with particular firmness in his "Eight Sermons" pronounced in Wittenberg in 1523. In stressing the ultimate inscrutability of the Divine will, Luther, according to Cassirer, disparaged the "objective form of religion" and, in light of human fallibility and mortality, he questioned the fundamental place that the Platonic-Stoic tradition had accorded to an ideal order of the universe arising through its participation in the "certitude of the Eternal that both illuminates and perdures beyond all existence in its necessary finitude."[258] In his novel twentieth century perspective, Heidegger presented a similar

256 Ernst Cassirer, *Das Mythische Denken, Philosophie der symbolischen Formen*, vol. 2, (Darmstadt: Wissenschaftliche Buchgesellschaft,1994), p. 300.

257 Ernst Cassirer, "Heidegger-Vorlesung," in *Davoser Vorträge, Vorträge über Hermann Cohen, Mit einem Anhang: Briefe Hermann und Martha Cohens an Ernst und Toni Cassirer, 1901–1929, Nachgelassene Manuskripte und Texte*, vol. 17, ed. Jörn Bohr (Hamburg: Meiner, 2014), pp. 3–76.

258 "[…] geht ihm die Gewissheit eines Ewigen auf, das alles Dasein, in seiner notwendigen Endlichkeit, überstrahlt u[nd] überdauert"; Ernst Cassirer, "Heidegger-Vorlesung," p. 67.

challenge to Platonic-Stoic assumptions concerning the fundamental status of an objective and autonomous cosmic order beyond the finitude of mortal perspectives. These assumptions, as Cassirer emphasized, had been a source of inspiration for a long tradition of Western thought extending to Kant's transcendental idealism and, in the debate with Heidegger at Davos, Cassirer centered his critique on Heidegger's aim to deconstruct Kant's quest for absolute ethical and theoretical truth beyond the fluctuating perspectives of mortal beings. In this context Cassirer emphasized what he took to be the danger for the idea of an *intrinsic* validity of truth of Heidegger's insistence that all truth is relative to finite human being.[259]

In his direct confrontation with Heidegger at Davos, Cassirer did not elaborate on what he had described in his preliminary lecture as the affinity between Heidegger's critique of the Platonic-Stoic heritage and the theological orientation inaugurated by Luther's "religious individualism."[260] Nonetheless, in the period following the Davos debate, the interpretation of the historical sources of the theological challenge directed against the Platonic-Stoic tradition was a focal point of Cassirer's ethical-political reflection. It is in his examination of the threat to the Platonic-Stoic heritage in the early modern period that Cassirer set the Platonic notion of the "good beyond essence" in a new light.

Cassirer's most detailed analysis devoted to an interpretation of the Platonic "good beyond essence" is found in the book *The Philosophy of the Enlightenment* (*Die Philosophie der Aufklärung*), first published in 1932. Appearing three years after the 1929 Davos debate with Heidegger, this work was written in a particularly tense political atmosphere—1931, and especially 1932 were years in which the Nazis began to score important victories in national elections. Indeed, this was the last book that

259 Cassirer, Heidegger, "Davoser Vorträge," Heidegger, *Kant und das Problem der Metaphysik, Gesamtausgabe*, vol. 3, pp. 276–277.

260 Independently from Cassirer's reflections, Karl Löwith investigated Heidegger's affiliation with Protestant theology, above all with Luther and Kierkegaard, and the path that led him toward finite choice in the face of nothingness and to the deconstruction of belief in eternal truths that had traditionally inspired the Christian faith. See Karl Löwith, "Der Okkasionale Dezisionismus von Carl Schmitt," *Heidegger – Denker in dürftiger Zeit. Zur Stellung der Philosophie im 20. Jahrhundert, Sämtliche Schriften*, vol. VIII (Stuttgart: Metzler, 1984), pp. 40–70. On the theological background to Heidegger's philosophy of existence and on the implications of Cassirer's critique of Heidegger at Davos, see my book *Martin Heidegger and the Problem of Historical Meaning* (New York: Fordham University Press, 2003). I have also dealt with this theme in my review article "Ernst Cassirer, Martin Heidegger and the Legacy of Davos," in *History and Theory*, vol. 51, 3, October, 2012, pp. 436–450. In it I deal with Peter Gordon's book, *Continental Divide: Heidegger, Cassirer, Davos* (Cambridge, MA: Harvard University Press, 2010).

Cassirer wrote in Germany; Hitler came to power several months after its publication, and Cassirer quickly emigrated from Germany to England, and subsequently to Sweden and to the United States.

In view of the dire political situation in Germany in the early thirties, the author of *The Philosophy of the Enlightenment* intended to present much more than a simple history of eighteenth-century thought. The book's theme and content are a plea in favor of the aspect of the German intellectual heritage that most glaringly contrasted with the contemporary situation. And it is in this context that he linked the political heritage of the seventeenth and eighteenth centuries to deeper sources revealed by the Platonic notion of a "good beyond essence."

Cassirer's analysis of seventeenth and eighteenth-century political ideas centered on theories of absolute state power that had emerged in modern conceptions of political sovereignty. Starting with Machiavelli and Bodin and culminating in the thought of Hobbes, such conceptions according to Cassirer began to assume ever more radical form, which increased in force over the course of the seventeenth century in response to the political claims of the radical religious reformers, who in the wake of Calvin's reform sought to establish a theocratic basis for absolute state power, founded not on what they took to be the fallibility and finitude of natural reason, but on the word of God interpreted by His representatives. As a reaction against religious fanaticism and the religious wars engendered by sects that each laid claim to a divinely inspired truth, Hobbes posited the absolute authority of the sovereign as the only means of maintaining peace. In view of the ongoing danger of civil war, an appeal either to natural law and natural right or to divine law and divine right was senseless and subversive because peace could be maintained neither by appeals to natural reason nor to divine authority but only by the sovereign will. As the avoidance of civil war is the ultimate good, the interpretation of what is just and lawful depends on the sovereign will alone, and nothing is sanctioned that is not in conformity with this will. In the extreme postulation of Hobbes, as Cassirer reminds us, the sovereign, by virtue of his absolute power, is conceived to be a "mortal God." Natural law and Divine law are valid only where they have been legitimated by the absolute sovereign authority, which it is unjust to resist collectively. What is most curious in this argument, as Cassirer stipulates, is that Hobbes's emphasis on the absolute legitimacy of the sovereign will as opposed to an autonomous order of truth, to a "good beyond essence" advanced by the Platonic-Stoic tradition, revealed a deep affinity between his political absolutism and the radical theological positions he placed in question. In rejecting the rationalism of the Platonic-Stoic tradition, both Hobbes and the theocrats, for opposite reasons, glorified brute sovereign force as the only answer to the radical problem posed by the quest for political order.[261] Thus the challenge raised against this tradition derived at once from the radical religious reformers and from the absolutist political philosophers who, as a means of subduing their religious adversaries, endowed the sovereign with absolute power analogous to divine omnipotence.

In his analysis of seventeenth and eighteenth-century political theories, Cassirer was surprisingly discrete when it came to drawing parallels to his contemporary world. In the context of the last years of the Weimar Republic, however, any politically minded reader would clearly discern the evident parallels to the contemporary situation. This period, after all, witnessed the rise both of absolutist social movements, with their creed of unconditional obedience to the leader, and of political theories advocating this creed. In the decade preceding the fall of the Weimar Republic, its opponents widely revitalized and radicalized the absolutist theories of Bodin and Hobbes as a means of justifying the unconditional character of sovereign power beyond any claims of natural law or other rationally grounded general norms. In this climate marked by a return of "political theology," the argument concerning the unconditional power of the sovereign sought legitimation in analogies drawn between this power and the absolute will of God.[262]

---

261 Ernst Cassirer, *Die Philosophie der Aufklärung* (Tübingen: Mohr, 1932), p. 319f.; Ernst Cassirer, *Die platonische Renaissance in England und die Schule von Cambridge* (Leipzig/Berlin: Teubner, 1932), pp. 53f.

262 One need only recall in this context the decisionist political theories of the late 1920s and 1930s in Germany, notably propounded by Carl Schmitt, that sought to revive and radicalize Hobbes's absolutist doctrine by seizing upon the traditional analogy between the sovereign and God to reinforce the idea of absolute sovereign power. Well beyond the limits of Hobbes's own thinking, Schmitt, in his work *Political Theology* (1922), emphasized that the sovereign's decisions can in no way be limited by natural right or any other pre-existing norms, for the norm depends, according to Schmitt's phrase, on the absolute sovereign's decision, born "out of nothingness" (*aus einem Nichts geboren*); Carl Schmitt, *Politische Theologie. Vier Kapitel zur Lehre von der Souveränität* (Berlin: Duncker and Humblot, 1985), p. 42. Carl Schmitt's questioning of both the traditional and rational basis of norms and his insistence that decision arises in the face of nothingness anticipates in a striking manner the philosophy of existence of Heidegger. In 1933, both Heidegger and Schmitt, who were in contact with each other at the time, joined the Nazi party and pledged allegiance to the Hitler regime. Although the argument has been recently advanced that Schmitt's attitude toward the Weimar regime was ambiguous during the last years of its existence, the doctrine of political decisionism, coupled with his implacable hostility to parliamentary democracy, were hardly compatible with the fundamental principles of the Weimar Republic.

In attacking the seventeenth and eighteenth-century absolutist theories, and, implicitly, also those who currently were extrapolating from and radicalizing Hobbes, Cassirer returned in *The Philosophy of the Enlightenment* to the political theories of Hobbes's predecessor and primary target—Hugo Grotius. Grotius, as Cassirer emphasized, opened the way to a major current of Enlightenment thought that culminated in the ethical-political theories of Leibniz and of Kant who, like Grotius, shared the presupposition that justice cannot depend on an arbitrary sovereign will. According to Grotius there are, indeed, ethical principles that are so fundamental and so irrevocable that their validity must be considered to be independent not only of the earthly sovereign but even of the Divine will. Ethical-political validity depends not on sheer will, be it even the will of God, but on what is *intrinsically* just and good. Even God cannot transform what is intrinsically wrong and unjust into something fair and good. In his analysis of Grotius, Cassirer situated this idea within a longstanding medieval and Stoic tradition extending back to the philosophy of Plato and the famous Platonic notion of a "good beyond essence." According to Cassirer's analysis: "What is lawful is valid neither because there is a God nor because it is supported by any kind of existence, whether empirical or absolute. It flows from the pure Idea of the Good—from the Idea which, for Plato, exceeds all else in power and dignity [...] the idea of a lawfulness that transcends in placing the just and the good above all being (*epekeina tês ousias*)."[263]

Cassirer and Levinas: The Problematic Relationship of Theology and Politics

In his book *Autrement qu'être: Au-delà de l'essence*, Levinas presented an interpretation that was at once different from that of Cassirer and curiously in harmony with his fundamental ethical-political persuasion. Cassirer, as we have seen, did not share the critical attitude of Hermann Cohen who, following Glaucon, manifested skepticism with regard to the hyperbole suggested by the idea of a "good exceeding essence in power and in dignity"; on the contrary, Cassirer affirmed this principle as a starting point for ethical-political reflection. Levinas, for his part, went beyond Cassirer, for he reinforced the exaggeration by radicalizing the distinction between the good and the essence or being which it transcends. For Plato, the idea

263 Ernst Cassirer, *Die Philosophie der Aufklärung*, p. 319f. The Platonic phrase "The good beyond essence" has been omitted from the English translation of the text.

of the good, if beyond essence, is nonetheless available to reminiscence. Reminiscence recalls the eternal being of the good in which the intelligible forms and, in an ephemeral way, the fleeting existence of terrestrial things participate. It recalls what is innately present, in at least implicit form, as fundamental a priori truth. For the Stoic and neo-Stoic tradition that inspired Grotius, and which Cassirer evoked, the good found its a priori basis in natural law. Levinas's radicalization of the Platonic phrase dissociated the good beyond essence from anything that might be represented or recalled in terms of a foundation in the Platonic or Stoic sense. Levinas, therefore, qualified the good, beyond being, as immemorial, as a transcendence that no reminiscence or memory might evoke. "The Good that reigns in its goodness," as Levinas wrote, "cannot enter into the presence of consciousness, even were it to be remembered."[264]

What, however, is the result of this radicalization of the Platonic dichotomy between the good and the immanent world of essence? Let us recall that in *Autrement qu'être* the immemorial and unrepresentable transcendence of essence by the good led to the evocation of God and of the sacred. Even if Levinas referred to God here with his characteristic discretion, such evocations come to the fore in the rare passages in this work that concern justice and the political, most notably where he described the bringing together of different subjectivities as citizens, through what he terms "synchronization." He wrote in this regard: "Synchronization is the act of consciousness which by representation and the spoken word [le Dit] institutes 'with the help of God,' the original place of justice, the common ground for me and for others, where I am counted among them; that is, where subjectivity is citizen with all measured and measurable duties and rights pertaining to the Me, which is equilibrated or equilibrates itself with the aid of duties and the concurrence of rights."[265]

And here we come to the crux of the matter. With the radicalization of the Platonic idea of transcendence of the good accompanied by this evocation of God, Levinas might seem to succumb precisely to the outpourings of moral feeling or religious fervor that Hermann Cohen identified as

264 "Le Bien qui règne dans sa bonté [...] ne peut entrer dans le présent de la conscience, fût-il remémoré"; Emmanuel Levinas, *Autrement qu'être. Au-delà de l'essence* (Dordrecht: Kluwer/Paris: Le livre de Poche, 1996), p. 88.

265 "La synchronisation est acte de conscience qui, par la représentation et le Dit, institue, 'avec l'aide de Dieu' le lieu originel de la justice, terrain commun à moi et aux autres où je suis compté parmi eux, c'est-à-dire où la subjectivité est citoyen avec tous les devoirs et droits mesurés et mesurables que comporte le Moi équilibré ou s'équilibrant par le concours des devoirs et la concurrence des droits"; Emmanuel Levinas, *Autrement qu'être. Au-delà de l'essence*, p. 250.

the danger inherent in the Platonic notion of the "good beyond essence" and which, to his mind, could only obscure genuine ethical purpose. Even Cassirer, who sought to rehabilitate the ethical meaning of the Platonic phrase, did so by carefully distinguishing it from any religious motive. As we saw, he related it to Grotius's claim that there are rules of justice and of goodness that are valid independently of any consideration of the divine will. As Grotius and later Cassirer interpreted the matter, this separation of theological questions from the realm of politics was the only means of finding common ground among the different religious persuasions, thereby avoiding either the politics of religious fanaticism, at one extreme, or the subordination of all theological matters to absolute political authority at the other. In short, both Grotius and Cassirer sought to distinguish, as clearly as possible, politics from religion in order to avoid the dangers latent in political theology.

In view of the discrete and careful way in which Levinas evoked God in his references to the political, there are no grounds for accusing him of promoting a form of political theology. Nonetheless, we may question whether, in initiating what Dominique Janicaud has aptly termed the "theological turn of French phenomenology,"[266] Levinas introduced a religious element into his philosophy, which long experience counsels us to keep separate from politics. Do we not encounter here a deeper source of the incompatibility between his reflections and the thought of predecessors such as Ernst Cassirer?

In order to understand what is at stake here, it is necessary to move beyond the framework of *Autrement qu'être* in order to focus more directly on Levinas's approach to the immanent domain of politics. In his view, if theological arguments represent a danger in the political sphere, this is because of the conflict that is engendered by attempts to ground political authority in particular interpretations of the sacred; it is, therefore, all the more important to search for a universal political criterion that, beyond the particular claims of a religious dogma, may accommodate a diversity of religious expressions and harmonize their claims.

Levinas examined the role of universal criteria in the ethical-political domain primarily in the thirteenth chapter of his book *Les imprévues de l'histoire*, entitled "La laïcité et la pensée d'Israël" ("Secularism and the thought of Israel"), in which he explored the possibility of moving beyond the particularism of Jewish religious practices to identify a universal

266 Dominique Janicaud, *Le tournant théologique de la phénoménologie française* (Paris: Editions de l'éclat, 1992).

message implicit in them that might also encompass other nations and other faiths in the modern social context. Here Levinas's reflections brought him in a curious way close to the fundamental inspiration of Cassirer's political philosophy. In this essay, Levinas introduced the Talmudic concept of the Noachian laws, which was reinterpreted and revitalized in the medieval philosophy of Maimonides. According to the Jewish religion, the Noachian laws comprise seven commandments considered by rabbinic tradition to constitute the essential moral duties required of all humans, regardless of nationality or culture.[267] According to Maimonides, the Hasid of the gentile nations who obeys these laws—the righteous "foreigner"—has a share in the world to come, even if he or she never converts to Judaism. Even among "idol worshippers," as Levinas reminded his readers, "there are just people [...] who participate in the world to come." And he concluded, "Jewish monotheism imbues God himself with the aspiration toward a universal society."[268]

What is particularly important for our present analysis is that Judaism's affirmation of the universal ideal became, as Levinas reminds us, not merely a utopian aspiration but a principal ancient source of modern theories of natural law:

> "The non-Jewish theorists of natural right, precursors of modern society, recognized, indeed, the way in which the idea of the foreigner developed into the idea of the Noachide and of the 'righteous among the gentiles.' They recognized the importance of this movement of thought for constituting the idea of natural right. John Selden (1584–1654), the great seventeenth-century English scholar, and one of the theoreticians of natural law, founded it on Hebrew law, notably in his work *De jure naturali et gentium juxta disciplinam Ebraeorum* [The law of nature and of peoples after the discipline of the Hebrews]. Hugo Grotius, founder of theory of the law of peoples, explicitly praised the Noachian institution."[269]

---

267 On this theme see Isidore Singer and Julius H. Greenstone, "The Noachian Laws" in *The Jewish Encyclopedia*, vol. 7 (New York/London: Funk and Wagnall's, 1901–1906), pp. 648–58. The references there are to "Sanh.," 56–60, "Yad," and "Melakhim," 8: 10, 10: 12. The seven Noachian Laws are as follows: the prohibition of idolatry, blasphemy, bloodshed, sexual sins, theft, eating from a living animal, and the injunction to establish a legal system. The just person or "hasid" among the non-Jewish populations is entitled to material support by the Jewish people and to the highest earthly honors, and also, according to Maimonides, a right to partake in life after death.

268 "Il y a des justes parmi les idolâtres qui participent au monde futur. [...] Le monothéisme juif met en Dieu même l'aspiration à une société universelle," Emmanuel Levinas, *Les imprévues de l'histoire* (Paris: Le livre de Poche, 1999), pp. 186–87.

269 "Les théoriciens non-juifs du droit naturel, précurseurs de la société moderne, connaissaient d'ailleurs la façon dont l'idée d'étranger s'épanouit en idée de noachide et de 'juste parmi les gentils' et l'importance de ce mouvement de pensée pour la constitution de l'idée du droit naturel. John Selden (1584–1654), le grand érudit du 17ème siècle

In thus alluding to Grotius and to Jewish sources of modern theories of natural law, Levinas returned to the same territory that Cassirer delineated in *The Philosophy of the Enlightenment*. In invoking a universal law valid for all religions, irrespective of the particular ways in which God reveals himself to them, Levinas provided an argument that was at once complementary to Cassirer's interpretation, while at the same time transforming its implication. Cassirer had recalled Grotius's famous argument to refute the claim that the sovereign's absolute will, analogous to God's, is the ultimate determinant concerning the criteria of goodness and justice; certain laws are so fundamental that their validity is independent of any particular divine fiat. Levinas subtly recast Grotius's argument, because, according to his perspective, even those theories that posit the validity of natural law irrespective of God are ultimately obliged to draw on religious sources. In its universal scope the ultimate source of natural law cannot be drawn from the reminiscence of an idea in the Platonic sense; its trace is refracted from an inscrutable transcendence. Even where we would like to secularize the political sphere and carefully separate theology from politics, we cannot escape from the insight that our political existence draws on profound sacred sources; in this sense it is impossible to "escape from God," as Levinas declared in *Autrement qu'être*.[270] If my analysis is correct, however, then Levinas enjoins us to reformulate the theological-political problem. If it is impossible to escape from God, even where we attempt to exclude theology from the political domain, then we are faced with only one alternative: radical transcendence. In denying the possibility of immanent representation or reminiscence, the notion of transcendence that radicalizes the Platonic notion of the "good beyond essence" introduces the possibility of "hearing a God who has not been contaminated by being," and cannot be invoked as "protector of all forms of egoism."[271] From this perspective, we have already forsaken the good when we draw the sacred into the sphere of being as a means of legitimating immanent interests in this world. In such cases we substitute an immanent basis, an interest, for what is radically transcendent and without basis, an-archic. In referring the sacred to the good's radical otherness beyond this world, Levinas aimed at denying a basis—an arche—to all traditional theological claims in the political sphere.

---

anglais, et l'un des théoriciens du droit naturel, le fonde sur la loi hébraïque, notamment dans son *De jure naturali et gentium juxta disciplinam Ebraeorum*. Hugo Grotius, fondateur de la théorie du droit des gens, loue expressément l'institution de noachide," ibid., p. 187.

270 Emmanuel Levinas, *Autrement qu'être. Au-delà de l'essence*, p. 165.

271 "[...] le protecteur de tous les egoismes," ibid., pp. 10, 250–51.

Conclusion

I shall conclude by returning to the Davos debate between Ernst Cassirer and Martin Heidegger that Levinas remorsefully recalled. Somewhat more bluntly than Levinas, Jürgen Habermas has also commented on Cassirer's role in this famous encounter. Although he was too young in 1929 to have attended the debate, Habermas claimed that Heidegger had wrested a "dubious victory" (*ein fragwürdiger Sieg*) from Cassirer. And if, according to Habermas, Cassirer had lost the debate, it was because he drew his inspiration from a vitiated German and European appeal to an ancient Greek heritage resuscitated by the neo-humanism of the eighteenth century. In the context of Weimar Germany, Jews' attempts to marshal support from the classical Greek heritage were flawed by "a certain impotence" (*etwas Kraftloses*). Habermas maintained that power for Jewish thinkers lay essentially in their own tradition, which he equated not with the Torah and the Talmud, but with the more esoteric doctrines of Kabbalah.[272]

In light of my analysis of Cassirer and of Levinas, Habermas's attitude toward Cassirer seems questionable. I am not convinced that Cassirer lost the Davos debate nor that speculation derived from the Jewish Kabbalah would have modified the essentially ethical nature of the arguments he presented against Heidegger, whose philosophy is perhaps best characterized by its utter indifference toward ethical concerns. If, indeed, there is strength in Cassirer's arguments, might it not be that they depended less on a foundation in a particular European or Jewish heritage—in an arche—than on the universality of an ethical reach which, in Levinas's perspective, ultimately derived from an anarchic trace "beyond essence" and "otherwise than being"?

272 "Ein Rückgang auf die Griechen, wo er von Juden versucht wurde, hat so immer etwas Kraftloses behalten—Kraft barg allein die Tiefe der eigenen Tradition, die Kabbala"; Jürgen Habermas, "Der deutsche Idealismus der jüdischen Philosophie" (1961), *Philosophisch-politische Profile. Erweiterte Ausgabe* (Frankfurt am Main: Suhrkamp, 1981), pp. 52–54.

Chapter 9

Gods without Faces: Emmanuel Levinas and the Question of Myth

The theme of myth and of mythical thinking, which has been a potent source of reflection since the beginning of the Western philosophical tradition, emerged in a new perspective over the course of the nineteenth and twentieth centuries following the gradual decline of the authority of traditional religion and the advent of secular forms of belief. In this chapter I will focus on Emmanuel Levinas's reflection on the theme of myth. My analysis will first identify the specific conception of myth that Levinas proposed in his work by distinguishing it from an important source of Jewish theological insight he acknowledged, the thought of Franz Rosenzweig. This will lead me to argue that Levinas's unique conception of myth sets in clear relief the central thrust of his critical reception of the philosophy of Martin Heidegger.

I

In a brief passage in his work *Totality and Infinity: An Essay on Exteriority* (*Totalité et infini. Essai sur l'extériorité*, 1961), Levinas evoked the topic of myth and related it to what he termed the "element" ("l'élément"). The "element" signifies for him what is utterly indeterminate and anonymous. It arises virtually out of nowhere, from the depths of wind, earth, and sky: "The depth of the element," as Levinas wrote, "extends and loses itself in the earth and sky, 'Nothing ends, nothing begins.'"[273] He pursued this reflection at a later point in this work in the following terms:

> "This coming out of nowhere opposes the element to what we describe as the face (*visage*), a being's presentation of itself in person. To be affected by an aspect (*face*) that comes upon me from nowhere is to tend toward the insecurity of tomorrow. The future of the element as insecurity is lived concretely as the mythical divinity of the element. Gods without faces, impersonal gods to which one does not speak designate the nothingness which, in its familiarity with the element, borders on the egoism of enjoyment. But it is thus that enjoyment achieves separation. The separated being

273 "La profondeur de l'élément le prolonge et le perd dans la terre et dans le ciel 'Rien ne finit, rien ne commence'"; Emmanuel Levinas, *Totalité et infini. Essai sur l'extériorité*, pp. 138–139.

> must run the risk of paganism that attests its separation and in which this separation is attained, until the moment when the death of these gods brings it to atheism and to true transcendence."[274]

Particularly noteworthy in this passage for the argument I will present in what follows is Levinas's opposition of the visage of the person to the anonymity of the faceless gods, the "gods of separation." These mythical gods, which are as impersonal as the limitless elements that surround us, are not inevitable and permanent features of human existence since the faceless beings perish and leave way for "true transcendence": the epiphany of the infinite in which the "visage," the face of the other, presents itself in person.

Two years prior to the publication of *Totality and Infinity*, in a speech entitled "Between two Worlds (The Way of Franz Rosenzweig)" ["Entre deux mondes (La voie de Franz Rosenzweig)," 1959], Levinas dealt in similar terms with the overcoming of the mythical gods in an interpretation of the philosophy of Franz Rosenzweig. In language that anticipated his later work, he alluded to Rosenzweig's depiction in *The Star of Redemption* (*Der Stern der Erlösung*, 1921) to the surmounting of the pagan gods—gods of "separation from the world"—through divine revelation before the "singularity of the person."[275] Here, as Levinas recalled, Rosenzweig interpreted revelation in the framework of what he termed the "New Thinking," which distinguished itself not only from the separation of the pagan gods from the world, but also from the perennial philosophical quest, from Thales to Hegel, to comprehend being as a totality. Rosenzweig's "New Thinking," as Levinas noted, focused on the temporal modes of human existence in its singularity which, following Rosenzweig himself, Levinas compared to Heidegger's insight in *Being and Time*, and he furthermore emphasized a revalorization of the irreplaceable personal

---

274 "Cette provenance de nulle part oppose l'élément à ce que nous décrivons sous le titre de visage, où précisément un étant se présente personnellement. Être affecté par une face venant sur moi de nulle part, c'est se pencher sur l'insécurité des lendemains. L'avenir de l'élément comme insécurité, se vit concrètement comme divinité mythique de l'élément. Dieux sans visage, dieux impersonnels auxquels on ne parle pas, marquent le néant qui borde l'égoïsme de la jouissance, au sein de sa familiarité avec l'élément. Mais c'est ainsi que la jouissance accomplit la séparation. L'être séparé doit courir le risque du paganisme qui atteste sa séparation et où cette séparation s'accomplit, jusqu'au moment où la mort de ces dieux, le ramènera à l'athéisme et à la vraie transcendance"; *Ibid.*, p. 151.

275 Emmanuel Levinas, "Entre deux mondes (La voie de Franz Rosenzweig)" in *Difficile Liberté. Essais sur le Judaïsme* (Paris: Albin Michel, 1976), pp. 283, 289.

dimension of human ethical relations.[276] The philosophy of totality, as Levinas concurred with Rosenzweig, could do justice neither to the singularity of human temporal existence nor to the personal core of ethical relations.

In his opposition to the concept of totality that had animated the traditional philosophical quest, Levinas stated in the opening pages of *Totality and Infinity* that Rosenzweig "was too often present in this book for me to cite it."[277] Yet, if Levinas insisted on this affinity of his orientation with Rosenzweig's rejection of the philosophies of totality, he did not mention Rosenzweig's interpretation of myth that, as we have seen, he had evoked in his earlier speech on Rosenzweig's thought. In this speech, Levinas reaffirmed with Rosenzweig that the traditional philosophies of totality had exhausted their significance and had been overtaken by the vital needs of the present. That is, as Levinas wrote, "perhaps the meaning itself of our epoch."[278] But if traditional philosophy had forfeited its significance, what of myth? In a world in which monotheistic revelation in its Jewish and Christian forms has weakened its hold, what are the prospects for pagan myth? Might the modern world not witness a recrudescence of myth, even if in a wholly new guise? As we will now see, Levinas's response to this question substantially diverged from that of Rosenzweig. And, while Rosenzweig, who died in 1929, never witnessed the rise to power of Hitler and the Nazi regime, Levinas faced the threat of a movement that directly appealed to pagan myth and he survived the catastrophe unfurled by this regime. Moreover, it is here, as I will argue, that Levinas's subsequent interpretation of myth and of the possibilities of its reemergence in modern form substantially colored his evaluation of Heidegger's philosophy and its relation to his political decision in favor of Hitler in 1933.

Rosenzweig addressed the problematic relation between myth and religion for modernity in his early essay "Atheistic Theology" ("Atheistische Theologie"), written in 1914. In this essay he examined the development of nineteenth and early twentieth century historical-critical studies of the Old and New Testaments by Jews and Christians alike, which

276 Rosenzweig's comments on Heidegger's conception of time in *Being and Time*, to which I will return below, were presented in 1929 in his brief essay "Vertauschte Fronten" ("Transposed Fronts") in Franz Rosenzweig, *Zweistromland. Kleinere Schriften zu Glauben und Denken, Gesammelte Schriften*, vol. 3, ed. Reinhold and Annemarie Mayer (Dordrecht: Martinus Nijhoff/Kluwer, 1984), pp. 236–37; Levinas, "Entre deux mondes," *Difficile liberté*, pp. 286, 287.

277 Emmanuel Levinas, *Totalité et infini*, p. 14.

278 Levinas, "Entre deux mondes," *Difficile Liberté*, pp. 277–78.

challenged the traditional biblical belief in God's transcendence and accounted for this belief in terms of merely human forms of representation, as the expression of collective myth-making of the ancient Jewish and Christian communities. The renowned early expression of this movement among Christians, as Rosenzweig noted, was articulated by David Friedrich Strauss in his work, *The Life of Jesus* (*Das Leben Jesu*, 1835) in which Strauss made the claim, on the basis of a critical scrutiny of the Gospels, that Jesus could have been nothing more than the product of the mythical imagination of the original Christian community.[279] This tendency, as Rosenzweig recalled, found a later echo among Jewish theologians who applied the category of myth to biblical studies.

In "Atheistic Theology," Rosenzweig indicated what he took to be a fateful consequence of this transformation of theology, which in its contemporary guise tended to disqualify all forms of transcendence as mere mythical productions of the collective imagination. The ultimate stage in this movement led to the deification of the collectivity itself. Under the influence of naturalistic theories, as Rosenzweig wrote, a growing de-spiritualization of the collectivity paralleled a metamorphosis in the idea of the nation which was conceived in terms of race (*Entgeistigung des Volks zur Rasse*).[280] In this early article, however, Rosenzweig could only express his doubts concerning the long-term viability of such mythical deifications of the collectivity for, once myth had been surpassed by revelation, purely human incarnations of the deity could only provide pale echoes of the transcendent God of true faith. Ultimately, the transcendent God of the fathers—as Rosenzweig concluded in evoking Jewish theology—could not be excluded (*ausgeschaltet*).[281] Here we see that the new forms of deification of the collectivity which come to ultimate expression in racial theories of national identity completely transform and pervert the traditional mythical distinction between God or gods and man.

---

279 David Friedrich Strauss' original exposition of this theme is found in his chapter "Der Begriff des Mythus," *Das Leben Jesu für das deutsche Volk bearbeitet* (Bonn: Emil Strauss, 1895), pp. 191–206.

280 Franz Rosenzweig, "Atheistische Theologie," *Zweistromland. Kleinere Schriften zu Glauben und Denken*, p. 691. On the topic of Rosenzweig's essay "Atheistische Theologie," see especially Leora Batnitzky, *Idolatry and Representation: The Philosophy of Franz Rosenzweig Reconsidered* (Princeton, NJ: Princeton University Press, 2000), pp. 193–94 and Samuel Moyn, *Origins of the Other: Emmanuel Levinas Between Revelation and Ethics* (Ithaca and London: Cornell University Press, 2005), pp. 117–32. On Levinas and Heidegger in France see especially Ethan Kleinberg, *Generation Existential: Heidegger's Philosophy in France, 1927–1961* (Ithaca and London: Cornell University Press, 2005), pp. 245–279.

281 Ibid., p. 697.

In his writings of the 1920s, Rosenzweig's interpretation of myth focused on its original role in antiquity, as a phase of human development prior to the revelation of the transcendent God. In this original period myth, far from limited to the sphere of human production, embraced at least one intrinsic truth, since it posited the primordial distinction between God and man.[282] In this interpretation, Rosenzweig referred to pagan myth as the "element" (*Element*) and "mystery" (*Geheimnis*), using the word "element" and "elementary" as synonyms for the invisible and unrevealed. Belief in the mythical gods was for Rosenzweig overtaken through monotheistic revelation which renewed and surpassed the pagan distinction between God and man through its new and profoundly ethical conception of the humanity of the other. Levinas' mythical gods, the "gods without faces" are, as we have seen, extensions of the "element" (of the "indeterminate" and "anonymous," in accord with his use of this term) and, as such, are objects of belief which are "outside of being and of the world."[283] As for Rosenzweig, for Levinas, even where belief situates the pagan gods outside the sphere of human production, only their demise can leave room for transcendence in the genuine sense. Yet Levinas, as I interpret him, evinced little interest in the historical process in which myth might have expressed some form of preliminary truth, for he concentrated his elucidation on the novelty of revelation.

Franz Rosenzweig, as I recalled above, died in 1929, before the unleashing of the catastrophic force of the political mythologies of the 1930s, and prior to World War II and the Shoah; by contrast, Levinas had to face these dark events and the recrudescence of the ominous and atavistic forces that propelled them. In his early essay "Reflections on the Philosophy of Hitlerism" ("Quelques réflexions sur la philosophie de l'hitlérisme"), published in 1934, Levinas attempted to account for the urgent threat posed by the conjuring up of elemental forces in the contemporary political context. In this brief article of 1934, Levinas did not refer to the phenomenon of myth as such; he cautioned that the "dreadfully dangerous" (*effroyablement dangereux*) Nazi movement had brought elementary sentiments to the fore which, in their racist character and their crude violence, had as little affinity with religious convictions bequeathed by the Judeo-Christian tradition as they did with attitudes that had been favored

---

282 "Das Heidentum ist also durchaus kein bloßer religionsphilosophischer Kinderschreck für Erwachsene […] Sondern es ist – nicht mehr und nicht weniger als die Wahrheit. Die Wahrheit freilich in elementarer, unsichtbarer, un-offenbarer Form." Franz Rosenzweig, "Das Neue Denken," in *Zweistromland*, p. 147.

283 "En dehors de l'être et du monde," Levinas, *Totalité et infini*, p. 151.

by the secular movements that had sought to replace this tradition.[284] Nazism, indeed, had brought about a break with all traditional conceptions of humanity that had predominated since antiquity.

In the aftermath of the experience of the Second World War and the Shoah, Levinas referred to pagan sentiments and to the elementary forces that animate them both in his assessment of twentieth century politics and society and in his analysis of twentieth century philosophy. It is here that the distinction of his position from that of Franz Rosenzweig becomes particularly clear. I would suggest, indeed, that the role which Levinas attributed to Rosenzweig's thought as a source of the basic conception of *Totality and Infinity* comes to light not only in those aspects of Levinas's thought which bear a resemblance to Rosenzweig's thinking, but also in passages in which he develops his interpretation well beyond the framework established by the master. I shall now turn to this latter aspect of Levinas's thought in order to identify what I take to be one particularly significant moment in its articulation: Levinas's critical appraisal, in light of his interpretation of myth, of what he qualified as the pagan philosophy of Martin Heidegger.

II

In one of his last writings, "Vertauschte Fronten" ("Transposed Fronts"), which was composed in the months before his death in 1929, during a period when he suffered from almost complete paralysis, Rosenzweig evoked the Davos debate that had recently taken place between Ernst Cassirer and Martin Heidegger. In this brief essay, Rosenzweig commented favorably on Heidegger's philosophy which, unlike that of Ernst Cassirer, seemed to him to announce the "New Thinking."[285] Rosenzweig did not

284 Emmanuael Levinas, "Quelques réflexions sur la philosophie de l'hitlérisme," *Les imprévus de l'histoire* (Paris: Fata Morgana, 1994), p. 26.

285 Franz Rosenzweig, "Vertauschte Fronten," *Zweistromland*, pp. 235–237. Where Rosenzweig, in his comments on the Davos debate in "Vertauschte Fronten," set Heidegger's philosophy on the side of the "New Thinking," he explicitly compared it to the last period of Hermann Cohen's work. Cohen died in 1918. In *Ethik des reinen Willens*, Cohen had highlighted what he took to be two principle aspects of the *difference* between myth and religion: first, prophetic religion broke beyond the limits of myth by virtue of its novel *temporal* orientation, for unlike myth the messianic time of the prophets was oriented toward the future. Second, Cohen highlighted the importance of ethical life (*Sittlichkeit*) for monotheistic faith. See *Ethik des reinen Willens*, p. 404–406, "In dieser Richtung auf die Zukunft entsteht die Religion im Unterschiede vom Mythos: die Religion der Propheten. Es gibt in der Tat einen Unterschied zwischen Religion und Mythos, obzwar die Religion aus dem Mythos entsprungen ist, und mit dem Mythos sich immer wieder zu vermischen trachtet. Bei den Propheten [...] wird der

elaborate on this point in his brief allusion to Heidegger, and one can wonder whether his physical condition might have prevented him from gleaning more than a very fragmentary account of the exchange between Cassirer and Heidegger. The young Levinas, who had attended this debate, also admired the force of Heidegger's presentation at a time when, as Levinas specified, Heidegger had not yet expressed his support for the Nazi party. If, as I briefly mentioned above, Rosenzweig had succinctly defined the "New Thinking" in relation two central points, the dissolution of traditional a-temporal ideas of truth and a fundamentally different approach to the other,[286] Levinas concurred in regard to the first point that Heidegger's philosophy of the temporality of truth ran parallel to Rosenzweig's fundamental conviction.[287] All the more striking in this context is the absence of reference to the second aspect of Rosenzweig's characterization of the New Thinking: "Need of the Other," which Rosenzweig himself did not specifically mention in his evocation of Heidegger. Nonetheless, Levinas's numerous critical reflections on Heidegger in *Totality and Infinity* made his own assessment of the matter abundantly clear, since he considered that Heidegger's reflections introduced, not a new philosophy of the Other, but a form of paganism that Levinas equated with denial of the Other. Let us examine this point more closely.

In one of his first critiques of Heidegger's philosophy in *Totality and Infinity*, Levinas noted that Heidegger's ontology "becomes an ontology of nature, the impersonal fertility of a generous mother without face." This "mother without face" engenders for Levinas "a philosophy of injustice," issuing from "pagan sentiments," which "subordinates the relation with the Other to the relation to being in general" and maintains "obedience to

---

Ursprung der Religion in ihrer Differenz vom Mythos darum so evident und so prägnant: dass sie durch den Begriff ihres neuen Einzigen Gottes in eine schroffe Opposition zu allem Mythos getrieben werden. Der neue Gott hat dem Menschen verkündet was gut sei. Und das ist Recht und Gerechtigkeit zu üben. Die Sittlichkeit allein ist, wie Luther sagen würde, das Amt dieses einzigen Gottes der Propheten." Evidently, the emphasis that Heidegger placed on the future concerned finite being toward death which singularizes Dasein in view of its finite end. This has little relation to messianic time.

286 "Bedürfen des Anderen und, was dasselbe ist, im ernstnehmen der Zeit"; Franz Rosenzweig, "Das Neue Denken," *Zweistromland, Kleinere Schriften zu Glauben und Denken*, pp. 151–52.

287 Emmanuel Levinas, *A l'heure des nations* (Paris: Éditions de Minuit, 1986), p. 177. As Levinas stated, this parallel between Rosenzweig's and Heidegger's conceptions of the temporal embodiment of truth had already been analyzed by Karl Löwith and set in relief by Stéphane Mosès. See Emmanuel Levinas, preface, Stéphane Mosès, *Système et révélation. La philosophie de Franz Rosenzweig* (Paris: Verdier, 2016), pp. 7–23.

anonymity, leading, fatefully [...] to imperialist domination and tyranny."[288]

Here we come to the decisive point. In this passage Levinas referred, not to "gods without faces," which he equated with myth, but to nature as a "mother without face" and to a philosophy issuing from "pagan sentiments." He was careful to avoid any allusion here, as in other evocations of Heidegger, to god or gods. He refrained from associating Heidegger's thought not only with the revealed God of monotheism, but even with the mythical gods. Indeed, in a later passage directly following Levinas's reference to mythical "gods without faces" I quoted earlier, he obliquely alluded to Heidegger in a way which is particularly significant for my present analysis. Levinas specified in this passage that the "gods without faces," the mythical divinities, are experienced as future insecurity, anticipating a future which is *not* projected from a position of "being thrown," *geworfen*,[289] evoking here Heidegger's concept of *Geworfenheit*, the existential facticity characterized by being thrown into a world in which one is immersed in present preoccupations and confronted with future death. Levinas, while directly qualifying Heidegger's philosophy as one of "pagan sentiments," at the same time carefully distinguished the Heideggerian concept of *Geworfenheit* from the elemental insecurity of the future which nourishes myth. How are we to understand Levinas's insistence on the incongruity between the experience evoked by the mythical gods and that associated with Heidegger's existential *Geworfenheit*?

A closer examination of Levinas's interpretation of Heidegger's concept of *Geworfenheit* makes his meaning clearer. Almost thirty years before the publication of *Totality and Infinity*, Levinas had dealt extensively with the concept of *Geworfenheit* in his essay "Martin Heidegger and ontology" ("Martin Heidegger et l'ontologie," 1932), one of the first discussions of Heidegger's philosophy to appear in the French language. In this context, Levinas described *Geworfenheit* as the fact of being "thrown into

---

288 "L'ontologie devient ontologie de la nature, impersonnelle fécondité, mère généreuse sans visage, matrice des êtres particuliers, matière inépuisable des choses [...] L'ontologie heideggerienne qui subordonne le rapport avec Autrui à la relation avec l'être en général—même si elle s'oppose à la passion technique, issue de l'oubli de l'être caché par l'étant—demeure dans l'obédience de l'anonyme et mène, fatalement, à une autre puissance, à la domination impérialiste, à la tyrannie." Levinas, *Totalité et infini*, p. 38.

289 "L'avenir de l'élément comme insécurité se vit concrètement comme divinité mythique de l'élément [...] Mais cet avenir ne prend pas le caractère d'une *Geworfenheit*"; *Ibid.* p. 151.

the world, abandoned, relinquished to oneself."[290] And, if Levinas dealt at length in this early essay with the concept of *Geworfenheit*, it must be remembered that this concept had played a central role not only in *Being and Time* (initially published in 1927), but also in the 1929 Davos debate between Heidegger and Ernst Cassirer, where Heidegger, in opposition to Cassirer's investigation of the symbolic configurations of mythical thinking, accorded a central role to existential *Geworfenheit* for the interpretation of myth.[291] It was precisely this role that *Totality and Infinity* denied in highlighting the incongruence between mythical experience and that of existential *Geworfenheit*. And, if this is the case, it is because for Levinas Heidegger's philosophy applies not to mythical experience, but to what he qualified as *absurd* existence. For his part, Levinas refused any possibility that the mythical world of the element, the world of uncertain primitive enjoyment (*jouissance*), might be reduced to a world of absurdity. This is why Heidegger's philosophy, if it expressed the "pagan sentiments" of a "mother without face," bears no essential relation to the mythical gods, let alone to the God of revelation: "The human being," as Levinas wrote, referring to *past* historical and pre-historical periods of human existence, "does not find itself in an absurd world into which it has been thrown, *geworfen*." Moreover, to emphasize this point, he added: "And this is true absolutely."[292] Far from engendering a new appreciation of the other which was a major aspiration of Rosenzweig's New Thinking, Heidegger's existential "being thrown" experiences the other as a "limit" and a "negation."[293] In other terms, enjoyment of life in the mythical extension of the element, if subjected to an uncertain future, is yet wholly unlike the absurd world of *Geworfenheit,* which evokes for Levinas the singular *contempo-*

290 "Avoir été jeté dans le monde, abandonné et livré à soi-même"; Emmanuel Levinas, *En découvrant l'existence avec Husserl et Heidegger* (Paris: Vrin, 1994), p. 69.

291 On the theme of "thrownness" in the Davos debate between Cassirer and Heidegger, see my essay "Ernst Cassirer's Theory of Myth. On the Ethico-Political Dimension of his Debate with Martin Heidegger," in J. A. Barash, ed., *The Symbolic Construction of Reality. The Legacy of Ernst Cassirer* (Chicago: University of Chicago Press, 2008), pp. 114–132; see also my review article of Peter Gordon's *Continental Divide: Heidegger, Cassirer, Davos*, titled "Cassirer, Heidegger, and the Legacy of Davos," in *History and Theory*, 51, October, 2012, pp. 436–450.

292 "L'être humain ne se trouve pas dans un monde absurde où il serait geworfen. Et cela est vrai absolument"; Levinas, *Totalité et infini*, p. 149. Levinas, in the 1959 lecture on Rosenzweig, "Entre deux mondes," to which I alluded earlier, after referring to Rosenzweig and Heidegger as two innovators of a new approach to time, presented critical comments on Heidegger's concept of *Geworfenheit*. See in this regard the essay "'Entre deux mondes': La voie de Franz Rosenzweig," *Difficile liberté*. pp. 246–247.

293 "La Geworfenheit heideggerienne, prise dans l'autre qui la limite et qui la nie." Levinas, *Totalité et infini*, p. 176.

rary situation of dire need bereft of enjoyment; it can thus only reflect "condemnation to the cursed labor of a proletarian condition, where the indigence of corporeal existence finds no home for refuge or for leisure."[294]

Levinas did not allude in this context to Rosenzweig's favorable appraisal of Heidegger in the 1929 essay "Vertauschte Fronten" and, if he agreed with Rosenzweig's judgment concerning the significance of Heidegger's philosophy of time, his critical rejection of the implications of this philosophy for that further aspect of the New Thinking, the approach to the Other, was emphatically clear. Beyond the horizon of mythical existence, and in a way that Rosenzweig could not have anticipated, Heidegger's philosophy was the ominous counterpart of absurd forms of existence that are specific to the modern world. And, where Rosenzweig in "Atheistic Theology" voiced his apprehensions in regard to twentieth century deifications of collective national existence, Levinas later identified and qualified in terms of Heidegger's philosophy the wholly unprecedented character of a modern situation that burst beyond all categorizations of an archaic mythical world.

294 "La condition prolétarienne condamnant au travail maudit et où l'indigence de l'existence corporelle ne trouve ni refuge, ni loisir chez soi, c'est là le monde absurde de la *Geworfenheit*"; Ibid., p. 156.

Chapter 10

The Reality of the Historical Past: The Heideggerian Turn in Paul Ricœur's Reflection on History

In recent decades, the question concerning our ability to comprehend the reality of the historical past has risen to the forefront of analysis not only in historiography or historical theory but, above all, in literary criticism. This question concerns the capacity of historical narratives based on documentary sources and other traces of actions and events that lie beyond the limits of all living memory to serve as reliable representations of a "true" historical past, and to attest the significance of its continuing existence in present awareness. In raising this question, schools of reflection that have emerged over previous decades in literary criticism and, in a different perspective, historical theory, have challenged traditional conceptions of historical representation: the emphasis they place on the rhetorical and literary aspects of historical writing has tended to blur the distinction between historical representation and fictional narrative. The aim of such theoretical orientations is by no means confined to the identification of points of similarity between the products of literature and of history, for it is through the comparison of the two modes of representation that suspicion is cast on the historian's claim to uncover the "reality" of the historical past.

This skeptical current, in turn, has led to a counter-critique by philosophers and historians. Through analysis of the specific difference between historical representation and literary fiction, this counter-critique has sought to understand how it might be possible for the historian to retrieve, even to a limited extent, something of the "reality" of the historical past. My analysis in this chapter will focus on the work of Paul Ricœur, and on the conception of the specific distinction he drew between literary fiction and historical representation to marshal support for the historian's claim to retrieve a measure of the past's reality. To this end, I will first focus on the challenge presented in literary criticism and historical theory to traditional conceptions of historical representation and proceed from there to an examination of Ricœur's response to this challenge in his major works of the late twentieth century. As I will illustrate, Ricœur's arguments on this topic changed substantially in different works over the course of this period. My purpose in bringing this change into focus, however, will be less to provide an exegesis of his conception of historical understanding, than to critically examine in the final section of this chapter the role that Martin Heidegger's philosophy came to assume for the theory of the "reality" of the historical past he elaborated in the last period of his œuvre.

I

The question concerning the relation between historical representation and fiction, and the problem this relation may pose for the claim concerning the possibility of grasping the reality of the historical past, has become a theme of animated debate since the 1970s. Nonetheless, the comparison of fiction and historical representation as a means of casting doubt on this claim is by no means of recent origin. In the eighteenth century, for example, the period in which the modern novel emerged, such comparisons became frequent vehicles for what had traditionally been termed historical pyrrhonism. Consider in this light the opinion of Denis Diderot, in his characterization of the English novelist Samuel Richardson: "Oh Richardson!," he wrote, "I will dare to say that the truest of histories is full of lies and that your novel is full of truths."[295] Jean-Jacques Rousseau, in affirming a similar attitude, advised in his book *Émile* against the inclusion of the writings of modern historians in his program of education. In comparing works of history with those of literary fiction, he wrote:

> "I see little difference between these novels and your histories, unless it is that the novelist resorts above all to his own imagination where the historian is subservient to that of others."[296]

In the early nineteenth century, a like-minded and highly influential doubt concerning the historian's claim to represent factual truth was elaborated in philosophical perspective by Arthur Schopenhauer in his work *The World as Will and Representation* (*Die Welt als Wille und Vorstellung*). Schopenhauer emphasized the irreducible singularity of historical facts which, in their infinite number, escape the historian's efforts to impose conceptual order on them. The more the historian's narrative attempts to encompass the singularity of past facts by means of general concepts, the

295 "O Richardson, j'oserai dire que l'histoire la plus vraie est pleine de mensonges, et que ton roman est plein de vérités"; Denis Diderot, "Éloge de Richardson," *Œuvres* (Paris: Gallimard, éditions de la Pléiade, 1951), p. 1067.

296 "Je vois peu de différence entre ces romans et vos histoires, si ce n'est que le romancier se livre davantage à sa propre imagination, et que l'historien s'asservit plus à celle d'autrui"; Jean-Jacques Rousseau, *Émile ou de l'éducation*, Book 4 (Paris: Garnier-Flammarion, 1966), p. 310.

further he or she moves away from their reality. Inversely, histories that focus on singularity, in the hope of remaining faithful to factual reality, above all in biographical and autobiographical narratives, are condemned to the incertitude that the myriad number of facts and the contingent relations between them makes manifest. These are at the same time the most "interesting" kinds of history for him, since it is here that history most resembles the novel.[297]

Friedrich Nietzsche, finally, in his unique way of comparing historical representation with the creations of fiction, formulated the most radical modern challenge to the historian's endeavor. Nietzsche's renowned critique of the modern preoccupation with historical understanding centered on what he took to be the modern incapacity to place it in the service of life in view of future creations. And, in the perspective of what he took to be vital needs, Nietzsche did not hesitate to identify the task of historical understanding less with a quest for factual reality than with creations modeled through the plastic force of the imagination: "[…] Only when historical writing bears being transformed into a work of art," as he wrote in the second of the *Untimely Meditations*, "can it perhaps maintain instincts or even arouse them."[298]

In a more recent period, renewed expressions of skepticism concerning the historian's capacity to retrieve the "reality" of the historical past have emerged over the course of the 1970s and 1980s following the so-called "linguistic turn" of literary theory. This movement took as its starting point the distance between linguistic meaning and the reality to which it refers to emphasize the radical incapacity of historical discourse to faithfully represent the historical past. Historical narrative, according to this hypothesis, through the very language it employs, produces meaning which it projects onto the past it interprets. "There are no facts in themselves," as Roland Barthes wrote, citing a passage from Nietzsche, "in order for facts to exist, one must always begin by introducing meaning." And he concluded that "the fact never has anything but a linguistic existence."[299] This sentence served as the epigraph to the collection of essays

297 Arthur Schopenhauer, "Über Geschichte," *Die Welt als Wille und Vorstellung*, vol. 2, 2 (Zurich: Diogenes, 1977), pp. 519–22.

298 "Nur wenn die Historie es erträgt, zum Kunstwerk umgebildet, also reines Kunstgebilde zu werden, kann sie vielleicht Instincte erhalten oder sogar wecken"; Friedrich Nietzsche, *Vom Nutzen und Nachteil der Historie für das Leben. 2. Unzeitgemässe Betrachtung, Sämtliche Werke, Kritische Studien Ausgabe*, vol. 1, p. 296.

299 "[…] Il n'y a pas de fait en soi. Toujours il faut commencer par introduire un sens pour qu'il puisse y avoir un fait"; "Le fait n'a jamais qu'une existence linguistique." Roland

of Hayden White, *The Content of the Form. Narrative Discourse and Historical Representation*—a fact which Paul Ricœur noted in his analysis of this theme in *Memory, History, Forgetting*[300]—and, indeed, it touches the heart of the problem of historical skepticism in its contemporary guise.

Be this as it may, the exact sense of Roland Barthes's pronouncement remains ambiguous. On one hand, he sought to emphasize that actions and events, in order to be remembered and communicated to others, must necessarily be translated into a linguistic medium which simplifies their real complexity. In transferring their representation from the sensuous manifold of immediate experience to the general categories of words, their reality is essentially transformed. But, as Ricœur justly noted in an essay of 1994, "Les philosophies critiques de l'histoire: Recherche, explication, écriture" ("The Critical Philosophers of History: Research, Explanation, Writing") and again in *Memory, History, Forgetting*, Barthes's claim is more radical. Since, for him, the reality of the historical past remains entirely at an extra-linguistic level, the historian's discourse can never succeed in reaching it.[301] In mobilizing Saussure's linguistic theory of the referent, the signifier, and the signified, Barthes argued that the historian forgets the extra-linguistic status of the real referent (*le référent*) and substitutes for it what is linguistically signified (*le signifié*). Rather than retrieve the reality of facts, the historian, through an act of imagination, linguistically constitutes this reality. By means of discourse the historian, according to Barthes, can at best create an "effect of the real" (*effet du reel*), in other words the illusory impression that it is not what has been linguistically reconfigured, but the past as such that is the object of his or her narrative. The real past, however, is radically incommensurable with the discourse through which the historian describes it. Indeed, the work of imagination that configures historical discourse produces a result that is no less fictive than the stories told in a novel. As Barthes noted in his essays "Le discours de l'histoire" ("The Discourse of History") and "L'effet du réel" ("The Effect of the Real"), the significance of the historian's illusory claim to recapitulate the *reality* of the historical past lies not in any truth this

---

Barthes, "Le discours de l'histoire," *Le Bruissement de la langue. Essais critiques IV* (Paris: Seuil, 1984), pp. 174–175.

300 Hayden White, *The Content of the Form. Narrative Discourse and Historical Representation* (Baltimore: Johns Hopkins, 1987), p. ii; Paul Ricœur, *La mémoire, l'histoire, l'oubli* (Paris: Seuil, 2000), p. 364.

301 Paul Ricœur, "Les philosophies critiques de l'histoire: Recherche, explication, écriture," *Philosophical Problems Today*, vol. 1, ed. G. Fløistad (Dordrecht, Kluwer, 1994), p. 168–69; *La mémoire, l'histoire, l'oubli*, pp. 322–323.

claim might have, but in its status as an *ideological* expression of the historian's own present epoch. "Historical discourse," as he wrote,

> "is an essentially ideological elaboration or, to be more precise, it is *imaginary*, if it is true that the imaginary is the language through which the enunciator of a discourse (a purely linguistic entity) 'fills' the subject of the enunciation (a psychological or ideological entity)."[302]

The American proponent of a similar kind of skeptical theory, Hayden White, reformulated the principal ideas of Roland Barthes in the perspective of a general theory of historiography, which he brought to expression in his book *Metahistory* (1973), and in his collections of articles, *Tropics of Discourse. Essays in Cultural Criticism* (1978), and *The Content of the Form. Narrative Discourse and Historical Interpretation* (1987). White's efforts were devoted above all to an analysis of historical discourse, which he related to different rhetorical forms or "tropes." On the basis of these rhetorical forms he, much like Barthes, identified what he took to be an abyss separating the language of historical representation from the reality of the historical past it purports to retrieve. In taking as the motto for his endeavor Barth's sentence, "the fact never has anything but a linguistic existence," Hayden White similarly assimilated the work of the historian to the creation of literary fiction. For him, historical narratives are essentially "verbal fictions, the contents of which are as much invented as found"; moreover, the contexts of historical narratives are "the products of the fictive capability of the historians who have studied them."[303] Even if Hayden White, in an article entitled "The Question of Narrative in Contemporary Historical Theory" (1984), hesitated to identify his own theoretical aims with those of Roland Barthes and if he recognized in Barthes's conception of historical interpretation what he took to be "a mass of highly problematical theories of language, discourse, consciousness, and ideology,"[304] the clear affinity he drew between the work of the historian and creations of literary fiction led him to adopt a similar skeptical attitude.

302 "[…] le discours historique est essentiellement élaboration idéologique, ou, pour être plus précis, *imaginaire*, s'il est vrai que l'imaginaire est le langage par lequel l'énonçant d'un discours (entité purement linguistique) 'remplit' le sujet de l'énonciation (entité psychologique ou idéologique)"; Roland Barthes, "Le discours de l'histoire," *Le bruissement de la langue*, p. 174.

303 Hayden White, "The Historical Text and Literary Artifact" (1974), *Tropics of Discourse. Essays in Cultural Criticism* (Baltimore: Johns Hopkins, 1978), pp. 82–89.

304 Hayden White, "The Question of Narrative in Contemporary Historical Theory," *The Content of the Form. Narrative Discourse and Historical Representation* (Baltimore and London: Johns Hopkins, 1987), p. 36.

The Nietzschean inspiration that Hayden White identified at the source of Barthes's historical conceptions is as characteristic of White's own methodology as of that Barthes himself had adopted. Historical skepticism, which an important modern current of thought had fueled through the likening of historiography to literary fiction, found powerful proponents both in Barthes's critique of the ideological language of historical representation and in White's analysis of the rhetorical forms of historical discourse.

II

Paul Ricœur developed his critical reflection on contemporary historical skepticism in publications that were elaborated over several decades, above all in volume three of *Time and Narrative, Narrated Time* (*Temps et récit, Le temps raconté* [1985]), in the 1994 essay "Philosophies critiques de l'histoire: recherche, explication, écriture" ("Critical Philosophies of History: Research, Explanation, Writing"), in an article published in 1998 in the *Revue de métaphysique et de morale*, entitled "La marque du passé" ("The Mark of the Past"), and finally in *Memory, History, Forgetting* (*La mémoire, l'histoire, l'oubli*), published in 2000.

Paul Ricœur presented his initial discussion of this theme in a section of volume three of *Time and Narrative* entitled "The Reality of the Historical Past." This theme, as he asserts, concerns the possibility of claiming not only that historical discourse "represents" the past in the sense of drawing a descriptive image of it, but also of being able, through this representation, to attest what *actually* existed in the past. Out of a multiplicity of heterogeneous facts in the past it is possible to produce all manner of different representations (its "représentation" or "Darstellung") but, beyond the narrative structure the historian confers on events, he or she seeks to produce a faithful narrative, even if it is limited in perspective, of what "really" happened. Beyond representation, the historian claims to present a sign that takes the place of what really happened, and this act of "taking the place of," of "lieutenance" or "Vertretung" which Ricœur terms "représentance," corresponds to the stronger claim, which historical skeptics underplay, that representation may indicate a past reality lying beyond the historian's discourse.

The capacity of "représentance" to take the place of past events and to attest their reality provides a well-known *leitmotiv* that runs throughout Ricœur's work from *Time and Narrative* until *Memory, History, Forgetting*. As I noted at the outset of this chapter, Ricœur's interpretation of this theme, however, changed considerably between these works. Underlying this change we find an important shift in focus from the accent he placed in *Time and Narrative* on the historical *imagination* as a means of uncovering the reality of the historical past toward a new emphasis that, without denying the importance of the historical imagination, comes to the fore in *Memory, History, Forgetting*: a notion of attestation of the reality of the historical past that draws more directly on the role of memory and of the witness. As we will see, this change has important implications for the theory of history Ricœur proposes.

In the chapter of *Time and Narrative* entitled "The Reality of the Historical Past," Ricœur dealt with the central theme of the historical imagination in his analysis of what he termed a plurality of conceptions of historical representation, each of which provides a partial approach to the "enigma" of "représentance" in its claim to uncover something of the reality of the historical past. In his well-known examination of this topic, Ricœur grouped these approaches to the historical past under the rubric of the three kinds (*genres*), the Same, the Other, and the Analogous, inspired by the great kinds of Being described in Plato's *Sophist* (254b–259d) and (for the Analogous) in the *Rhetoric* of Aristotle. These three approaches to the past, none of which, for Ricœur, is by itself adequate to account for its reality, correspond to three fundamental attitudes: the Same, represented by the British historical theorist R. G. Collingwood, emphasized the central role of the historical imagination as a means of overcoming the temporal distance that separates the historian from the past and, on the basis of documentary evidence and imaginative reconstruction, of "reenacting" it in the present; the Other, characterized by French theorists Paul Veyne and Michel de Certeau insisted, on the contrary, on the insurmountable character of the temporal distance between present and past, rendering the original sense of the past essentially alien and opaque; the third kind, the Analogous, exemplified by Hayden White, emphasized an approach to the past that treats it "as if" it might really be made to correspond to his or her account of it. Hayden White, however, as Ricœur notes, interpreted this analogy as an exercise of the historical imagination that, far from capable of reenacting the past in Collingwood's sense, is limited in scope to the rhetorical images and linguistic representations produced by the historian's narrative activity. As plausible and coherent as these accounts might be, the historian's analogical mode of understanding, for White, can never truly grasp the heterogeneous multiplicity of possible stories that might be drawn out of the past itself. For his part, Paul Ricœur, while accepting the idea that the historian, in giving the past narrative form, considers it "as if" it existed in reality, at the same time seeks to break out of the limits that White imposed on historical discourse: here Ricœur intends to restore a thickness to the scope of analogy in order to support a limited claim, ascertained through critical scrutiny of documentary evidence, to "représentance" capable of uncovering meaning lying in the past itself.[305] Hence the analogical approach to the past, where correctly understood, permits us to navigate between the Same and its too ready assumption that the historical imagination is capable of reenacting the past, and the presupposition of the Other that the reality of the past lies entirely outside its grasp.

Without limiting my analysis to an exegesis of Ricœur's theory, my task is above all to clarify its implications in seeking beyond what he himself explicitly acknowledged. In this vein, if in *Time and Narrative* Ricœur referred to theories of the historical imagination elaborated by his predecessors R. G. Collingwood and Hayden White, he did not evoke the specific differences in their respective theories of the imagination. Moreover, he did not mention the fact that Hayden White developed his theory of the historical imagination which, by virtue of the affinity he drew between history and fiction, led him to skeptical conclusions by means of a critical appraisal of Collingwood's reflections on the same faculty. As I will attempt to illustrate, it is nonetheless in light of such important nuances in interpretation that a number of tacit presuppositions come to light which will permit us to scrutinize more closely Ricœur's theory of the reality of the historical past.

In a footnote found in the chapter of *Time and Narrative* III entitled "The Reality of the Historical Past," where Ricœur refers to the act of the historical imagination that, according to Collingwood, makes it possible to reenact the past in the present, Ricœur evoked the underlying source of Collingwood's theory of the historical imagination. Ricœur mentioned in passing Collingwood's reference, in his work *The Idea of History* (1946), to Kant's theory of the transcendental imagination, and to Kant's statement that this faculty "is as blind as it is necessary." It is this theory of the transcendental imagination, as Ricœur stated, that Collingwood applied more specifically to the realm of historical understanding.[306]

Kant's theory of the transcendental schematism, I recall, concerned the capacity of the pure imagination to lend structure to temporal experience. In Kant's interpretation it is the schematism, the faculty of pure

305 Paul Ricœur, *Temps et récit*, vol. 3 (Paris: Seuil, 1985), p. 225.
306 Ibid., p. 209n.

imagination, which adapts the heterogeneity of sense data to a general conceptual structure and, in so doing, patterns sense experience in time. In the second of his "epilogomenes" presented in *The Idea of History*, Collingwood extrapolated from Kant's interpretation of this aspect of the transcendental imagination. He extended its function beyond the acts through which temporal form is conferred on experience to identify the ways in which the imagination lends structure to historical time. Through this interpretation of Kant's theory, Collingwood developed a salient insight for which his work *The Idea of History* is justly famous: in lending temporal structure to human experience in general, the transcendental imagination lies at the source of the coherence not only of the factual events of history but also of the imaginary creations of fiction. Nonetheless, this common temporal structure at the root of history and of fiction does not lead Collingwood to equate their representations; rather, the time-configuring activity of the transcendental imagination, when correctly understood, also provides us with the possibility of *distinguishing* historical narratives from fiction.

In his interpretation of the specific difference between fictive creations and historical representations, Collingwood's reasoning pursued a path established by Kant's logic which he applied at the level of historical time. In the "Transcendental Analytic" of the *Critique of Pure Reason*, Kant had asked how, if the structuring activity of the transcendental imagination underlies *all* experience, it might be possible to distinguish dreams and hallucinations from reality. And, in his detailed response to this question, Kant asserted that it is the necessary coherence and regularity in terms of which the whole of our experience is articulated that permits us to determine what is real and what is not. Following an analogous logic, Collingwood enumerated three general rules that permit us to distinguish historical reality from literary fiction: 1. The coherence in the historian's manner of localizing historical representations in time and space; 2. The intrinsic consistency of historical representation; 3. Faithfulness to historical evidence.[307] In his account of Collingwood, it would appear that Ricœur overlooked this aspect of Collingwood's analysis, for he reached the puzzling conclusion that Collingwood proceeded toward a "quasi-identification of the work of the historian with that of the novelist."[308]

---

307 R. G. Collingwood, *The Idea of History* (Oxford: Oxford University Press, 1956), p. 246.

308 Paul Ricœur, *Temps et récit*, vol. 3, p. 209n.

For his principal work, entitled *Metahistory*, Hayden White chose as the subtitle, *The Historical Imagination in the Nineteenth Century*. Nonetheless, the term "historical imagination" refers to a very different idea of its function than that Collingwood had proposed. In his essays, White subsequently criticized Collingwood's theory and completely reformulated it. In the essay "The Historical Text as Literary Artifact," White took to task Collingwood's theory of the imagination that operated in analogy to Kant's transcendental schematism. Much like the logic and temporal pattern imposed by Kant's transcendental schematism, Collingwood's constructive principles of historical imagination, as White pointed out, presuppose a general sense that different kinds of human situations can take. Reality can be inferred where the evidence fits into the coherent pattern prescribed by these situations.[309]

Against Collingwood, Hayden White proposed a radically different approach to the imagination. Collingwood's theory, as Hayden White noted, was not only inspired by Kant's philosophy, but it blended Kant's conception with a nineteenth century tradition that interpreted the historical imagination, on a psychological level, in terms of empathy.[310] Empathy concerned the historian's ability to transpose himself into a foreign historical context in order to comprehend it. Against this tradition, however, White underlined what he took to be the insurmountable limits of empathy, as of historical discourse, in face of the reality of the historical past. In his article "The Politics of Interpretation. Discipline and De-Sublimation" (1982), White warned his readers against the "dangerous" character of imagination for the historian. According to his interpretation, the historian is never able to determine to what extent the activity of the imagination, as it is directed toward a foreign context in the past, in fact corresponds to what "really" took place in this context or, on the contrary, derives from imaginary creations that are as fictive as literary productions. After citing with approval Roland Barthes' essay "The Discourse of History" ("Le Discours de l'histoire") in a footnote, White explained his conception of the historical imagination in the following terms:

> "[…] Imagination is dangerous for the historian, because he cannot know that what he has 'imagined' was actually the case, that it is not a product of his 'imagination' in the sense in which that term is used to characterize the activity of the poet or writer of fiction. Here, of course, the imagination is disciplined by its subordination to the rules of evidence which require that whatever is imagined be consistent with

309 Hayden White, "The Historical Text as Literary Artifact," *Tropics of Discourse. Essays in Cultural Criticism*, p. 227.

310 Ibid., p. 84.

> what the evidence permits one to assert as a 'matter of fact.' Yet 'imagination,' precisely in the sense in which it is used to characterize the activity of the poet or novelist, is operative in the work of the historian at the last stage of his labors, when it becomes necessary to compose a discourse or a narrative in which to represent his findings, that is, his notion of 'what really happened' in the past. It is at this point that what some theorists call the style of the historian, considered now as a writer of prose, takes over and an operation considered to be exactly like that of the novelist, an operation that is openly admitted to be literary, supervenes."[311]

In *Time and Narrative*, Paul Ricœur, much like Collingwood, appealed to Kant's theory of the transcendental schematism as a source for his own theory of historical understanding.[312] In the chapter of *Time and Narrative* III entitled "The Interlinking of History and of Fiction" ("L'entrecroisement de l'histoire et de la fiction"), Ricœur, much like Collingwood, related the transcendental schematism to the capacity to give temporal structure to human experience in general, which is conceived less in the guise of the abstract Kantian *cogito*, than as a framework for symbolic and linguistic structures that lend coherence both to the imaginary plots of fictive creations and to the factual events of history. And in lending configuration to historical *time*, the imagination lies not only at the common root of fictive accounts and historical narratives but, as Collingwood had earlier asserted, permits us to distinguish historical narratives from fiction.

In the three volumes of *Time and Narrative*, Ricœur's extrapolation from Kant's idea of the transcendental schematism for his own idea of the imaginative configuration of time leads his work in a new direction. The originality of Ricœur's interpretation lies above all in the celebrated opposition he delineated between two traditions of temporal interpretation in Western thought; between the tradition that accords a fundamental status to cosmic time, the measurable time made up of successive moments, and the tradition that situates lived or phenomenological time at the fundamental temporal level. According to Ricœur's well-known hypothesis in this work, neither of these two theoretical approaches can account for the phenomenon of time as such. Neither of them is reducible to the other. And yet, we may designate points of connection (*connecteurs*) between the two fields of cosmic time and phenomenological time. Ricœur designated three such points of connection that he identified with calendar time, the series

311 Hayden White, "The Politics of Interpretation. Discipline and De-Sublimation," *The Content of the Form*, pp. 67–68.

312 Paul Ricœur, *Temps et récit*, vol. III, p. 268. On the broader theme of imagination in the work of Ricœur, see especially Richard Kearney, "Between Imagination and Language," *On Paul Ricœur. The Owl of Minerva* (Aldershot, Hampshire, England: Ashgate, 2004), pp. 35–58.

of generations, and the trace. According to the chapter of *Time and Narrative* on the "interlinking of history and fiction" these three points of connection fulfill, on the level of human historical time, the schematizing function of the imagination, bringing together as a unity at three different levels time which is measured and time which is lived. In accounting for historical time which is "thinkable and manipulable" (*pensable et maniable*), these points of connection in time lend configuration, through acts of imagination, both to fiction and to historical representation.

In the argument that Ricœur drew from this theory in favor of the possibility of moving beyond the mere linguistic representations of the historian toward signs capable of retrieving a measure of the reality of the historical past, Ricœur's critique centered in particular on the reflection of Hayden White. He criticized Hayden White's restriction of the historian's representations to the figures of historical discourse, and reproved what he described as a "certain tropological arbitrariness," referring to the rhetorical figures of Hayden White through which the historian organizes his or her discourse; these figures, according to Ricœur, should "not make us forget the constraints that the historical past, through available documents, imposes on historical discourse."[313]

Beyond this critique, Ricœur also evoked what he took to be deeper motives that animate the historian's will to be faithful to documentary evidence and to follow the logical coherence of narratives: enunciated at the beginning of the chapter "The Reality of the Historical Past," this idea is summed up by Ricœur's conviction that the historian has a debt to the dead of the past, a debt that obliges him to "restitute what is due to them."[314] This idea of the debt to the dead of the past, which is poetically eloquent and theologically suggestive, was inspired in *Time and Narrative* by the work of Michel de Certeau, and provided Ricœur with a central theme that he would develop in a different way in later years, above all in *Memory, History, Forgetting*.

III

As Paul Ricœur noted in his essay "La marque du passé," initially published in 1998 in the *Revue de Métaphysique et de Morale*, he later found unsatisfactory the theory of the reality of the historical past he had

313 "[…] il ne faut pas qu'un certain arbitraire tropologique fasse oublier la sorte de contrainte que l'événement passé exerce sur le discours historique à travers les documents connus"; Ibid.

314 Ibid., pp. 203, 228.

elaborated in *Time and Narrative* concerning the distinction between history and the creations of fiction.[315] This essay adumbrated the central idea of the project that Ricœur would bring to fruition two years later in *Memory, History, Forgetting*. In it he announced the abandonment of such sweeping categories of analysis presented in *Time and Narrative* as the three kinds of approach to the past modeled on the Same, the Other, and the Analogous.[316] At the same time, the theory of imagination deployed in analogy with Kant's transcendental schematism and applied to the temporal structure of both history and fiction lost its prominence in his method of analysis. Nonetheless, the question itself concerning the reality of the historical past retained its earlier significance. Indeed, in defending the historian's ability to restitute a measure of the reality of the historical past, Ricœur intensified his combat against historical skepticism. In the section of *Memory, History, Forgetting* entitled "History/Epistemology" ("Histoire/épistémologie"), he elaborated on critical analysis he had presented in his 1994 essay, "Les philosophies critiques de l'histoire: Recherche, explication, écriture," in which he had attacked historical skepticism and the proposition that "facts never have anything but a linguistic existence," as it oriented the work of Roland Barthes and Hayden White. He argued that this skeptical current focused too exclusively on the final moment of literary "mise en forme" of historical discourse while neglecting other phases of the historian's work, above all documentary proof and causal/purposeful explanation which this final phase presupposed.[317] Here he extended and systematized arguments that were adumbrated in *Time and Narrative*.

In this triple articulation of the historical account—documentary proof, causal/purposeful explanation, literary *mise en forme*—which Ricœur presented as the "secret of historical knowledge,"[318] it seems legitimate to wonder whether, even after he abandoned the idea of the schematizing function of the historical imagination, his thought did not pursue a goal similar to that which Collingwood had advocated in his theory of historical representation. If not identical with Collingwood's three principles of historical understanding enumerated above—the coherence in the historian's manner of localizing historical representations in time and space; the intrinsic consistence of historical representation; faithfulness to

315 Paul Ricœur, "La marque du passé," *Mémoire, Histoire, Revue de Métaphysique et de Morale*, ed. Jeffrey Andrew Barash, 1, March 1998, pp. 7–32.

316 Ibid., p. 16.

317 Paul Ricœur, *La mémoire, l'histoire, l'oubli* (Paris: Seuil, 2000), pp. 320–339.

318 Ibid., p. 323.

historical evidence—Ricœur's triple articulation of the historical account was certainly consonant with these principles.

This indeed brings us to the heart of the matter: if Ricœur did not discuss Collingwood's epistemological principles, he did return to Collingwood's theory of reenactment of the past. This discussion of Collingwood is not included in the section of *Memory, History, Forgetting* entitled "History/Epistemology," which deals with historical knowledge and method; it is placed, rather, in the section of Ricœur's book entitled "The Historical Condition," which turned from historical reflection (*la pensée historique*) toward *ontology* and examined the question of historical being. In referring to the "reality" of the historical past in *Time and Narrative*, Ricœur had already broached the field of ontological analysis.[319] In his later work, however, the ontological claim moved to the center of his endeavor, as he focused more resolutely not only on the question of *knowing* the reality of the past, but on that of its ongoing significance for our own later historical *being*. Beyond the ability to attest the death of those who lived in the past and to assist in placing them in their tombs (*la mise au tombeau*), Ricœur's analysis centered on their significance for us as they once lived, as "acting and suffering beings" in the past.[320]

At this point in his analysis Ricœur, in evoking Collingwood's theory of historical time, leveled against him in the later ontological perspective *of Memory, History, Forgetting* a similar objection to the one we encountered in *Time and Narrative* in the section on the reality of the historical past. He once again questioned Collingwood's assumption that, through an act of the historical imagination, the historian might be able to "reenact" the past. Without calling attention to the methodology through which Collingwood aimed to critically control this concept, Ricœur equated it, in a loose manner, with the nineteenth century romantic idea of Jules Michelet, according to which the historian might "resurrect" the past. Both of the concepts of re-enactment and resurrection must be placed in question according to Ricœur, for both neglect "the moment of alterity of the past."[321] And, to compensate for this weakness, he introduced the concept of "repetition" (*Wiederholung*), which he drew from Heidegger's fundamental ontology in *Being and Time*.

In a number of his previous writings Ricœur had devoted lengthy analyses to Heidegger's philosophy, above all to his reflection on

319 Paul Ricœur, *Temps et récit*, vol. 3, p. 12.
320 Paul Ricœur, *La mémoire, l'histoire l'oubli*, p. 495.
321 Ibid., p. 496.

temporality in volume three of *Time and Narrative* and, in the work *Oneself as Another* (1990), to the problem posed by the absence of an ethical perspective in *Being and Time*. However, it is in *Memory, History, Forgetting*, notably in the section of this work "The Historical Condition," that Heidegger's philosophy assumed a central role in the orientation of Ricœur's thought, above all in regard to his approach to the alterity of historical being. Ricœur at the same time proposed to enlarge and rectify Heidegger's perspective in view of his own approach to historical time. From Ricœur's new standpoint in *Memory, History, Forgetting*, repetition permits us to compensate for the constantly shifting horizons of historical time and, in view of the irreducible difference between past temporal horizons and our own, to retrieve a measure of the temporal structure in which past experience was framed. In this light, the theme of repetition of past possibilities led Ricœur to reintroduce one of the central themes of *Time and Narrative*, according to which it is the *debt* we owe to those who have lived in the past that motivates our faithfulness to its factual reality. Here, beyond the framework of his discussion of the debt in *Time and Narrative*, Heidegger's concept of being-in-debt (*Schuldigsein*) in *Being and Time* served as the basis of his analysis. Acceptance of the debt, as he interpreted Heidegger, marks the capacity to repeat possibilities implicit in the past in relation to a heritage taken up in the present and projected toward the future.

Ricœur's adoption of the Heideggerian conceptions of repetition and of being-in-debt in his elaboration of an historical ontology in *Memory, History, Forgetting* is curious, above all in view of the critique that, on ethical grounds, he had directed against these same conceptions ten years earlier in *Oneself as Another*. This critique had been voiced in the framework of his interpretation of the moral implications of conscience (*Gewissen*) and the sense of "being-in-debt" that it elicits. In *Being and Time*, Heidegger had sought to dissociate conscience from its traditional moral connotations and to establish an original basis through which moral topics might subsequently be placed in what he claimed to be a fundamental perspective. Heidegger never went farther in the clarification of this claim and, in *Oneself as Another*, Ricœur contested Heidegger's suspension of moral questions in the domain of fundamental ontological analysis. According to Ricœur, Heidegger had brought about what he termed a "demoralization of conscience" (*dé-moralisation de la conscience*). Ricœur contrasted Heidegger's demoralization of conscience, and of the "being-in-debt" (*Schuldigsein*) it brought to light, to what he took to be a more appropriate conception of conscience which engaged ethics at the fundamental level through the fact of being called upon by the other. And Ricœur concluded:

> "[...] Here we find the legitimate notion of the *debt*, which Heidegger ontologized too quickly at the expense of the ethical dimension of indebtedness."[322]

In the context of Ricœur's subsequent ontology of history elaborated in *Memory, History, Forgetting*, his interpretation of indebtedness toward the past in terms of Heidegger's notion of "being-in-debt" (*Schuldigsein*) in *Being and Time* clearly represents an important shift in his orientation. As Ricœur acknowledged in a footnote,[323] Heidegger identified the debt (in the double German sense of *Schuld*, signifying both debt and guilt), in terms of the openness of finite existence (*Dasein*) to the possibility of nothingness in the face of the singularity of death, and it was for him choice in the face of nothingness—stripped of all traditional ethical connotations—that makes possible a grasp of what may be authentically repeated in the past. Ricœur justified his newfound appreciation for Heidegger in stipulating that the historian, at the preliminary stage of research, must formulate a "morally neutral" concept (*un concept moralement neutre*), before proceeding toward evaluation of the ethical dimension of the debt.[324]

What interests me here is less the question concerning the historiographical implications of Ricœur's ideal of "morally neutral concepts," formulated in the light of Heidegger's existential analytic, than the revision that the introduction of this Heideggerian element represents for Ricœur's overall theory of the reality of the historical past. Here too in according a central role to Heidegger's conception of "being-in-debt," Ricœur revised his earlier theory: "being-in-debt," in a Heideggerian perspective, now accounted for the existential possibility of "représentance," of retrieving what really existed in the past which, as repeatable, continues

---

322 "Ainsi serait fait droit à la notion de *dette*, que Heidegger a trop vite ontologisée aux dépens de la dimension éthique de l'endettement"; Paul Ricœur, *Soi-même comme un autre* (Paris: Seuil, 1990), p. 404. Compare also in this context Ricœur's critique of Heidegger in his contemporary review of Jeanne Hersch's translation of the book of Karl Jaspers, *Philosophie*, where he raised the following question in regard to Heidegger: "What is a philosophy worth in the last analysis if it is not capable of better arming us for moral decision and for political judgment? "; ("Que peut valoir, en fin de compte, une philosophie qui n'arme pas mieux pour la décision morale et pour le jugement politique?"); Paul Ricœur, "Éclairer l'existence," (1986) *Lectures 1. Autour du politique* (Paris: Seuil, 1991), p. 156.

323 Paul Ricœur, *La mémoire, l'histoire, l'oubli*, pp. 472–73n.

324 Ibid., p. 473.

to have significance for us. And "being-in-debt" at the same time accomplished more than this, for it not only concerns repetition of the past, but it at the same time underlies the synthesis of the temporal modes of historical existence guiding our focus on the past in view of the future. In Ricœur's words, strongly marked by Heideggerian vocabulary:

> "Being-in-debt constitutes in this way the existential possibility of 'taking the place of' (*représentance*). Whereas the notion of 'taking the place of' remains dependent, in regard to its significative structure, on the deliberately retrospective standpoint of historical knowledge, 'being-in-debt' constitutes the reverse side of resolute anticipation."[325]

Ricœur provides here a noteworthy reading of Heidegger, which to my mind places his manner of interpreting the reality of the historical past in a thoroughly problematic light. Where existence is conceived on the basis of radical *singularity* in the face of death, the question must be raised concerning the possibility of adequately accounting for its *communal* dimension, in its past, present, and future articulations. Aside from Heidegger's remarks in *Being and Time* on communal, public existence as an inauthentic means for diverting finite existence from its irreducible singularity, his interpretation of authentic community remained entirely vague. And, in an earlier period of his reflection on historicity, Ricœur himself had acknowledged this vagueness in Heidegger's philosophy. Moreover, he also affirmed that in regard to the question concerning the possible link between national communities and historical epochs that been raised in previous German historical reflection, Heidegger's philosophy in *Being and Time*, "renders more opaque the transfer of the authentic choice of *Dasein* that we each are to a historical community and to the destiny of a people."[326]

---

325 "L'être-en-dette constitue à cet égard la possibilité existentiale de la représentance. Alors que la notion de représentance reste dépendante, quant à sa structure de sens, de la perspective délibérément retrospective du savoir historique, l'être-en-dette constitue l'envers de la résolution devançante"; ibid., p. 473.

326 "[…] rend plus opaque le transfert du choix authentique du Dasein que nous sommes chacun à une communauté historique et à la destinée d'un peuple"; Paul Ricœur, Préface à "Heidegger et le problème de l'histoire" (1988) *Lectures 2. La contrée des philosophes* (Paris: Seuil, 1989), p. 300; see also in this regard Ricœur's critique of Heidegger at the end of *Temps et récit*, vol. III, p. 368: "Yet, although Heidegger only envisions, at least at the most original level, the transmission of a heritage from oneself to oneself, traditionality (*la traditionalité*) involves the avowal of a debt that is fundamentally contracted in regard to another. Heritages are principally transmitted by way of language and, more generally, on the basis of symbolic systems that imply the sharing of a minimum of commonly held beliefs and of agreements concerning the rules permitting the deciphering of signs, symbols, and norms acknowledged by the group." ("Mais, alors que Heidegger ne conçoit, du moins au plan le plus originaire, qu'une transmission d'héritage de soi-même à soi-même, la traditionalité comporte l'aveu d'une dette qui

In view of this difficulty of accounting for communal existence on the basis of the singular finitude of *Dasein*, how might "repetition" in light of finite singularity permit us to open a horizon for approaching the *alterity* of the collective past in its real distance from the present? I am not convinced that the Heideggerian concept of repetition provides Ricœur with a less problematic approach to the reality of the historical past than Collingwood's concept of re-enactment.

Evidently, as I mentioned above, Ricœur, in *Memory, History, Forgetting*, did not simply adopt the interpretation Heidegger developed in *Being and Time*, but he proposed to enlarge and to rectify its perspective. He did not hesitate to criticize Heidegger's position where he found it questionable. Above all, Ricœur himself called attention to what he took to be Heidegger's exaggerated focus on the singularity of death, which accorded too limited a place to the themes of solicitude for the death of others and of fear of violent death that others may inflict.[327] In accord with the interpretation of Jean Greisch, Ricœur invoked Hannah Arendt's concept of natality and of the necessary plurality it introduces in the sphere of political action as a corrective to what he took to be Heidegger's too-exclusive focus on being-toward-death.[328]

Nonetheless, these doubts concerning Heidegger bring us to the crucial point: in view of Ricœur's call for sweeping correctives to Heidegger's existential ontology, we may question the legitimacy of his insistence on Heidegger's method and his use of concepts of debt and guilt that are elaborated in its perspective, for an interpretation of the historical condition and of the "reality" of the historical past.

At many points in his analysis in *Memory, History, Forgetting*, Ricœur referred to Reinhart Koselleck's reflection on historical time, above all in his book *Futures Past* (*Vergangene Zukunft*). In this work, Koselleck developed his well-known theory that human historicity finds its root in the different ways of anticipating the future in regard to the present and the past, of relating the space of experience (*Erfahrungsraum*) to the horizon of expectation (*Erwartungshorizont*). Koselleck, however, questioned the adequacy of Heidegger's philosophy of singular finite

est fondamentalement contractée à l'égard d'un autre; les heritages transmis le sont principalement par la voie langagière et le plus généralement sur la base de systems symboliques impliquant un minimum de partage de croyances communes et d'ententes sur les règles permettant le déchiffrage des signes, symboles et normes en vigueur dans le groupe").

327 Paul Ricœur, *La mémoire, l'histoire, l'oubli*, pp. 461–471.

328 Ibid., p. 465.

existence for an attempt to understand the past and to retrieve a measure of its "reality." In his debate with Hans-Georg Gadamer, Koselleck took Heidegger's philosophy to task, not only for what he took to be the inadequacy of its account of relations with others, but for the weakness of its interpretation of the common space lying between human beings that is continually transformed over the course of time. "The times of history," as he wrote, in reference to Heidegger,

> "are not identical and they are also not derivable from the existential modalities that have been developed in regard to human beings as 'Dasein.' Right from the start, the times of history are constituted in an inter-human manner; it is always a matter of simultaneity of the unsimultaneous, of delineations of difference, that contain their own finitude, and cannot be referred back to an 'Existenz.'"[329]

In these sentences Reinhart Koselleck presents what I take to be the principle consideration which must serve as the starting point for reflection on what we term the "reality of the historical past": historical finitude cannot simply be derived from the singular finitude of mortal beings, nor identified on this basis with the quest to repeat what is implicit in the past, for the distance of the past, its "alterity," is situated at another fundamental level of finitude that has its own unique modes of being. This level may be designated by the intermediary symbolic space through which human beings communicate. All expressions in this symbolic space emerge in the limited perspective through which, as historical beings, they share a common world.

329 "Die Zeiten der Geschichte sind nicht identisch und auch nicht ableitbar aus den existentiellen Modalitäten, die an dem Menschen als 'Dasein' entwickelt worden sind. Die Zeiten der Geschichte sind von vornherein zwischenmenschlich konstituiert, es handelt sich immer um Gleichzeitigkeiten des Ungleichzeitigen, um Differenzbestimmungen, die ihre eigene Endlichkeit enthalten, die nicht auf eine 'Existenz' zurückführbar ist"; Reinhart Koselleck, "Historik und Hermeneutik," *Zeitschichten. Studien zur Historik. Mit einem Beitrag von Hans-Georg Gadamer* (Frankfurt am Main: Suhrkamp, 2000), p. 101. This text was originally published in 1987 as a separate work alongside Gadamer's contribution to the debate; cf. *Historik und Hermeneutik* (Heidelberg: Carl Winter, 1987).

Conclusion

In the introduction to this book I called attention to Heidegger's claim in his 1919–1921 review of Karl Jaspers's *Psychology of World-Views* that the predominant philosophical orientations of his period had evaded the fundamental task of thought. Instead of reclaiming a heritage of original questions, they had become preoccupied with secondary matters, positing as essential what was in truth only incidental. If in the works that followed, beginning with *Being and Time*, Heidegger steadily claimed that the *Seinsfrage* revealed this more fundamental path for thought, I have raised the question whether Heidegger's manner of rethinking the past heritage of Western intellectual traditions, in both his earlier and later periods, made good on his promise to set it in a more fundamental direction.

Any attempt to answer this question faces a seemingly insurmountable difficulty from the start, for it presupposes the capacity to identify *what* is fundamental and to distinguish it from the secondary and incidental. How then might we make such a distinction?

In the analyses I have undertaken in the preceding chapters, which have benefitted from the insight of the different thinkers whose respective critical perspectives I have taken into consideration, the touchstone for revealing what is fundamental lies in its appropriateness for interpreting human historical experience and for revealing in it a meaningfulness that is not readily evident in view of elucidating the ethico-political conditions of human co-existence in a common world. As I conceive of it, Heidegger's claim that the *Seinsfrage* as he conceived of it provides an adequate basis for interpreting human historical experience proves particularly problematic in both the earlier and later periods of his thought, and this comes to light above all in its relation to ethico-political considerations. I will limit my comments in this conclusion to the central facets of what I take to be an essential shortfall in his claim in regard both to the period of *Being and Time* and to his later work.

I

In *Being and Time* Heidegger claimed that *Dasein*'s manner of conferring sense on being—on what it means *to be*—through its finite choices of a way of being provides the foundation for all anthropological interpretation. The shortfall of his claim, as it has been subjected to analysis in the various perspectives proposed in this book, lies in its approach to human co-existence in the public realm and in the broader context of the historical world.

The problematic character of Heidegger's analysis comes most vividly to light if we recall his conception of the specifically *public* aspect of *Dasein*'s being-in-the-world. According to Heidegger's well-known conception of being-in-the-world in *Being and Time*, *Dasein*'s public way of being concerns first and foremost its everyday world comprising the different systems of tools and signs with which it is preoccupied, as well as co-*Dasein* that shares its everyday concerns. Tools draw their meaningfulness from a totality of references (*Verweisungen*) in which each particular tool finds its place. Like tools, the different sign systems *Dasein* employs fit into a totality of references from which the meaning of each individual element is drawn. The publicly interpretable character (*öffentliche Ausgelegtheit*) of *Dasein*'s being-in-the-world lies in the generality and replaceability of the functions of tools and signs which are the objects of its everyday preoccupations, as well as of other *Dasein* who are co-participants in these preoccupations. In this everyday context, *Dasein*'s preoccupations orient its ontological self-interpretation: "Dasein finds 'itself' most immediately in what it operates, needs, awaits, avoids."[330]

Heidegger's analysis of *Dasein*'s being-in-the-world in the framework of a publicly interpretable everyday world draws a sharp distinction between this everyday world in which the meaningfulness of each element depends on its relation to the whole and the singularity of *Dasein* that is incommensurable with any such system. The public interpretability of *Dasein*, like that of the tools and signs and of fellow *Dasein*, which is focused on the generality and interchangeability of its function, can only be indifferent to each *Dasein*'s finite singularity. Unlike this finite singularity, the public realm in its generality reveals itself to everyone in the same manner. Where particular tools or signs eventually become outmoded and the *Dasein* that employs them dies, the way of being of public functions comprises an undying temporal continuity. According to Heidegger's famous depiction, *Dasein*'s everyday preoccupation with things and other *Dasein* in the context of a publicly interpretable world provides the occasion for it to forget the finite singularity of its being and discharge the burden of its being-toward-death. Heidegger equates its publicly interpretable way of being with this quest for dissimulation and forgetfulness. This

330 "Dasein findet 'sich selbst' zunächst in dem was es betreibt, braucht, erwartet, verhutet," Martin Heidegger, *Sein und Zeit*, *GA*, vol. 2, p. 159; *Being and Time*, p. 155, trans. modified.

interpretation of the public realm as a way of being providing for *Dasein*'s flight into inauthentic dissimulation led him to the conclusion I noted in chapter seven in regard to Hannah Arendt's penetrating analysis: "The public obscures everything …" ("Die Öffentlichkeit verdunkelt alles").

The radical dichotomy Heidegger established in the early sections of *Being and Time* between *Dasein*'s singular finite existence and the undying perdurability of the public realm guided his ontological analysis not only of *Dasein*'s being in an everyday world, but of what he took to be the hidden expression of *Dasein*'s everyday quest that tacitly oriented Western theoretical preoccupations since antiquity. The interpretation of *Dasein*'s tacit quest to dissimulate its finitude by virtue of its participation in the undying functions of a publicly interpretable world led him to radically revise traditional ideas of the subject which, on a theoretical level, *Dasein*'s everyday forgetfulness of its finitude brought to expression. Whether posited in terms of the Cartesian cogito, the Kantian "consciousness in general," or the Hegelian Spirit, the traditional subject, far from situating *Dasein*'s finite being as the basis for its grasp of truth, had discounted its finitude in identifying it with a capacity to establish absolute, universally valid criteria of truth to identify the undying permanence of what truly "is." This tendency to overlook the finitude of the subject extended the assumption of an ancient metaphysical tradition centered on the human rational capacity to glean immutable, eternal truth.

On the basis of his analysis of *Dasein*'s being-in-the-world and of the ramifications of its publicly interpretable preoccupations in the theoretical sphere, Heidegger applied his interpretation of the public realm in the later sections of *Being and Time* to the broad articulations of *Dasein's* temporal and historical existence. At the basis of the general functions comprising the public character of *Dasein*'s everyday being-in-the-world, the temporality of the public realm resides in its continuity as an infinitely extendible series, a "public time," that is open to all in the same way. The time of the public realm provides the paradigmatic structure for the chronology of world-time—the time that in Heidegger's words "makes itself public" (*sich veröffentlichende Zeit*). Public time also provides the basis for the temporal cohesion of world-history.[331] The dichotomy between *Dasein*'s finite time and publicly intelligible world time served as a potent argument that Heidegger brandished to question a tradition of historical reflection inaugurated by Hegel's philosophy of history.

---

331 Heidegger, *Sein und Zeit*, *GA*, vol. 2, pp. 547–548; Eng. trans., p. 467.

Hegel, as Heidegger argued, provided the epoch-making conception of the temporal cohesion of history elaborated through the deepening self-understanding of the Spirit that brings together as a unity the different moments of its experience in the movement of world-history. Hegel's identification of the meaning of history with the ongoing continuity of the Spirit was rooted for Heidegger in the tacit appropriation of the temporal paradigm of the undying permanence of world-time. Through this paradigm, Hegel conferred on *Dasein*'s everyday quest to look away from its finite singularity a central theoretical role in the framework of a philosophy of history.[332] Heidegger's conception of historicity sought to radically subvert Hegel's assumption that historical meaning resides in the objective, self-sustaining cohesion of a continuous process endowed with universal significance.

A half century after Hegel's death, Wilhelm Dilthey, whose historical reflection was a focus of Heidegger's ontological interpretation in the period of *Being and Time*, came under the spell of Hegel's influence. Even after contesting the absolute metaphysical foundation of Hegel's philosophy of history, Dilthey centered his interpretation of human historical life on the cohesion of history (*Zusammenhang der Geschichte*), which he identified with the continuity of the different articulations of the historical development of the human spirit. Against this assumption, Heidegger proclaimed in his 1928–29 Freiburg course lectures, *Introduction to Philosophy* (*Einleitung in die Philosophie*), that Dilthey's concentration on objective cultural expressions as the key to understanding the historicity of human life, could only blind him to the ontological source of the cohesion of history in the fundamental structure of *Dasein* itself.[333]

In opposition to these predominant currents of historical reflection, Heidegger deflected the quest for meaning in history from the objective cohesion of cultural and world-history to focus on the modes of appropriation of the past by the one who interprets it. This shift in perspective recalls an assumption that had animated Friedrich Nietzsche's historical reflection in the second of his *Untimely Meditations*, which Heidegger cited with admiration in *Being and Time*. Nietzsche stipulated that the quest for meaning in the past that is endowed with a universal validity for all to behold can only misconstrue its essential significance, which reveals itself uniquely to those who know how to interpret it. The meaning of the past,

332 Ibid., p. 565–575; Eng. trans., pp. 480–486.

333 Martin Heidegger, *Einleitung in die Philosophie* (1928–29), *GA*, vol. 27, ed. Otto Saame and Ina-Saame-Speidel (Frankfurt am Main: Klostermann, 2001), pp. 349–350.

as Nietzsche wrote, "is always a dictum of the oracle: only as the architect of the future, the knower of the present will you understand it."[334]

From Heidegger's standpoint in *Being and Time*, the approach to history as a continuous process of development endowing *Dasein* with a meaningfulness extending beyond its finite existence reflected nothing other than the tacit ontological subservience to the public world and to the temporal permanence of its function. By contrast, fidelity to the past and to its authentic significance depended on *Dasein*'s way of uncovering and repeating its possibilities through its choice of a way of being in light of the finite future.

The temporal paradigm of the public world, as it runs through the different levels of Heidegger's ontological analysis in *Being and Time* from the depiction of *Dasein*'s being-in-the-world to the interpretation of temporality and historicity, draws its ontological significance solely from its role as a *counterpart* to *Dasein*'s singular being-toward-death. But can this reduction of all that is public to the role of a mere counterpart justify Heidegger's bold assertion that his ontology establishes the basis for interpretation of the complex ontic modalities of human co-existence in a common world?

It is here, I believe, that we uncover the principle shortfall in Heidegger's claim that analysis of *Dasein*'s thrownness into the world in which it is preoccupied with everyday affairs and confronted with the necessity of choosing a way of being in the face of its finite future might provide an adequate basis for analysis of the intermediary space configuring the public world of human interaction and the realm of human historical existence. In view of the radicalism of the dichotomy he established between public time and the finite time of singular *Dasein*, how might it be possible to account for the cohesion over time of the interspace of customs, institutions, and practices? In the chapter of *Being and Time* on temporality and historicity Heidegger briefly evoked the possibility of an authentic group existence in the guise of contemporaneous generations and of the people (*das Volk*). Nonetheless, he never provided anything but a vague assertion to support this claim. He offered no clarification in *Being and Time* for the possible articulations of the finite temporal mode of these realms of collective authenticity in their distinction from what he took to be the darkness of the public realm.

334 Friedrich Nietzsche, *Vom Nutzen und Nachteil der Geschichte für das Leben*, *Unzeitgemässe Betrachtungen*, II, *Kritische Studienausgabe*, ed. Giorgio Colli and Mazzino Montinari (Munich/Berlin-New York: DTV/de Gruyter: 1988), vol. 1 p. 294.

One of the principle indications of this shortfall in Heidegger's ontological analysis, as I conceive of it, lies in his restriction of the *symbolic* sphere of human interaction to the narrow function of signs (*Zeichen*) in the everyday world. In regard to Heidegger's disregard for the symbolic sphere, Hans Blumenberg ventured the insightful remark that Heidegger's concentration on the question of the "sense of being" was hardly conducive to the elaboration of a theory of the symbol.[335] Indeed, in his course lectures, *Prolegomena to the History of the Concept of Time* (*Prolegomena zur Geschichte des Zeitbegriffs*), presented two years before the publication of *Being and Time*, Heidegger bruskly rejected the possibility that signs or symbols in the sense of Ernst Cassirer's *Philosophy of Symbolic Forms* might, as modes of spatio-temporal and conceptual configuration, serve to mediate human experience as a whole.[336] As Heidegger made clear in his review of the second volume of Cassirer's *Philosophy of Symbolic Forms*, *Mythical Thought* (1925), and then later in the debate between them at Davos, he strongly opposed the Kantian and neo-Kantian basis of Cassirer's model of consciousness and the original re-orientation of it he proposed in terms of the symbolic configuration of a shared, historically evolving cultural world.

Nonetheless, does insight into the symbolic sphere of human co-existence necessarily depend on Kantian or neo-Kantian models of consciousness any more than it does on the Hegelian Spirit or on objectifications of human life-experience in the sense of Dilthey? And does the assertion of an ongoing, trans-generational meaningfulness, notably of political symbols, not draw on truth claims endowed with an *intrinsic* validity which, in the course of their historical re-elaboration, reveal a cohesion of a fully different order than *Dasein*'s choices in light of its finite being-toward-death? The intrinsic meaningfulness claimed by fundamental principles—notably of political justice and equity—does not *result* from *Dasein*'s finite ontological decisions, but provides in each epoch an anthropological *prerequisite* for viable political co-existence. If the contents of such fundamental principles call for continuous rethinking in light of

335 "Wer nach dem Sinn von Sein fragen kann, wird für das Symbol nicht viel halten"; Hans Blumenberg, *Die Verführbarkeit des Philosophen*, (Frankfurt am Main: Suhrkamp, 2000), p. 78.

336 In a quip that hardly provides a serious rebuttal of Cassirer's philosophy, Heidegger wrote in regard to the symbol that "what is a suitable approach for aesthetic phenomena, may for other phenomena bring about anything but an elucidation and interpretation." Martin Heidegger, *Prolegomena zur Geschichte des Zeitbegriffs* (1925), *GA*, vol. 20, pp. 178–179.

the historicity of political outlooks and institutions, their ongoing meaningfulness over time, beyond the inauthentic "looking away from finitude" in the narrow scope of the Heideggerian ontology, gives testimony to a continuity in the conditions of human co-existence itself. The fundamental status of this continuity comes to expression where a past symbolic order resonates in the present and, notwithstanding essential historical discontinuities, serves to elucidate the contours of a present situation.

The dearth of political thought in Heidegger's early philosophy that is illustrated by the quasi-absence of reflection in *Being and Time* on what he took to be the authentic community of *Dasein* is the most evident sign of the aporetic character of his attempt, on the basis of *Dasein*'s radically singular choices, to account for human being-together in a common world.

II

As I illustrated from different points of view in the preceding chapters, Heidegger reoriented his *Seinsfrage* in the aftermath of *Being and Time*. Following his political engagement as rector of Freiburg University in 1933–34, he displaced the *Seinsfrage* from *Dasein*'s ways of conferring meaning on being in light its finite temporal and historical existence to focus on the history of Being. In the aftermath of this reversal or *Kehre* of the 1930s, Being itself, which he radically distinguished from all history attributed to human action, calls forth the historicity of the different perspectives on truth that rise to predominance in each epoch. Where *Being and Time*, by virtue of the radically singular existence of *Dasein*, challenged the privilege traditionally accorded to world history and to cultural development as the source of meaning in history, Heidegger's later work deepened this challenge and pursued it from another direction. Heidegger's historical thought in this later period shifted the focus of his analysis from *Dasein*'s mostly tact quest, through its search for stability and continuity in cultural and world-history, to displace the burden imposed by the finitude of its existence; his *Seinsfrage* later set as its central target what he took to be the tendency to identify all meaning in history with the objects of human production.

I have underlined from different perspectives in this book what I consider to be the salient traits of Heidegger's interpretation: in each epoch, the mutations of truth called forth by Being constitute the foundation of human history in relation to which all other forms of historical reflection remain entirely tributary. At the culmination of this long trajectory of Being punctuated by the history of Western metaphysics, the modern incapacity to conceive of a history more fundamental than that of humanity itself culminates in the era of technology. In this epoch, humanity seeks assurance, through its technical domination of beings, that it is capable of mastering its own historical becoming.

The history of Being aims toward a radical shift in the fulcrum of thought itself. Interpretation of the cohesion of history (*Zusammenhang der Geschichte*) upon which the philosophy of history had centered reflection since Hegel continually obfuscated the opacity of the source of this cohesion. All previous methods of historical reflection, since they interpreted the past in relation to manifest contexts of development, remained blind to Being that is the hidden source of the movement underlying these contexts. In this manner they bring to expression the central trait of what Heidegger terms modern "historical-technical consciousness."[337] In excluding Being as the opaque foundation of history, it denies all historical veracity to what cannot be made an object of human representation.

In the final analysis, Heidegger's history of Being, where it interprets the modern epoch in the *single* perspective of the advent of the will to technical mastery, shies away from the ultimate paradox it brings to the fore. The radical challenge Heidegger addresses to traditional conceptions of historical cohesion founded on the development of cultural and of world-history raises the question of how, given the opacity of the source of history, it might be possible to grasp the history of Being as a *unified* movement. Does Heidegger's monolithic conception of a unified history of Being—the presumption, according to Heidegger's expression, that it is possible to "envision the totality of history" (*das Ganze der Geschichte [...] erblicken*)[338]—not itself succumb to a quest for order and continuity that his conception of the radical opacity of Being would only seem to undermine? Heidegger never seriously engages in critical reflection on the problem posed by the plurivocity and ambiguity of all historical phenomena that resist the kind of all-encompassing schema he imposes on them. In deflecting reflection from the plenitude of a shared human world and

337 Martin Heidegger, *Nietzsche*, vol. 2, *GA*, vol. 6, 2, p. 27; Martin Heidegger, "Überwindung der Metaphysik," *Vorträge und Aufsätze*, *GA*, vol. 7, p. 71.

338 Martin Heidegger, *Identität und Differenz*, *GA*, vol. 11, ed. Friedrich-Wilhelm von Herrmann (Frankfurt am Main: Klostermann, 2006), p. 59. Werner Beierwaltes has cogently argued that Heidegger's *Seinsgeschichte* attains its vision of the unity of the Western metaphysical tradition by excluding those exemplary moments in its elaboration that do not correspond to his preconceptions. This becomes evident for Beierwaltes above all through a closer examination of the philosophies of Proclus and of Plotinus. See Werner Beierwaltes, *Identität und Differenz. Zum Prinzip cusanischen Denkens* (Opladen: Westdeutscher Verlag, 1977), pp. 31–42.

the complex historicity of its articulations, Heidegger's vision of an all-encompassing unity commanded by the hidden call of Being assumes that it is capable of surmounting the essentially limited character of human understanding as it is marked by plurality, contingency, and finitude. It is directly here that the history of Being assumes a mythological guise. According to Hans Blumenberg's apt characterization, the mythological vision of Heidegger's *Seinsgeschichte* proposes "total schemata" that in eliminating the "desire to ask for more [...] makes it seem as if there were nothing more to ask."[339]

Heidegger's mythology embellished its account of the unity of the history of Being through a narrative of God and the gods. Over the course of this history, the monotheistic God of the Judeo-Christian tradition assumes a singular role. The deepening forgetfulness of Being as the opaque ground of history and the gradual exclusion of all that could not be grasped in terms of human representation is accompanied by the eclipse of the extra-human province of monotheistic religious belief. Paradoxically, however, as we saw in chapter six, this eclipse is prepared by the appropriation by the metaphysical tradition of the doctrine of the *creator* God, the omnipotent God who *makes* the world. The God of metaphysics, in portraying this world as the *ens creatum*, foreshadowed its successive reconfigurations leading to the identification of the created world with the objects of human production. Over the centuries, the work of divine creation gave way to its identification with a human capacity in the era of technical mastery.[340]

In the movement of the history of Being, as religion forfeits its extra-human reference, it is reduced to an object of lived experience (*Erlebnis*) in the realm of historical culture. The forgetfulness of Being corresponds to the disappearance of the primordial intermediary opening—"the opening in which gods and human beings become recognizable to each other."[341] At the culmination of the contemporary age, technological activism tends toward nihilism: the advent of what Heidegger identified with the global "machination" or *Machenschaft*. In this ultimate phase, Heidegger counseled disengagement and *Gelassenheit*, an awaiting of the

339 Hans Blumenberg, *Arbeit am Mythos* (Frankfurt am Main: Suhrkamp, 2006), p. 319; English translation, *Work on Myth*, trans. Robert M. Wallace (Cambridge, MA and London: MIT Press, 1985), p. 288, translation modified.

340 Martin Heidegger, *Beiträge zur Philosophie (Vom Ereignis) (1936–1938)*, *GA*, vol. 65, pp. 107, 124.

341 Martin Heidegger, *Überlegungen VII–XI (Schwarze Hefte)*, *GA*, vol. 95, § 29, p. 25.

call of Being to the event or Ereignis—the "other beginning" (*anderer Anfang*) and the emergence of another divinity—the "last god."[342]

Heidegger's recently published *Black Notebooks*, which completed the series of one hundred and two volumes of his collected works that began to appear in 1975, most clearly reveal the political thrust of his mythology of Being. Like Oswald Spengler or Ernst Jünger, he considered democratic principles of mass organization to be the sign of modern decline. In his writings of the period of World War II, Heidegger impugned the principles of popular sovereignty. Democracy to his mind incarnates the political form of the *Machenschaft*. It participates in the illusion that humans make their history and favors the quest for human domination in a technical age. By contrast, as I have stressed in previous chapters, Heidegger lauded the greatness of dictators (*Diktatoren*): they alone are able to discern the "hidden necessity" of the machination that Being calls forth and to resist all its seductions in view of accompanying modernity to the consummation (*Vollendung*) of its supreme essence (*ihr höchstes Wesen*).[343] Although he states his disappointment with the direction Nazi politics had taken, the wholesale arbitrariness of the acts of which absolute dictators are capable never seemed to weigh on his judgment: as we have seen in chapter five, leaders (*Führer*) bear no responsibility for catastrophes and only the hidden call of Being ultimately brings to pass the dawn of the new beginning.

If Heidegger in this period emphasized the decline inscribed in the movement of the history of Being, his anticipation of "another beginning" held out the promise of a special mission for the German nation. As I highlighted this conviction in chapter 1, Heidegger stated in the first volume of the *Black Notebooks* in the years before the war: "Only the German can express Being in a novel and original way." And this is because in an epoch of "complete loss of the historical" (*völlige Geschichtslosigkeit*), as he explained in a letter to Kurt Bauch in May, 1942, only the Germans have maintained the original determination of the Greeks (*anfängliche Bestimmung des Griechentums*) and have retained an intimation of the

342 Heidegger, *Beiträge zur Philosophie*, *GA*, vol. 65, pp. 24, 70, 403–510.

343 Martin Heidegger, *Überlegungen VII–XI (Schwarze Hefte, 1938–39)*, *GA*, vol. 95, § 47, p. 404; on Heidegger's affirmation of what he portrayed as Nietzsche's opinion that democracy is a "degenerate form of nihilism" spelling the "death of Europe," see his 1936 lectures on Nietzsche, *Der Wille zur Macht als Kunst*, *GA*, vol. 43, ed. Bernd Heimbüchel (Frankfurt am Main: Klostermann, 1985), p. 193; on this point see Ronald Beiner, *Dangerous Minds: Nietzsche, Heidegger, and the Return of the Far Right* (Philadelphia, PA: University of Pennsylvania Press, 2018), pp. 48–49.

historical (*Ahnung des Geschichtlichen entfaltet*).[344] In chapter six, I alluded to the mythical terms according to which, during the darkest moments of World War II, Heidegger sketched the outlines of this mission:

> "Once again—and how often will it be—the German essence (*das deutsche Wesen*) is thrown far back into an uncanny concealment; it still lacks the clarity and courage to dominate from out of the calm conferred by the supreme struggle in Being itself, which is the origin retained of the final god."[345]

Since the appearance of the five volumes of the *Black Notebooks* between 2014 and 2018, much analysis has focused on the legacy of his thought in light of the political orientation he chose to bring to the forefront in these final volumes of his works. In view of the political mythology Heidegger elaborated in the *Black Notebooks*, one can legitimately wonder in regard to his own perception of this legacy what motivated him to save them to provide the crowning touch to his massive *Gesamtausgabe*. The existence in these volumes of what is undoubtedly the most troubling element in his ruminations was unknown to all but the direct administrators of his *Nachlass*, mostly members of his family, until their publication began in 2014—forty years after his death! In a period following the disappearance of his generation and of all living memory of the war and the Shoah, might it be that he anticipated a radical shift in the political climate of Europe and the world, the ripening of a more fertile situation for the reception of the political mythology he spun out during the darkest years of World War II? The answer to this question can only remain a matter of speculation. Be this as it may, the intense preoccupation with Heidegger on a global scale among right-wing extremists lends a troubling side to this question and underscores the importance of scrutinizing Heidegger's legacy anew in the perspective of political theory and historical reflection.[346]

As I interpret it, the ultimate challenge of Heidegger's later thought lies in the key assumption that he expressed in his later works as a whole: the affirmation that the future course of human history lies entirely beyond

---

344 Martin Heidegger, *Überlegungen II–VI (Schwarze Hefte 1931–1938)*, *GA* vol. 94, §71, p. 27; letter to Kurt Bauch, 1 May 1942, in Martin Heidegger – Kurt Bauch, *Briefwechsel, 1932–1975*, p. 78; see in this light the insightful article of Marion Heinz, "Seinsgeschichte und Metapolitik," in *Martin Heideggers "Schwarze Hefte." Eine philosophisch-politische Debatte*, ed. Marion Heinz and Sidonie Kellerer (Frankfurt am Main: Suhrkamp, 2016), pp. 122–143.

345 Martin Heidegger, *Überlegungen XII–XV (Schwarze Hefte, 1939–41)*, *GA*, vol. 96, § 27, p. 48.

346 On this point see the illuminating analyses of Ronald Beiner in *Dangerous Minds: Nietzsche, Heidegger, and the Return of the Far Right*, pp. 35–53.

human choice. If, as I have continually stressed in this volume, Heidegger identified the central illusion of modernity with the presupposition that humanity makes its history and determines its future course, the surmounting of this illusion foresees the birth of a new capacity to listen to the call of Being and of piety toward a new divinity. To my mind, the mythological vision in which this affirmation is couched, in propagating a wholly fatalistic outlook that denies human responsibility for the future course of history, risks incurring weighty future consequences. Against this presumption, I can only reaffirm my conviction that any judgment concerning Heidegger's historical legacy cannot forego a consideration of its practical consequences. In this light, it is important to reiterate as a final argument the conclusion inspired by Hans Jonas to which I alluded in chapter five: the fatalism that renounces any possible recourse to a principle of responsibility ultimately runs the risk of promoting a self-fulfilling prophecy.[347] In inspiring mass credulity, fatalism only makes more probable the outcome it claims to foresee.

347 Hans Jonas, "Fatalismus wäre die eine Todsünde des Augenblicks. Berliner Ansprache (Juni 1992)," in *Fatalismus wäre Todsünde. Gespräche über Ethik und Mitverantwortung im dritten Jahrtausend*, ed. Dietrich Böhler (Münster: LIT Verlag, 2005), pp. 53–56.

Bibliography

Aquinas, Thomas, Saint, *Summa contra gentiles. De veritate catholicae fidei*, (Naples, Tipographia Virgiliana, 1846), p. 7; Eng. trans. *On the Truth of the Catholic Faith. Summa contra gentiles*, trans. Anton C. Pegis. Garden City, NY: Douleday, 1955.

Arendt, Hannah, *Between Past and Future*. New York: Viking, 1954.

…, *Essays in Understanding (1930–54)*, ed. Jerome Kohn. New York: Harcourt Brace and Co., 1994.

…, *The Human Condition*. Chicago: University of Chicago Press, 1958.

…, *The Life of the Mind*. New York/London: Harvest/Harcourt-Brace Jovanovich, 1978.

…, "Martin Heidegger at Eighty," *New York Review of Books* vol. 17, 6, 21 October, 1971, pp. 50–54, reprinted in Michael Murray, ed., *Heidegger and Modern Philosophy*. New Haven: Yale University Press, 1978, p. 293–303.

…, *Men in Dark Times*. Harmondsworth: Penguin, 1973.

…, "Philosophy and Politics, (1954)," in *Social Research*, vol. 57, number 1, 1990, pp. 73–103.

Arendt, Hannah, Jaspers, Karl, *Briefwechsel*. Munich: Piper, 1985.

Arrien, Sophie-Jan, *L'inquiétude de la pensée. L'herméneutique de la vie du jeune Heidegger (1919–1923)*. Paris: Presses Universitaires de France, 2014.

Arrien, Sophie-Jan and Sommer, Christian, eds., *Heidegger aujourd'hui. Actualité et postérité de sa pensée de l'événement*. Paris: Hermann, 2021.

Astrada, Carlos, ed., *Heideggers Einfluss auf die Wissenschaften. Aus Anlass seines sechsigsten Geburtstags*. Bern: Francke, 1949.

Augustine of Hippo, Saint, *The City of God*, Books 17–22, trans. Gerald G. Walsh, S.J. and Daniel J. Honan, in *Writings of St. Augustine*, vol. 8. Washington, D.C.: The Catholic University of America Press, 2008.

…, *Confessions*, vol. 2, trans. W. Watts. Cambridge, MA: Loeb Classical Library, Harvard University Press, 1988.

Barash, Jeffrey Andrew, *Collective Memory and the Historical Past*. Chicago and London: University of Chicago Press, 2016.

…, "Ernst Cassirer's Theory of Myth. On the Ethico-Political Dimension of his Debate with Martin Heidegger," in J. A. Barash, ed., *The Symbolic Construction of Reality. The Legacy of Ernst Cassirer*. Chicago: University of Chicago Press, 2008, p. 114–132.

…, "Ernst Cassirer, Martin Heidegger and the Legacy of Davos," in *History and Theory*, vol. 51, 3, October, 2012, p. 436–450.

…, *Martin Heidegger and the Problem of Historical Meaning*. New York: Fordham University Press, 2003.

…, *Temps de l'Être, temps de l'histoire: Heidegger et son siècle*. Paris: Presses Universitaires de France, 1995.

…, "Ueber den geschichtlichen Ort der Wahrheit. Hermeneutische Perspektiven bei Wilhelm Dilthey und Martin Heidegger," *Martin Heidegger: Innen- und Aussenansichten.*, ed. Peter Rohs, Siegfried Blasche, Wolfgang R. Köhler, Wolfgang Kuhlmann. Frankfurt/M: Suhrkamp, 1989, pp. 58–74.

Barthes, Roland, *Le Bruissement de la langue. Essais critiques* IV. Paris: Seuil, 1984.

Batnitzky, Leora, *Idolatry and Representation: The Philosophy of Franz Rosenzweig Reconsidered.* Princeton, NJ: Princeton University Press, 2000.

Beierwaltes, Werner, *Identität und Differenz. Zum Prinzip cusanischen Denkens.* Opladen: Westdeutscher Verlag, 1977.

Beiner, Ronald, *Dangerous Minds: Nietzsche, Heidegger, and the Return of the Far Right.* Philadelphia, PA: University of Pennsylvania Press, 2018.

Bernasconi, Robert, "Heidegger's alleged challenge to the Nazi concepts of race," in *Appropriating Heidegger*, ed. James E. Faulconer and Mark A Wrathall. Cambridge, UK/New York: Cambridge University Press, 2000, p. 50–67.

Blumenberg, Hans, *Arbeit am Mythos*. Frankfurt am Main: Suhrkamp, 2006; English translation, *Work on Myth*, trans. Robert M. Wallace. Cambridge, MA and London: MIT Press, 1985.

…, *Die Verführbarkeit des Philosophen.* Frankfurt am Main: Suhrkamp, 2000.

Bultmann, Rudolf, "Die liberale Theologie und die jüngste theologische Bewegung" (1924), *Glauben und Verstehen, Gesammelte Aufsätze*, vol. I. Tübingen, Mohr/Siebeck, 1966, pp. 1–25.

Bultmann, Rudolf, Heidegger, Martin, *Briefwechsel, 1925–1975*, ed. Andreas Grossmann and Christof Landmesser. Frankfurt am Main/Tübingen: Klostermann/Mohr Siebeck, 2009.

Camilleri, Sylvain, *Heidegger et les grandes lignes d'une phénoménologie herméneutique du christianisme primitif.* Cham, Switzerland: Springer, 2017.

Cassirer, Ernst, *Davoser Vorträge, Vorträge über Hermann Cohen, Mit einem Anhang: Briefe Hermann und Martha Cohens an Ernst und Toni Cassirer, 1901–1929, Nachgelassene Manuskripte und Texte*, vol. 17, ed. Jörn Bohr. Hamburg: Meiner, 2014.

…, *Das Mythische Denken, Philosophie der symbolischen Formen*, vol. 2. Darmstadt: Wissenschaftliche Buchgesellschaft,1994.

…, *Die Philosophie der Aufklärung.* Tübingen: Mohr, 1932.

…, *Die platonische Renaissance in England und die Schule von Cambridge.* Leipzig/Berlin: Teubner, 1932.

Cohen, Hermann, *Ethik des reinen Willens.* Berlin: Cassirer, 1921.

Collingwood, R. G., *The Idea of History.* Oxford: Oxford University Press, 1956.

Di Cesare, Donatella, *Heidegger e gli ebrei. I "Quaderni neri."* Torino: Bollati Boringhieri, 2014.

Diderot, Denis, *Œuvres.* Paris: Gallimard, éditions de la Pléiade, 1951.

Farias, Victor, *Heidegger et le nazisme.* Paris: Verdier, 1992.

Farin, Ingo and Malpas, Jeff, eds., *Reading Heidegger's Black Notebooks, 1931–1941*. Cambridge, MA: MIT Press, 2016.

Faye, Emmanuel, *Heidegger, L'introduction du nazisme dans la philosophie. Autour des séminaires inédits de 1933–1935*. Paris: Albin Michel, 2005.

Fédier, François, ed., *Heidegger à plus forte raison*. Paris: Fayard, 2007.

Figal, Günter, *Zu Heidegger: Antworten und Fragen*. Frankfurt am Main: Klostermann, 2009.

Fischer, Eugen, *Die Rehobother Bastards und das Bastardierungsproblem beim Menschen: anthropologische und ethnographische Studien am Rehobother Bastardvolk in Deutsch-Südwest-Afrika*. Jena: Fischer, 1913.

Fried, Gregory, *Heidegger's Polemos: From Being to Politics*. New Haven and London: Yale University Press, 2008.

Gadamer, Hans-Georg, Introduction to Martin Heidegger, *Der Ursprung des Kunstwerkes*. Stuttgart: Reclam, 1962, pp. 102–107.

…, "Philosophie und Religion des Judentums," *Gesammelte Werke*, vol. 4. *Neuere Philosophie*, 2, *Probleme – Gestalten*. Tübingen: Mohr, 1987, p. 68–77.

Gander, Hans-Helmuth and Striet, Magnus, eds., *Heideggers Weg in die Moderne: Eine Verortung der "Schwarzen Hefte."* Frankfurt am Main: Klostermann, 2017.

Gordon, Peter Eli, *Continental Divide: Heidegger, Cassirer, Davos*. Cambridge, MA: Harvard University Press, 2010.

Günther, Hans F. K., *Rassenkunde des deutschen Volkes*. Munich: Lehmann, 1922, 1933.

Habermas, Jürgen, *Philosophisch-politische Profile. Erweiterte Ausgabe*. Frankfurt am Main: Suhrkamp, 1981.

Harries, Karsten, *Art Matters. A Critical Commentary on Heidegger's "The Origin of the Work of Art."* Berlin/New York: Springer, 2009.

Hegel, *Vorlesungen über die Geschichte der Philosophie*, vol. 2, in *Works*, vol. 19. Frankfurt am Main: Suhrkamp, 1971.

Heidegger, Martin, *Anmerkungen I–V (Schwarze Hefte 1942–48)*, *GA*, vol. 97, ed. Peter Trawny. Frankfurt am Main: Klostermann, 2015.

…, *Der Begriff der Zeit* (1924), *GA*, vol. 64, ed. Friedrich Wilhelm von Herrmann. Frankfurt am Main: Klostermann, 2004.

…, *Beiträge zur Philosophie: Vom Ereignis,* 1936–38, GA, vol. 65, ed. Friedrich-Wilhelm von Herrmann. Frankfurt am Main: Klostermann; English trans. *Contributions to Philosophy: (From Enowning)*, trans. Parvis Emad and Kenneth Maly. Bloomington and Indianapolis: Indiana University Press, 1999.

…, *Zur Bestimmung der Philosophie*, *GA*, vol. 55/56. Frankfurt am Main: Klostermann, 1987.

…, *Einführung in die Metaphysik* (1935), *GA*, vol. 40, ed. Petra Jaeger. Frankfurt am Main: Klostermann, 1983.

..., *Einleitung in die Philosophie* (1928–29), *GA*, vol. 27, ed. Otto Saame and Ina-Saame-Speidel. Frankfurt am Main: Klostermann, 2001.

..., *Zu Ernst Jünger*, *GA*, vol. 90, ed. Peter Trawny. Frankfurt am Main: Klostermann, 2004.

..., *Die Frage nach dem Ding. Zu Kants Lehre von den transzendentalen Grundsätzen* (1935–36), *GA*, vol. 41, ed. Petra Jaeger. Frankfurt am Main: Klostermann, 1984.

..., *Die Geschichte des Seyns. 1. Die Geschichte des Seyns (1938/40). 2. Koinón. Aus der Geschichte des Seyns (1939/40)*, *GA*, vol. 69, ed. Peter Trawny. Frankfurt am Main: Klostermann, 1998.

..., *Grundbegriffe* (1941), *GA*, vol. 51, ed. Petra Jäger. Frankfurt am Main: Klostermann, 1991.

..., *Die Grundbegriffe der Metaphysik. Welt – Endlichkeit – Einsamkeit (1929–30)*, *GA* 29/30, ed. Friedrich-Wilhelm von Herrmann. Frankfurt am Main: Klostermann, 1983; English trans. *The Fundamental Concepts of Metaphysics. World, Finitude, Solitude*, trans. William McNeill and Nicholas Walker. Bloomington and Indianapolis: Indiana University Press.

..., *Grundprobleme der Phänomenologie* (1919/20), *GA*, vol. 58, ed. Hans-Helmuth Gander. Frankfurt am Main: Klostermann, 1993.

..., *Die Grundprobleme der Phänomenologie* (1927), *GA*, vol. 24, ed. Friedrich-Wilhelm von Herrmann. Frankfurt am Main: Klostermann, 1975.

..., *Hölderlins Hymne "Andenken,"* *GA*, vol. 52, ed. Curd Ochwadt. Frankfurt am Main: Klostermann, 1992.

..., *Hölderlins Hymne "Der Ister,"* *GA*, vol. 53, ed. Walter Biemel. Frankfurt am Main: Klostermann, 1984, p. 68; English translation, *Hölderlin's Hymn "The Ister."* trans. William McNeill and Julia Davis. Bloomington and Indianapolis: Indiana University Press, 1996.

..., *Holzwege*, *GA*, vol. 5, ed. Friedrich-Wilhelm von Herrmann. Frankfurt am Main: Klostermann,1977.

..., *Identität und Differenz*, *GA*, vol. 11, ed. Friedrich-Wilhelm von Herrmann (Frankfurt am Main: Klostermann, 2006.

..., *Kant und das Problem der Metaphysik*, *GA* vol. 3, ed. Friedrich-Wilhelm von Herrmann. Frankfurt: Klostermann, 1991.

..., *Logik: Die Frage nach der Wahrheit* (1925–26), *GA*, vol. 21, ed. Walter Biemel. Frankfurt am Main: Klostermann, 1976.

..., *Metaphysische Anfangsgründe der Logik im Ausgang von Leibniz*, *GA*, vol. 26, ed. Klaus Held. Frankfurt am Main: Klostermann, 1978.

..., *Nietzsche*, *GA*, vol. 6, 2, ed. Brigitte Schillbach. Frankfurt am Main: Klostermann, 1997.

..., *Nietzsche: Der europäische Nihilismus*, *GA*, vol. 48, ed. Petra Jaeger. Frankfurt am Main: Klostermann, 1986.

…, "'Only a God Can Save Us': The *Spiegel* Interview" (1966), trans. W. Richardson, *Heidegger: The Man and the Thinker*, ed. Thomas Sheehan. Chicago: Precedent, 1981, pp. 45–72.

…, *Ontologie. Hermeneutik der Faktizität*, *GA*, vol. 63. Frankfurt am Main: Klostermann, 1988.

…, *Parmenides* (1942–43), *GA*, vol. 54, ed. Manfred Frings. Frankfurt am Main: Klostermann, 1992.

…, *Phänomenologie der Anschauung und des Ausdrucks. Theorie der philosophischen Begriffsbildung*, *GA*, vol. 59, ed. Claudius Strube. Frankfurt am Main: Klostermann, 1993.

…, *Phänomenologie des religiösen Lebens*, *GA*, vol. 60, ed. Matthias Jung, Thomas Regehly, and Claudius Strube. Frankfurt am Main: Klostermann, 1995; English trans., *The Phenomenology of Religious Life*, trans. Matthias Fritsch and Jennifer Anna Gosetti-Ferencei. Bloomington and Indianapolis: Indiana University Press, 2004.

…, *Phänomenologische Interpretationen zu Aristoteles. Einführung in die Phänomenologische Forschung* (1921–22), *GA*, vol. 61, ed. Walter Bröcker and Käte Bröcker-Oltmanns. Frankfurt am Main: Klostermann, 1994.

…, Preface, William J. Richardson, *Through Phenomenology to Thought*. New York: Fordham University Press, 2003, p. viii–xxiii.

…, *Prolegomena zur Geschichte des Zeitbegriffs*, *GA*, vol. 20, ed. Petra Jaeger. Frankfurt am Main: Klostermann, 1979.

…, *Reden und andere Zeugnisse eines Lebensweges, 1910–1976*, ed. Hermann Heidegger, *GA*, vol. 16. Frankfurt am Main: Klostermann, 2000.

…, *Schelling: Vom Wesen der menschlichen Freiheit, (1809) (1936)*, *GA*, vol. 42, ed. Ingrid Schüssler. Frankfurt am Main: Klostermann, 1988.

…, *Sein und Wahrheit*, *GA*, vol. 36–37. Frankfurt am Main: Klostermann, 2001.

…, *Sein und Zeit*, *GA*, vol. 2, ed. Friedrich-Wilhelm von Herrmann. Frankfurt am Main: Klostermann, 1977.

…, *Seminare, Hegel – Schelling*, *GA*, vol. 86, ed. Peter Trawny. Frankfurt am Main: Klostermann, 2011.

…, *Überlegungen II–VI (Schwarze Hefte 1931–1938)*, *GA* vol. 94, ed. Peter Trawny. Frankfurt am Main: Klostermann, 2014.

…, *Überlegungen VII–XI (Schwarze Hefte, 1938–39)*, *GA*, vol. 95, ed. Peter Trawny. Frankfurt am Main: Klostermann, 2014.

…, *Überlegungen XII–XV (Schwarze Hefte, 1939–41)*, *GA*, vol. 96, ed. Peter Trawny. Frankfurt am Main: Klostermann, 2014; English translation, *Ponderings, XII–XV. Black Notebooks, 1939–41*, trans. Richard Rojcewicz. Bloomington, IN: Indiana University Press, 2014.

…, *Vorträge und Aufsätze*, *GA*, vol. 7, ed. Friedrich-Wilhelm von Herrmann. Frankfurt am Main: Klostermann, 2000.

…, *Was heisst Denken?*, *GA*, vol. 8, ed. Paola-Ludovika Coriando. Frankfurt am Main: Klostermann, 2002.

…, *Wegmarken, GA*, vol. 9, ed. Friedrich-Wilhelm von Herrmann. Frankfurt am Main: Klostermann, 1976; English trans. *Pathmarks*, ed. William McNeill. Cambridge, UK: Cambridge University Press, 1998.

…, *Der Wille zur Macht als Kunst, GA*, vol. 43, ed. Bernd Heimbüchel. Frankfurt am Main: Klostermann, 1985.

Heidegger, Martin, Bauch, Kurt *Briefwechsel, 1932–1975*, ed. Almuth Heidegger. Freiburg im Breisgau: Alber, 2010.

Heidegger, Martin, "Mein liebes Seelchen!" Briefe *Martin Heideggers an seine Frau Elfride, 1915–70*, ed. Gertrud Heidegger. Munich: Deutsche Verlagsanstalt, 2005.

Heidegger, Martin, Jaspers Karl, *Briefwechsel, 1920–1963*, ed. Walter Biemel and Hans Saner. Frankfurt am Main: Klostermann/Munich/Zurich: Piper, 1990.

Heidegger, Martin, Löwith, Karl, *Briefwechsel, 1919–1973*, ed. Alfred Denker. Freiburg/Munich: Alber, 2017.

Heidegger, Martin, Rickert, Heinrich, *Briefe (1912–33) und andere Dokumente*, ed. Alfred Denker. Frankfurt am Main: Klostermann, 2002.

Heinz, Marion and Kellerer, Sidonie, eds., *Martin Heideggers "Schwarze Hefte." Eine philosophisch-politische Debatte*. Frankfurt am Main: Suhrkamp, 2016.

Heisenberg, Werner, "Grundlegende Voraussetzungen in der Physik der Elementarteilchen," *Martin Heidegger zum siebzigsten Geburtstag*. Pfullingen: Neske, 1959, pp. 291–97.

Herder, Johann Gottfried, *Briefe zu Beförderung der Humanität*, *Werke*, vol. 7, ed. Hans Dietrich Irmscher. Frankfurt am Main: Deutscher Klassiker Verlag, 1991.

Herrmann, Friedrich-Wilhelm von, "Wirkungen der Martin-Heidegger-*Gesamtausgabe*," in Markus Happel, ed., *Heidegger-neu gelesen*. Königshausen und Neumann: Würzburg, 1997, p. 87–96.

Herrmann, Friedrich-Wilhelm von and Alfieri, Francesco, *Die Wahrheit über die Schwarzen Hefte*. Berlin: Duncker and Humblot, 2017.

Humboldt, Wilhelm von, *Ideen zu einem Versuch, die Gränzen der Wirksamkeit des Staates zu bestimmen, Werke*, vol. 1. Stuttgart: Cotta, 1960.

Janicaud, Dominique, *Le tournant théologique de la phénoménologie française*. Paris: Editions de l'éclat, 1992.

Jaran, François, *La métaphysique du Dasein: Heidegger et la possibilité de la métaphysique (1927–30)*. Bucharest: Zeta Books, 2010.

Jaspers, Karl, *Max Weber. Politiker, Forscher, Philosoph*. Bremen: Storm, 1946.

…, *Notizen zu Heidegger*. Munich: Piper, 1978.

…, *Die Schuldfrage*. Heidelberg: L. Schneider, 1946.

Jollivet, Servanne, *L'Historisme en question. Généalogie, débats et réception (1800–1930)*. Paris: Honoré Champion, 2013.

Jonas, Hans, "Fatalismus wäre die eine Todsünde des Augenblicks. Berliner Ansprache (Juni 1992)," in *Fatalismus wäre Todsünde. Gespräche über Ethik und Mitverantwortung im dritten Jahrtausend*, ed. Dietrich Böhler. Münster: LIT Verlag, 2005, p. 53–56.

Jonas, Hans, Stern, Fritz, *Reflexionen finsterer Zeit*. Tübingen: Mohr, 1984.

Jünger, Ernst, *Der Arbeiter*, *Werke*, vol. 6, *Essays* II. Stuttgart: Klett, 1960, p. 9–328.

…, "Über die Linie," *Werke*, vol. 5, *Essais* I, *Betrachtungen zur Zeit*. Stuttgart: Klett, 1960, p. 245–289.

Kant, Imanuel, *Die Religion innerhalb der Grenzen der blossen Vernunft*, in *Die Metaphysik der Sitten*, *Werkausgabe*, vol. 8, ed. Wilhelm Weischedel. Frankfurt am Main, Suhrkamp, 1982, p. 645–879.

Kierkegaard, Søren, *Die Wiederholung, Die Krise*, *Werke*, vol. II, trans. L. Richter. Reinbeck bei Hamburg: Rowohlt, 1961.

Kisiel, Theordor, "Edition und Übersetzung. Unterwegs von Tatsachen zu Gedanken, von Werken zu Wegen," in Dietrich Papenfuss and Otto Pöggeler, eds., *Zur philosophischen Aktualität Heideggers*, vol. 3, *Im Spiegel der Welt: Sprache, Übersetzung, Auseinandersetzung*. Frankfurt am Main: Klostermann, 1992, p. 89–107.

…, *The Genesis of Heidegger's Being and Time*. Berkeley and Los Angeles: University of California Press, 1993.

Kleinberg, Ethan, *Generation Existential: Heidegger's Philosophy in France, 1927–1961*. Ithaca and London: Cornell University Press, 2005.

Klibansky, Raymond, "Das Sagbare hat seine Grenzen. 50 Jahre Reichspogrommnacht," *Unispiegel* (Universität Heidelberg), June, 1988, pp. 3–4.

Kolbenheyer, Guido, "Lebenswert und Lebenswirkung der Dichtkunst in einem Volke," in *Werke* vol. 8, *Aufsätze, Vorträge und Reden*. Munich: Langen/Müller, 1941, p. 63–86.

Koselleck, Reinhart, "Historik und Hermeneutik," *Zeitschichten. Studien zur Historik. Mit einem Beitrag von Hans-Georg Gadamer*. Frankfurt am Main: Suhrkamp, 2000), p. 97–118.

Krell, David Farrell, *Ecstasy, Catastrophe. Heidegger from Being and Time to the Black Notebooks*. Albany, NY: SUNY Press, 2015.

Krieck, Ernst, "Germanischer Mythos und Heideggersche Philosophie," *Volk im Werden*, vol. 2, 1934, pp. 247–49.

Levinas, Emmanuel, *Autrement qu'être. Au-delà de l'essence*. Dordrecht: Kluwer/Paris: Le livre de Poche, 1996.

…, *En découvrant l'existence avec Husserl et Heidegger*. Paris: Vrin, 1994.

…, *Difficile Liberté. Essais sur le Judaïsme*. Paris: Albin Michel, 1976.

…, *A l'heure des nations*. Paris: Éditions de Minuit, 1986.

…, *Les imprévus de l'histoire*. Paris: Fata Morgana, 1994.

…, preface, Stéphane Mosès, *Sytème et révélation. La philosophie de Franz Rosenzweig*. Paris: Verdier, 2016.

…, *Totalité et infini. Essai sur l'extériorité.* Paris: Le livre de Poche, 1991/Dordrecht: Kluwer, 1971.

Levinas, Emmanuel, Poiré, François, *Essai et entretiens.* Paris: Actes Sud, 1996.

Löwith, Karl, *Der Europäische Nihilismus: Betrachtungen zur geistigen Vorgeschichte des europäischen Krieges, Sämtliche Schriften*, vol. 2, *Weltgeschichte und Heilsgeschehen.* Stuttgart: Metzler, 1983.

…, *Heidegger. Denker in dürftiger Zeit. Zur Stellung der Philosophie im 20. Jahrhundert, Sämtliche Schriften*, vol. 8. Stuttgart: Metzler, 1984.

…, "Les implications politiques de la philosophie de l'existence chez Heidegger," in *Les Temps Modernes*, vol. 2, 1946, p. 343–60.

…, *Mein Leben in Deutschland vor und nach 1933. Ein Bericht.* Stuttgart: Metzler, 1986.

Luther, Martin, "De Lege et Fide conclusiones xxviii cum resolutionibus (Heidelberger Disputation)," in *Werke. Kritische Gesamtausgabe.* Weimar: Böhlau, 1883, vol. 1, p. 350–374; English translation, Martin Luther, "Theses for the Heidelberg Disputation," in *Basic Theological Writings*, ed. John Dillenberger, Garden City, NY: Doubleday, 1961, p. 500–503.

Marcuse, Herbert, "Beiträge zu einer Phänomenologie des historischen Materialismus" (1928), *Der deutsche Kunstlerroman. Frühe Aufsätze, Schriften*, vol. 1. Frankfurt/M: Suhrkamp, 1978, pp. 347–384.

Massin, Benoît, "L'anthropologie raciale comme fondement de la science politique. Vacher de Lapouge et l'échec de l''anthroposociologie' en France," Claude Blanckaert, ed., *Les Politiques de l'anthropologie: discours et pratiques en France (1860–1940).* Paris: L'Harmattan, 2003, p. 269–334.

Mazzarella, Eugenio, *Il mondo nell'abisso. Heidegger e i Quaderni neri.* Milan: Neri Pozza, 2018.

Mehring, Reinhard, *Heideggers "Grosse Politik." Die semantische Revolution der Gesamtausgabe.* Tübingen: Mohr/Siebeck, 2016.

Meinecke, Friedrich, *Die deutsche Katastrophe: Betrachtungen und Erinnerungen.* Wiesbaden: E. Brockhaus, 1946.

…, *Die Idee der Staatsräson in der neueren Geschichte*, in *Werke*, vol. 1, ed. Walther Hofer. Munich/Vienna: Oldenbourg, 1976.

…, *Politische Schriften und Reden, Werke*, vol. 2, ed. Georg Kotowski. Darmstadt: Toeche-Mittler, 1958.

Mitchell, Andrew J. and Trawny, Peter, eds., Heidegger's *Black Notebooks: Responses to Anti-Semitism.* New York: Columbia University Press, 2017.

Moyn, Samuel, *Origins of the Other: Emmanuel Levinas Between Revelation and Ethics.* Ithaca and London: Cornell University Press, 2005.

Naumann, Friedrich, *Mitteleuropa.* Berlin: Reimer, 1915.

Nietzsche, Friedrich, Ecce homo, Werke, vol. 3, ed. Karl Schlechta. Frankfurt am Main: Ullstein, 1979.

…, *Die Geburt der Tragödie, Unzeitgemässe Betrachtungen 1–4, Nachgelassene Schriften, 1870–73*, Sämtliche Werke, Kritische Studien Ausgabe, vol. 1, ed. Giogio Colli and Mazzino Montinari. Berlin/New York: DTV/de Gruyter, 1988.

…, *Götzen-Dämmerung, Kritische Studienausgabe*, vol. 6, ed. Giorgio Colli and Mazzino Montinari. Berlin/New York: DTV/de Gruyter, 1988.

Norton, Robert E., *The Crucible of German Democracy. Ernst Troeltsch and the First World War*. Tübingen: Mohr/Siebeck, 2021.

Ott, Hugo, *Martin Heidegger. Unterwegs zu seiner Biographie*. Frankfurt/M: Campus, 1988.

Overbeck, Franz, *Christentum und Kultur. Gedanken und Anmerkungen zur modernen Theologie*, ed. Carl Albrecht Bernoulli. Basel: Schwabe, 1919.

Plato, *Phaedon*, trans. F. Schleiermacher, *Works*, vol. 3. Darmstadt: Wissenschaftliche Buchgesellschaft, 1977.

Plato, *The Republic*. Cambridge, MA: Loeb Classical Library/Harvard University Press, 1980.

Pöggeler, Otto, "Den Führer führen? Heidegger und kein Ende," *Philosophische Rundschau*, vol. 32, 1985, pp. 26–67.

…, *Philosophie und Politik bei Heidegger*. Freiburg: Alber, 1972.

…, *Der Denkweg Martin Heideggers*. Pfullingen: Neske, 1990.

Ranke, Leopold von, "Ueber die Epochen der neueren Geschichte," *Geschichte und Politik*, ed. H. Hofmann. Stuttgart: Kröner, 1940, pp. 138–347.

Ricœur, Paul, "La marque du passé," in *Mémoire, Histoire, Revue de Métaphysique et de Morale*, ed. Jeffrey Andrew Barash, 1, March, 1998, p. 7–32.

…, *La mémoire, l'histoire, l'oubli*. Paris: Seuil, 2000.

…, *Lectures 1. Autour du politique*. Paris: Seuil, 1991.

…, *Lectures 2. La contrée de philosophes*. Paris: Seuil, 1989.

…, "Les philosophies critiques de l'histoire: Recherche, explication, écriture," *Philosophical Problems Today*, vol. 1, ed. G. Fløistad. Dordrecht, Kluwer, 1994, p. 139–201.

…, *Soi-même comme un autre*. Paris: Seuil, 1990.

…, *Temps et récit*, 3 vols. Paris: Seuil, 1983–85.

Rolland, Jacques, *Parcours de l'autrement: Lecture d'Emmanuel Levinas*. Paris: Presses Universitaires de France, 2000.

Rosenberg, Alfred, Der Mythus des 20. Jahrhunderts. Eine Wertung der seelisch-geistigen Gestaltenkämpfe unserer Zeit. Munich: Hoheneichen, 1930.

Rosenzweig, Franz, "Vertauschte Fronten," in *Zweistromland. Kleinere Schriften zu Glauben und Denken, Gesammelte Schriften*, vol. 3, ed. Reinhold and Annemarie Mayer. Dordrecht: Martinus Nijhoff/Kluwer, 1984, pp. 235–37.

Rousseau, Jean-Jacques, *Émile ou de l'éducation*. Paris: Garnier-Flammarion, 1966.

Ruin, Hans, *Enigmatic Origins. Tracing the theme of Historicity through Heidegger's Works*. Stockholm: Almqvist and Wiksell International, 1994.

Schleiermacher, Friedrich, *Brouillon zur Ethik* (1805–06). Hamburg: Meiner, 1981.

…, *Die Lehre vom Staat. Aus Schleiermachers handschriftlichem Nachlass, Sämtliche Werke*, vol. 8, 3. Berlin: Reimer, 1845.

…, *Über die Religion: Reden an die Gebildeten unter ihren Verächtern*. Hamburg: Meiner, 1958.

Schmitt, Carl, *Der Begriff des Politischen*. Berlin: Duncker and Humblot, 1963.

…, *Politische Theologie. Vier Kapitel zur Lehre von der Souveränität*. Berlin: Duncker and Humblot, 1985.

Schopenhauer, Arthur, *Die Welt als Wille und Vorstellung*, 4 vols. Zurich: Diogenes, 1977.

Schorcht, Claudia, *Philosophie an den bayerischen Universitäten, 1933–45*. Erlangen: Fischer, 1990.

Schwan, Alexander, "Heideggers 'Beiträge zur Philosophie' und die Politik," in *Zeitschrift für philosophische Forschung*, vol. 43, 1989, p. 593–617.

…, *Politische Philosophie im Denken Heideggers*. Wiesbaden: VS Verlag, 1989.

Sieg, Ulrich, "Die Verjüdung des deutschen Geistes," *Die Zeit*, 52, 22 December, 1989, p. 50.

Singer, Isidore and Greenstone, Julius H., "The Noachian Laws" in *The Jewish Encyclopedia*, vol. 7. New York/London: Funk and Wagnall's, 1901–1906, p. 648–58.

Sommer, Christian, *Heidegger, Aristote, Luther: Les sources aristotéliciennes et néo-testamentaires d'Être et temps*. Paris: Presses Universitaires de France, 2015.

Spengler, Oswald, *Der Untergang des Abendlandes*, vol. 1, *Gestalt und Wirklichkeit*. Vienna: Braumüller, 1918; vol. 2, *Welthistorische Perspektiven*. Munich: Beck, 1922.

Spinoza, Benedict, *Theological-Political Treatise*, in *Collected Works of Spinoza*, vol. 2, trans. Edwin Curley. Princeton and Oxford: Princeton University Press, 2016.

Spranger, Eduard, "Über Rickerts System," in *Logos*, vol. 12, 1923–24, p. 183–198.

Strauss, David Friedrich, *Das Leben Jesu für das deutsche Volk bearbeitet*. Bonn: Emil Strauss, 1895.

Thomä, Dieter, "Heidegger und der Nazionalsozialismus. In der Dunkelkammer der Seinsgeschichte," Dieter Thomä, ed., *Heidegger Handbuch. Leben-Werk-Wirkung*. Stuttgart: Metzler, 2003, p. 141–61.

…, *Die Zeit des Selbst und die Zeit danach: Zur Kritik der Textgeschichte Martin Heideggers, 1910–1976*. Frankfurt am Main: Suhrkamp, 1990.

Trawny, Peter, *Heidegger und der Mythos der jüdischen Weltverschwörung*. Frankfurt am Main: Klostermann, 2015.

…, "Heidegger und das Politische: Zum "Rechtsphilosophien"-Seminar," in *Heidegger-Studies*, vol. 28, 2012, p. 47–66.

Troeltsch, Ernst, Aufsätze zur Geistesgeschichte und Religionssoziologie, Gesammelte Schriften, vol. 4, Tübingen: Mohr (Paul Siebeck), 1925

…, *Der Historismus und seine Probleme. Werke*, vol. 3. Tübingen: Mohr, 1922.

…, "Naturrecht und Humanität in der Weltpolitik," *Deutscher Geist und Westeuropa. Gesammelte Kulturphilosophische Aufsätze und Reden*, ed. Hans Baron. Aalen: Scientia, 1966, pp. 3–30.

Uexküll, Jacob von, *Staatsbiologie. Anatomie – Physiologie – Pathologie des Staate*. Hamburg: Hanseatische Verlagsanstalt, 1933.

Weber, Max, *Gesammelte Aufsätze zur Religionssoziologie*, vol. 1. Tübingen: Mohr, 1947.

…, *Gesammelte politische Schriften*. Munich: Drei Masken Verlag, 1921.

…, *Verstehende Soziologie und Werturteilsfreiheit. Schriften und Reden, 1908–17, GA*, section. 1, vol. 12, ed. Johannes Weiss and Sabine Frommer. Tübingen: Mohr/Siebeck, 2018.

…, *Wissenschaft als Beruf 1917/1919 Politik als Beruf, 1919, GA*, section 1, vol. 17, ed., Wolfgang J. Mommsen, Wolfgang Schluchter, and Birgitt Morgenbrod. Tübingen: Mohr/Siebeck, 1992.

Weingart, Peter, Kroll, Jürgen and Bayertz, Kurt, *Rasse, Blut und Gene. Geschichte der Eugenik und Rassenhygiene in Deutschland.* Frankfurt am Main: Suhrkamp, 1992.

Weismann, August, *Aufsätze über Vererbung und verwandte biologische Fragen.* Jena: Gustav Fischer, 1892.

…, "Germinal Selection," *The Evolution Theory*, vol. 2, trans. J. Arthur Thomson and Margaret R. Thomson. London: Edward Arnold, 1904, p. 113–158.

…, *Über die Vererbung. Ein Vortrag*. Jena: Gustav Fischer, 1883.

Werner, Judith, *Poesie der Vernichtung: Literatur und Dichtung in Martin Heideggers Schwarzen Heften*. Stuttgart: Metzler, 2018.

White, Hayden, *The Content of the Form. Narrative Discourse and Historical Representation*. Baltimore: Johns Hopkins, 1987.

…, *Tropics of Discourse. Essays in Cultural Criticism*. Baltimore: Johns Hopkins, 1978.